A WOMAN'S HEART

GOD'S DWELLING PLACE

BETH MOORE

LifeWay Press®
Nashville, Tennessee

ISBN 978-1-4158-2590-7
Item 005076821

This book is the text for course CG-0114 in the subject area MINISTRY
in the Christian Growth Study Plan.

Dewey decimal classification: 220.07
Subject heading: BIBLE STUDY \ WOMEN—RELIGIOUS LIFE

Unless otherwise noted, Scripture quotations are from the Holy Bible, New International Version, copyright © 1973, 1978, 1984 by International Bible Society. Scripture quotations marked HCSB® are taken from the Holman Christian Standard Bible®, copyright © 1999, 2000, 2001, 2002 by Holman Bible Publishers. Used by permission. Scripture quotations marked KJV are from the King James Version of the Bible. Scripture quotations marked NASB are taken from the New American Standard Bible®, copyright © 1960, 1962, 1963, 1968, 1971, 1973, 1975, 1977, 1995 by the Lockman Foundation. Used by permission. (www.lockman.org)

To order additional copies of this resource: WRITE LifeWay Church Resources Customer Service; One LifeWay Plaza; Nashville, TN 37234-0113; FAX order to (615) 251-5933; CALL toll-free 1-800-458-2772; E-MAIL orderentry@lifeway.com; ORDER ONLINE at www.lifeway.com; or VISIT the LifeWay Christian Store serving you.

Printed in the United States of America

Leadership and Adult Publishing
LifeWay Church Resources
One LifeWay Plaza
Nashville, TN 37234-0175

To Keith,

Years ago I dedicated the original version of this Bible study to you, thanking you for making room in our marriage for me to enter the holy of holies. To date, and to our absolute astonishment, eleven more Bible studies have followed. You, my Darling, are a wonder. I cannot imagine another man on earth providing more support, more love, more faith in a woman, and more material than you! I'd have no ministry without you…nor do I think I'd want one. Of the people I love most on this earth, you are my dearest.

I love you more than ever,

Beth

The Author

Beth Moore has written best-selling Bible studies on Daniel, David, John, Paul, and Jesus. Her books *Breaking Free, Praying God's Word,* and *When Godly People Do Ungodly Things* have all focused on the battle Satan is waging against Christians. *Believing God* and *Living Beyond Yourself* have focused on how Christians can live triumphantly in today's world. Beth has a passion for Christ, a passion for Bible study, and a passion to see Christians living the lives Christ intended.

Beth is an active member of First Baptist Church of Houston, Texas. The wife of Keith and mother of two young adult daughters, Beth serves a worldwide audience through Living Proof Ministry. Her conference ministry, writing, and videos reach millions of people every year.

Contents

Introduction

Welcome to *A Woman's Heart: God's Dwelling Place!* I'm pleased God led you to choose this book as a tool to dig deep into His precious Word. The months I originally spent with God preparing this study were some of the most meaningful, maturing months of my life. When we decided to update the study, I wondered if God would speak to me again through it. I'm pleased to report that God again showed Himself in magesty. I pray with all my heart that everyone who completes this study will encounter Christ in an unforgettable way, just as I did.

An in-depth, 10-week Bible study, *A Woman's Heart: God's Dwelling Place* contains five daily lessons each week. Each lessson requires about 45 minutes, and their completion is crucial.

Each week's introduction includes Principal Questions. Their answers alert you to look for information as you study and prepare you for each week's discussion group.

Each lesson begins with a Today's Treasure that represents the lesson's theme. Claim the treasure as your verse for the day; ask God to bring it to your mind often during the day.

Each day's study consists of reading assignments and learning activities. Each activity specifically assists you to reap full benefit from the study. Please do not omit them. They will contribute immeasurably to your retention.

Questions designated by a heart (♥) signify personal questions that will help you apply what you learn. They ensure this study accomplishes its priority goal: to get God's Word into your heart! Your weekly group will discuss these, and you may share your answers if you wish.

God wants you to take His Word very personally! I pray you will expect to hear a fresh word from God every day. Your lessons should be personal times you share with God. By the conclusion of each, you should be able to identify something you believe He was saying directly to you. Look and listen for God to draw out certain truths He wants to underscore for you.

Begin each day's study in prayer, asking God to give you "the mind of Christ" (see Phil. 2:5) to comprehend the riches of His Word. (See Eph. 1:18; 1 Cor. 2:10.) Your answers will often differ from those of other group members, and comparing your answers will enrich your weekly discussion time.

A Woman's Heart: God's Dwelling Place primarily employs the New International Version of the Bible, but I have frequently made reference to the King James Version and the Holman Christian Standard Version. Use any version you prefer for personal study, but keep a NIV nearby for times when I ask you to note a particular word or phrase.

Although individuals can certainly enjoy this study of God's Word, a group environment is effective for studying this and most in-depth Bible studies. Members meet for weekly accountability and discussion and also watch video segments that enhance the book's material and conclude with additional truths and challenges. I hope you make the group meetings a priority throughout this study.

Please know that I have prayed for you. I have asked God to pour His Spirit, ensuring with the riches of His glory that your heart will find Him irresistible and will forever be His dwelling place. Now commit this study in prayer to God, asking Him to give you His passion for finished works (see Phil. 1:6). I am honored to have the opportunity to escort you as we examine the most vivid portrait of God's Son in the Old Testament: the tabernacle. Come walk with me through the wilderness wanderings, where we will surely discover streams in the desert.

Viewer Guide

Read Exodus 25:1-2,8-9. Open your spiritual eyes to:

1. The _____ of God's _____ of man.

      God asked, _____ _____ _____ (Gen. 3:8-9)?

2. The _____ of God's _____.

- According to *Anchor Bible Dictionary,* "more _____ of the Pentateuch are _____ to it [the tabernacle] than any other _____."

- Compare Exodus 25:8-9 and 25:40. The phrase 'the pattern shown you on the mountain' (also translated "which is being shown you") "means literally 'which you are _____ _____ _____.' "

- Compare Hebrews 8:5. The Old Testament tabernacle was a _____ and shadow of a _____ reality. Strong's definition of the Greek word *hupodeigma,* translated "copy," is "an _____ for _____ … a pattern." Lenski's Commentary on the New Testament offers these synonyms: "a _____ , _____, outline."

See Revelation 15:5.

3. The _____ of God's _____. See Luke 24:25-27,44-45.

May these words become our constant plea throughout the next 10 weeks: *"Lord, open my mind that I might have understanding."*

The Greek word for "understand" is *suniemi* which "strictly denotes the collecting together of the individual features of an object into a whole, as collecting the pieces of a puzzle and putting them together."

Lord Jesus, _____ my _____ so I can understand the Scriptures.

Broken Hearts, Broken Ties

DAY 1 • AN EMPTY GARDEN

DAY 2 • A PERFECT HEART

DAY 3 • A PEOPLE FOR HIS NAME

DAY 4 • THE ORIGINAL LOVE STORY

DAY 5 • ON THE MOVE

WEEK 1

The consistent theme of *A Woman's Heart: God's Dwelling Place* is the desire of a holy God to dwell among mortals. We will explore this theme by concentrating on one vital method by which God's desire took action: the Old Testament tabernacle. Week 1 lays a strong biblical foundation on which we will build the entire study. This week we will span the entire history of humankind from creation to the exodus as we seek answers to the following questions.

Principal Questions

1. Why were the Israelites to build the tabernacle?
2. What is the human heart like apart from fellowship with God?
3. How did God respond to what He saw at the tower of Babel?
4. What did God preach to Abraham?
5. By what name did God tell Moses to call Him to the Israelites?

If you've studied God's Word for a long time, you may be tempted to skim over the historical background this week provides. But you have probably never studied the early history of humanity in specific relationship to the Old Testament tabernacle. Don't let the seeming familiarity of this material cheat you of countless treasures. Ask God to open your mind to a fresh understanding of these age-old accounts so you come to appreciate with great intensity God's revolutionary words: "Have them make a sanctuary for me, and I will dwell among them" (Ex. 25:8).

Day 1
An Empty Garden

Read Today's Treasure and pray that God will speak to you through His Word.

See the first occasion in God's perfectly-inspired Scripture that the word *tabernacle* appears.

 Read Exodus 25:1-2,8-9. According to verse 8, why were the Israelites to build the tabernacle?

_____

When I originally wrote this Bible study, I was in the throes of the wildest and busiest years of parenting. Our older daughter, Amanda, had just entered middle school. Melissa, three years her junior, was in elementary school, and our house was splitting at the seams with a hyperactive pint-sized boy.

Michael entered our lives when he was four years old, and we were utterly convinced we'd raise him to adulthood. We were wrong. God left him with us for seven years of laughter, hard work, confusion, fears, and at least a thousand gallons of tears. Then God had other plans. Though Michael's time with us was abbreviated, he marked our lives forever. Stories of him were sprinkled throughout the original edition of this study. Though my own personal examples are updated in this edition, I can't bring myself to remove all the Michael stories. He's simply too tangled in my heartstrings. I also do not believe my journey with God through the wilderness of Exodus would have been the same had I not had Michael at the time. My ears were shocked clean. With your blessing I will, therefore, begin this study just as I did the first time: with one of a million Michael stories.

The child had an uncanny habit of taking apart any gadget he could get his hands on. One day when he was five years old, I was expecting an important long-distance phone call. I had busied myself with some work around the house to decrease my anticipation, and Michael was playing quietly—my first signal that mischief was lurking. When the phone finally rang, I sprouted wings and flew toward it, only to find that the three cords connecting the phone were plugged into different places. A two-inch cord now connected the receiver to the base. In other words, when I picked up the phone, I picked up the whole phone. The long cord that usually plugs into the wall was connected by two inserts on the back of the phone, and the extra long, curly cord was connected to the wall. Just try having a conversation with an entire phone hanging at your chin and a five-year-old boy laughing hysterically at your feet. And would you believe it worked?

I am convinced that God was sparing my son's dear flesh. He seemed to get a kick out of Michael. And Michael seemed to get a kick out of me. Still does, as a matter of fact. He loves to hear stories of how he baffled me. Even

"THERE, ABOVE THE COVER BETWEEN THE TWO CHERUBIM THAT ARE OVER THE ARK OF THE TESTIMONY, I WILL MEET WITH YOU AND GIVE YOU ALL MY COMMANDS FOR THE ISRAELITES."
Exodus 25:22

as a preschooler, he relentlessly took apart radios, tape players, and video games and managed to live to boast about it. Every time I'd catch him, I always asked the same question: "Why did you take this apart?" Hopelessly enthusiastic, his response never varied. "So I can see how it works!" Throughout this study we will take apart Scripture verses and a certain tent of meeting for exactly the same reason—so we can see how they work.

Look back at Exodus 25:1-2,8-9 and let's begin building a crucial foundation for our study.

Discover who is involved. Who is talking? _____

Whom is He addressing? _____

Who is "them" in verse 8? _____

What is Moses to have them do?
❑ build themselves a sanctuary ❑ build God a sanctuary
❑ build a church

How are they to construct it? _____

_____

What two names does God call this structure in verses 8-9?

_____

The tabernacle had to meet God's standard rather than a human one. The Hebrew word for *sanctuary* is *miqdash*, a masculine Hebrew noun meaning *a consecrated or holy thing or place; a hallowed part, like a chapel; an asylum; an area devoted to the sphere of the sacred.* It is derived from the word *qadhash*, which means *to be clean, to make clean, to pronounce clean (ceremonially or morally); to hallow, to dedicate, to purify.*

The Hebrew word for *tabernacle* is *mishkan*, carrying the basic meaning of residence. The word does not often mean a place of physical splendor; rather, it could be a shepherd's hut, an animal's lair, or the grave. Most often in the Scriptures *mishkan* refers specifically to the tabernacle in the wilderness, which we are studying. It was the place where God chose to dwell with His people.

Review the definitions of *sanctuary* and *tabernacle*. Considering them jointly, check any of the following that apply to the tabernacle.
❑ a simple structure ❑ an asylum ❑ a dwelling place
❑ a place of splendor ❑ a holy place ❑ a place of purity
❑ devoted to sacred things ❑ a mansion ❑ a storehouse

SANCTUARY

a consecrated or holy thing or place; a hallowed part, like a chapel; an asylum; an area devoted to the sphere of the sacred

TABERNACLE

residency

Each of these Scriptures pertains to the tabernacle: Exodus 25:22; 29:42-43; 30:6,36. What is the obvious purpose of the structure?

_____

God's glorious, incomprehensible desire to meet with humans is the cornerstone on which we will build over the next 10 weeks. What did God have in mind when He wanted to meet with man? The Hebrew word for *meet* is *ya'adh*, meaning *to appoint, fix (a place or time); to betroth, give in marriage; to meet by agreement, come together.*

 Read in 2 Corinthians 5:18 a beautiful definition of what the tabernacle in the wilderness represented. What has God given us?

_____

Through Christ, God has given us the incomparable ministry of reconciliation. The tabernacle is a marvelous Old Testament picture of God's ministry of reconciliation. Through the course of our study we will see these parallel verses become even more vital in our understanding of God's ministry to His people through the tabernacle.

> Through Christ, God has given us the incomparable ministry of reconciliation.

We will conclude our lesson today by reviewing our need for reconciliation. Why was a place where God could dwell among people necessary? What had happened to separate God and man?

_____

We began today tracing God's activity in the lives of His prized creation. At the end of our first week we will arrive at the point in the wilderness where God issued the command to build a dwelling place. To paint a landscape of events leading from the creation of man to the command to build a tabernacle, we need to cover a significant amount of scriptural ground. Therefore, your Scripture reading will be lengthier this week than those that follow. Ask God to help you carve out the time because the more you participate, the more you'll grasp what, to me, became one of the most fascinating concepts in all Scripture: God dwelling among men.

Read Genesis 1:26–3:24 aloud if possible to help you focus. You may have read these chapters dozens of times but probably not with the goal of understanding the tabernacle's purpose. I like the way Tony Evans, the pastor of Oak Cliff Bible Church in Dallas, summed up the events in Genesis 3 on a radio broadcast: "It wasn't the apple in the tree that was the problem. It was the pear [pair] on the ground." In the midst of all the excitement in the garden, it is easy to miss the extreme significance of Genesis 3:8-9.

What was God doing in Genesis 3:8-9? _____

Can you imagine? The lofty feet of His Highness leaving prints on the lowlands of earth. He asked the question in Genesis 3:9 that became significant to us in our introductory session: "Where are you?"

In our introductory session I posed this very question to you as I pondered it for myself. I believe God appoints our journeys through His Word to correspond with our current life seasons. Where does this study find you right now?

Just as God sought the fellowship of His first children in the garden, He chooses yours. Right here and now. Whatever state you're in. The God of the universe is seeking you. Think back on that first couple and their unparalleled glimpses of Him. Obviously God's practice was to meet with them side by side, walking and talking with them in their paradise-world. This time He found His children hiding because they'd sinned.

Recall the curse that fell on the ground because of Adam in Genesis 3:18: "It will produce thorns and thistles for you." The weight of that curse eventually fell on the head of Another. Read Matthew 27:29 in the margin. Thorns have a way of working themselves into the flesh, don't they? In the Apostle Paul's terminology, you might say that Christ asked that His "thorn in the flesh" be removed (see Luke 22:42). Heaven's angels must have stood afraid to breathe as the Father had to respond, "No, My Son." You see, His thorn was the curse of our sin.

In 2 Corinthians 12:7-9 Paul stated that his thorn remained because God wanted him to know the sufficiency of His grace. The day our Savior bore the thorns in His flesh was the day God perfected the ultimate sufficiency of grace: "God made him who had no sin to be sin for us, so that in him we might become the righteousness of God" (2 Cor. 5:21).

[They] twisted together a crown of thorns and set it on his head. They put a staff in his right hand and knelt in front of him and mocked him. "Hail, king of the Jews!" they said.

Matthew 27:29

What did God do to cover Adam's and Eve's nakedness (Gen. 3:21)?

_____

What must happen to an animal when it is skinned?

_____

Our immutable God still covers sin the same way—by the bloodshed and death of the Innocent: "What shall we say, then? Shall we go on sinning so that grace may increase? By no means!" (Rom. 6:1-2).

Glance ahead to Genesis 4:6-7. According to these verses, check each word that accurately describes sin.
❑ passive   ❑ unaware   ❑ watching   ❑ aggressive

Let's beware of walking on the wrong path this week. We just might step on a thorn. You are off to a great start! Don't dismay if today's lesson was a review for you. I assure you that throughout the next 10 weeks God will have plenty of fresh insights to share with us!

Day 2
A Perfect Heart

Begin your study by reading Today's Treasure and praying that God will speak to you through His Word.

Questions like "Who am I?" and "Why am I here?" have placed many people on psychologists' couches. Such preoccupation seems to measure the onset of middle age. Mainstream Christianity has traditionally rejected these personal queries as far too self-centered for the truly spiritual to ask aloud. Oddly, if such a curiosity is out of line for the believer, God has certainly dedicated an impressive amount of ink to His response. Let's take a look at a few of His answers:

> "You are worthy, our Lord and God, to receive glory and honor and power, for you created all things, and by your will they were created and have their being" (*Rev. 4:11*).

> "Everyone who is called by my name, whom I created for my glory, whom I formed and made" (*Isa. 43:7*).

So who are you and why are you here? You are God's chief creation, and you are here for His pleasure and His glory. God did not create us so that He could have the front-row seat at an ongoing saga of our follies and failures. He created us because He delights in us. Let's do a brief word study of the terms *pleasure* and *glory* to deepen our understanding.

The Greek word for *pleasure* in Revelation 4:11 is *thelema*. It means "the result of the will ... not to be conceived as a demand, but as an expression or inclination of pleasure towards that which is liked, that which pleases and creates joy."[1]

Several years ago while I was teaching a midweek class at my church, someone from the office notified me that my husband, Keith, needed to speak to me right away on the telephone. My heart pounded frantically as I ran to the office, because I knew only an emergency would cause Keith to summon me from class. To my surprise, I was greeted by a congenial voice that said, "How about taking your husband to lunch today?"

Still suspicious that something had to be wrong, I answered, "I had plans with a friend, but I can cancel if you really need me." I will never forget his response: "I don't need to have lunch with you, Honey; I just wanted to."

I promptly rescheduled with my friend. As long as we've been married, if my husband chooses to be with me from the pure desire of his heart, I'll be there!

Far greater, that is why God created us: not because He needed us but because He wanted us. The act was based on the pleasure of His will. Reread the definition of *thelema* and try to fathom that God doesn't just love us. He also likes us!

Today's Treasure

"THE EYES OF THE LORD RANGE THROUGHOUT THE EARTH TO STRENGTHEN THOSE WHOSE HEARTS ARE FULLY COMMITTED TO HIM."

2 Chronicles 16:9

THELEMA

the result of the will ... not to be conceived as a demand, but as an expression or inclination of pleasure towards that which is liked, that which pleases and creates joy.

13

The word for *glory* in Isaiah 43:7 is *kavodh* and means *weight, honor, esteem, majesty, abundance, wealth.* At first glance *weight* may seem an odd synonym for *glory* until we recall that, in ancient times, all value was estimated on the basis of weight. Everything from gold to grain was placed on a scale. The heavier the item, the higher the value. We were created to be God's abundance—estimations of His value!

I come from a large family. One day when my older daughter was about two years old, she snuggled in her beloved grandmother's lap and asked, "Are you rich, Nanny?" She certainly had reason to assume so after copious trips to the dollar store. My mother responded, "Oh, yes, Darling, I am very rich—rich in kids!" Of all the grandeur heaven could boast, God measures His riches by His children. We are His wealth, the apple of His eye, created to be His treasure.

♥ **What does Matthew 6:21 tell you about God's heart?**

_____

_____

What does God measuring His wealth by His children mean to you?

_____

_____

Of all God's creation, we are closest to His heart! God placed man and woman in the garden, surrounded by splendor, as precious objects of His delight. They enjoyed the standing invitation of perpetual access. So splendid was their existence that they were vastly unacquainted with problems that plague humans today.

Psalm 8:4-8 records the position of humans in comparison to all other creation. List what was over them and under them.

over: _____

under: _____

God created us higher than any other creature with the possible exception of angels. All of Adam and Eve's needs were met. No sickness. No hunger. No danger. No drought. No floods. No demands. No stress. (No kids.) No bills. No irreconcilable differences. No tree of knowledge. And that was just one no too many.

How often we surmise that we could easily make Christ our first priority and lead spiritual lives if not for the mate we married, the handicapped child we birthed, the financial burden we face, the job we perform, or the incredible stress we bear. This couple had it all. They did not sin because of their circumstances. Sin is not the product of our haves and have-nots. It is a product of the heart.

 What is the human heart like apart from fellowship with God?

_____

Jeremiah 17:9 says, "the heart is more deceitful than anything else" (HCSB). The Hebrew word for *deceitful* means *fraudulent, crooked, one who lies in wait.* Adam and Eve let their hearts convince them that they deserved the one thing they had been denied and that taking it would do them no harm. Hearts easily buy into Satan's lies. Your heart often lies to you, just as my heart often lies to me. "Follow your heart" is the stuff of fairy tales and the stuff of many a nightmare.

Nothing is more misleading than an unsanctified heart. For this reason God exhorts us continually throughout His Word to give Him our whole hearts. We might occasionally be able to change our circumstances, but only God can change our hearts. "If only ..., then I could be happy" are words that often invade our thoughts. Attaining all of our "if onlys" simply gives birth to a new set. Just as we get what we thought we had to have, all of the rules seem to change. Isn't it frightening that we could finally talk God into giving us all we desire? Psalm 106:15 says, "He gave them their request; but sent leanness into their soul" (KJV).

Since sin began inside the garden, imagine what sin became outside the garden. With the multiplication of humanity came the multiplication of sin. As we continue to research the background events that led to the tabernacle in the wilderness, let's discover what the populated earth eventually became.

Read Genesis 6:1-9 and answer the following questions.

What did God see according to Genesis 6:5? _____

_____

What was His response in verse 6?
- ❑ God decided to destroy humanity from the earth.
- ❑ God regretted making man and grieved what they had become.
- ❑ God decided to send Jesus to die for humanity's sins.

What was His plan of action in verse 7? _____

_____

How does Genesis 6:8-9 describe Noah? _____

_____

The scenario had changed significantly from the time of Adam and Eve. They had been surrounded by purity and splendor. They had been set for spiritual success and "equipped for every good work" (2 Tim. 3:17). Yet, in the midst of all the right circumstances, they made the wrong choices.

Enter Noah who lived in a society of rampant wickedness. Sin ruled. Perversion prevailed. Righteousness was as rare as a perfect gem. People followed every evil inclination without restraint. The only absolute was absolute depravity.

In the midst of all the wrong circumstances, Noah made right choices. How? Noah walked with God. Surrounded by a perverse generation, Noah knew that righteousness could not be attained and could not persist on the basis of a one-time commitment. Scripture does not even say that Noah religiously renewed his commitment every Sunday. He walked with God. He was in a constant state of habitual fellowship—day by day, hour by hour.

Joshua 24:15 says, "Choose for yourselves this day whom you will serve, whether the gods your forefathers served beyond the River, or the gods of the Amorites, in whose land you are living. But as for me and my household, we will serve the LORD." God has applied this verse to my heart by leading me to make that choice daily. Committing to His lordship on Easter, at revivals, or even every Sunday is not enough. We must choose this day—and every day—whom we will serve. This deliberate act of the will is the inevitable choice between habitual fellowship and habitual failure.

> We must choose this day—and every day—whom we will serve.

The word *covenant* and its concept become crucial to our study this week. Search Genesis 6:10–9:19 for every reference and phrase containing the word *covenant* and record each here. I'll give you a head start with its first appearance in Scripture.

Reference   Phrase

<u>Genesis 6:18</u>   <u>"I will establish my covenant with you"</u>

_____   _____

_____   _____

_____   _____

_____   _____

_____   _____

_____   _____

As we conclude our study today, answer the following based on the Scripture passage you completed. Your answers will prepare you for day 3.

Check Noah's response to God in Genesis 6:22.
❑ responded hesitantly   ❑ argued   ❑ obeyed

What did the rainbow represent? _____

_____

What parties were involved in the covenant (Gen. 9:17)?

_____

Noah provides us a wonderful example. Our culture surrounds us with every conceivable practice of sin and the continual mockery of God. We can be victorious only if we walk with God. We have seen God was faithful to Noah, and the One who never changes will be faithful to us. If you have not already met God in absolute surrender, give Him your whole heart today. No other hands are safer.

Day 3
A People for His Name

I'm so glad you're back today! Begin by reading Today's Treasure and praying that God will speak to you through His Word. I hope God is revealing some new treasures to you as we identify the bridge between the garden and God's command to build a tabernacle. If you'll persevere, I promise all of this will start coming together by session 1. OK, day 2 concluded with a brief consideration of the covenant God made between Himself and "all life on the earth" (Gen. 9:17).

Read Genesis 9:1. What command did God give Noah and his sons?

_____

Now, contrast Genesis 11:1-5, answering the following questions.

What unified the people? _____

For what specific reason did they build the city and the tower?
❏ God had commanded them to build it.
❏ They sought a closer relationship with God.
❏ They wanted to make a name for themselves.
❏ They hungered for a place to call home.

Why did the people want to build the city and make a name for

themselves? _____

Today's Treasure

"REMEMBER THE FORMER THINGS, THOSE OF LONG AGO; I AM GOD, AND THERE IS NO OTHER; I AM GOD, AND THERE IS NONE LIKE ME. I MAKE KNOWN THE END FROM THE BEGINNING, FROM ANCIENT TIMES, WHAT IS STILL TO COME. I SAY: MY PURPOSE WILL STAND, AND I WILL DO ALL THAT I PLEASE. FROM THE EAST I SUMMON A BIRD OF PREY; FROM A FAR-OFF LAND, A MAN TO FULFILL MY PURPOSE. WHAT I HAVE SAID, THAT WILL I BRING ABOUT; WHAT I HAVE PLANNED, THAT WILL I DO."

Isaiah 46:9-11

Did you see how the tower stood in direct opposition to God's command in 9:7? Then behold the result: "The LORD came down" (Gen. 11:5). Try to digest those four profound words. The Hebrew word for *came down* is *yarad*, meaning to descend abundantly. This verse does not dispute God's attribute of omnipresence, (see Ps. 139). But God's presence everywhere does not mean His fullness of presence. The Lord descended on Shinar in His power and glory, and He was not happy.

Read Genesis 11:6-9. How did God respond to what He saw?

_____

The word translated _impossible_ in verse 6 is _batsar_, which means _isolated_ or _inaccessible._ It does not mean humans would be all powerful. It means, "If they try this, they will try anything!" This would not be an isolated incident.

In Genesis 11:7 exactly who "went down"? _____

Glance back at Genesis 1:26-27. Verse 26 describes the Creator as "Us," and verse 27 expounds that the "Us" is God. In fact, from the first mention of God's name in Genesis 1:1, "In the beginning God," we see evidence of the Trinity. The Hebrew word for _God_ in this reference and in most Old Testament uses of the term is _Elohim_, a plural proper noun. Though some scholars insist the plural is only a way of showing the majesty of God, it certainly hints at more. The same blessed Trinity dramatically and individually involved in creation dramatically and corporately revisited planet Earth in Genesis 11:7!

What action did the Lord take against the people?
❑ He rebuked them verbally.   ❑ He crumbled the tower.
❑ He confused their language and scattered them over the earth.

Now consider these events together. Review God's command, the people's reaction, and God's response.

In Genesis 9:1 God told them to _____

In Genesis 11:4 the people built a tower and a city to make a name for themselves so that they would not ...

_____

In Genesis 11:8 the Lord _____

What does Isaiah 46:9-11, Today's Treasure, say about God's will?
❑ It will be accomplished.   ❑ It is subject to change.
❑ It depends on the people's cooperation.

How often it occurs to me, as it must to you, that it is far easier simply to cooperate with God! We can be either a part of His program or a part of the problem.

One way or another, God will perform His will. He may change the process or the person, but He will not change the plan. We are blessed immeasurably, however, when we learn to agree with God and to participate in His plan.

The occurrences at the tower of Babel resulted in nations, races, and languages—in a word, division. Therefore, at this point in history God began to set apart one people through whom to bring forth the Messiah.

According to Revelation 13:8, Christ is the "Lamb slain from the foundation of the world" (KJV). God's breathing a soul into Adam signed His precious Son's death certificate. The moment the decision was made to create humankind, Christ was, in simple terms, as good as dead. We had to have a Redeemer. Although God grieved over people's sin, He was not surprised. The plan was intact prior to the people, and no one could thwart that plan!

Recall Genesis 9:18-19. Because of God's faithfulness to His covenant, He has never judged the whole earth again as He did in the flood, no matter how wicked and perverse people have been; therefore, all the earth's population has descended from either _____, Ham, or Japheth.

Glance over Genesis 11:10-32 and let your eyes rest on a vital introduction in the midst of all these "begats." List every piece of information about Abram offered in this passage.

♥ Have you truly accepted that Christ died not only for you but also instead of you? ❑ yes ❑ no If so, explain what that means to you.

_____

_____

_____

At the top of your list did you note that Abram was a descendent of Shem, one of Noah's three sons? Not coincidentally, the Hebrew word *shem* means *name.* You see, God desired to set apart a people devoted to His name, not their own: "If my people, who are called by my name" (2 Chron. 7:14).

Hang in here with me for one last reading assignment for today! It's critical that you see these events in reference to one another as we bridge the garden to the tabernacle. Read Genesis 12:1-9, the call of Abram, carefully and with reverence. The single most important nation in all of history discovers its deepest roots in this passage. What a turning point in history! Every nation of the world will be affected by Abram's descendants.

In conclusion let me ask one question based on Genesis 12:1—Have you noticed that God often requires us to leave our comfort zones to answer our calling? That through which God hones us is rarely within the parameters of the familiar. You may be thinking: Thank goodness I'm not important enough to be called by God. I don't like new territories and unfamiliar assignments. Think again, my beloved friend! According to Romans 8:30, if you consider yourself a

Christian, consider yourself called. No amount of comfort is worth missing the greatest adventure humankind can experience. "Pay attention to the ministry you have received in the Lord, so that you can accomplish it" (Col. 4:17, HCSB).

The Original Love Story

"TAKE YOUR SON, YOUR ONLY SON, ISAAC, WHOM YOU LOVE, AND GO TO THE REGION OF MORIAH. SACRIFICE HIM THERE AS A BURNT OFFERING ON ONE OF THE MOUNTAINS I WILL TELL YOU ABOUT."

Genesis 22:2

Read Today's Treasure and ask God to speak to you through His Word.

We are building a bridge composed of Scripture connecting the garden and the tabernacle. We concluded our previous lesson with the call of Abram and the promises God made him in Genesis 12:1-9. Our bridge is roughly two-thirds complete. Glance back over days 1-3 and label on the bridge below the significant events we've studied in Scripture between the garden and Genesis 12:1-9. We will fill in the remaining events at the conclusion of day 5.

Call of Abram

The Garden of Eden   The Tabernacle

Today we will look more in-depth at the call of Abram and the road it entailed. Fill in the columns according to Genesis 12:1-3.

God's Instructions   God's Promises

_____   _____

_____   _____

_____   _____

_____   _____

_____   _____

_____   _____

Want to see something exciting? Get a load of Galatians 3:8! "The Scripture, foreseeing that God would justify the Gentiles by faith, preached the gospel beforehand to Abraham, saying, 'ALL THE NATIONS WILL BE BLESSED IN YOU'" (NASB).

What did God preach to Abraham? _____

Galatians 3:8 is the only reference in all Scripture that uses the exact Greek word *proeuaggelizomai.* The first three letters mean *beforehand.* The remainder of the word means to preach the gospel or the good news, hence to proclaim the gospel before-hand. Can you imagine? God was the preacher, Abram was the congregation, and the message was a prophecy of something that had not yet happened.

What was the gospel? It was the good news of God's blessing on mankind. Tighten your spiritual seat belt and take a look at this next word study. The Hebrew word for *bless* in Genesis 12 is *barakh,* meaning "to bend the knee, kneel down; to bless." Though the Hebrew root is only translated "to kneel" three times, consider the connection. "There was a close association felt between kneeling and receiving a blessing."[2] Whether or not the association is always intended when the word *bless* is used, the final fulfillment of God's promises to Abram will undoubt-edly be received by his spiritual descendants on their knees!

Philippians 2:8-11 says that after Christ humbled Himself and gave His life on the cross, God "highly exalted Him and gave Him the name that is above every name, so that at the name of Jesus every knee should bow—of those who are in heaven and on earth and under the earth—and every tongue should confess that Jesus Christ is Lord, to the glory of God the Father" (HCSB).

What action does Philippians say everyone will take?

_____

Just the mention of His name is all it will take! Ultimately the gospel God shared with Abram's descendants was the message of His own Son, God's supreme bless-ing to humanity, a message that will finally bring every living being to our knees!

God's promise to Abram was emphatic: "I will." Let's consider those two words, keeping in mind a very important rule of thumb: anything God does, Satan attempts to counterfeit. Isaiah 14:12-14 offers audacious statements that can ultimately be ascribed to Satan alone.

In the following passage, circle every time the Enemy said, "I will."

"I will ascend to the heavens; I will set up my throne above the stars of God. I will sit on the mount of the gods' assembly ... I will ascend above the highest clouds." The final statement voices the ultimate blasphemy: "I will make myself like the Most High" (Isa. 14:12-14, HCSB).

Beloved, what you have before you is Satan's own unholy "gospel." Being the anointed cherub was not enough for Lucifer (Ezek. 28); he wanted to be God. The temptation in the garden makes more sense now, doesn't it? Isn't it interest-ing that our every sin finds its roots in the words of the original author of sin?

Whether or not we realize it, all sin is born of those same words, "I will," while obedience is found in the opposite words, "Thy will." God willed from the very beginning to bless His people. Satan's "gospel" is to thwart God's blessing by tempting us to seek and demand our own will.

We will spend the remainder of today's lesson on the covenant God cut with Abram, sealing the promise He gave in Genesis 12.

Read Genesis 15, a chapter with paramount importance as we build our bridge.

Fill in the blanks from Genesis 15:18 "On that day the LORD

_____ a _____ with Abram."

The men who have violated my

covenant and have not fulfilled

the terms of the

covenant they made before

me, I will treat like the calf

they cut in two and then

walked between its pieces.

Jeremiah 34:18

The Hebrew word for *covenant* is *beriyth,* a compact, treaty, or alliance made by passing through pieces of flesh or the divided parts of a victim. The word translated *made* in verse 18 is *karath,* meaning *to cut.* God literally passed through the pieces of the sacrifices to seal His covenant with Abram and his descendants.

How does verse 17 portray God's presence?
❏ **as a blinding light**   ❏ **as a smoking fire pot**
❏ **as a pillar of fire by day and cloud by night**

Jeremiah 34:18 described the primary idea behind the passing through the pieces. Violators of such a covenant are like the animals cut in half. In other words, when they "cut" the covenant, they guaranteed it with their lives. Thus, when God Himself acted out the ritual, He guaranteed it with His life.

What was Abram doing while God cut the covenant?

_____

What does Abram's lack of participation imply to you?

_____

This was God's covenant; its ultimate end was unconditional. The faithfulness of God's promise had nothing to do with Abram and everything to do with God.

Let's examine the stunning portrait of the gospel that God painted for Abram many years later. Bear with me, Dear One! I need to ask you to read one more segment today that is crucial to our background information.

Write a sentence describing the contents of Genesis 22:

_____

Throughout God's Word He progressively sheds light on the gospel revealed to Abram. The test God gave Abram in Genesis 22 is the Old Testament's most vivid portrayal of the avenue to blessing.

Note several important words and phrases in this chapter. God called Abram by the new name He had given him (Gen. 17:5), Abraham, and said, "Take your son … your only son Isaac, whom you love, go to the land of Moriah, and offer him there" (v. 2, HCSB). God determined that the first use of the Hebrew word *ahab*—meaning "to love, desire, delight"—would appear in this very context in Scripture.[3] God chose this exact moment in all of history to introduce delighting love. Far from coincidentally, the word is used first to describe the immense feelings a father has for his son—his only son.

I love Abraham's response when Isaac asked, "Where is the lamb for the burnt offering?" He answered, "God will provide *himself* a lamb" (Gen. 22:8, KJV; emphasis added). And indeed He did: "Behold the Lamb of God, which taketh away the sin of the world" (John 1:29, KJV). "God so loved the world" that He offered in sacrifice His one and only Son, whom He loves (see John 3:16)!

God was faithful to Abraham as he passed this humanly incomparable test: "Abraham looked up and there in a thicket he saw a ram caught by its horns. He went over and took the ram and sacrificed it as a burnt offering instead of his son. So Abraham called that place The LORD Will Provide" (Gen. 22:13-14).

Notice that Abraham "looked up" into the thicket. Ordinarily, the bushes in the region of Mount Moriah were comparatively small, not the height to which a man would have to look up. Could it be that the reason Abraham looked up into a small bush was because he had fallen on his face before God? Furthermore, a thicket in the Middle Eastern terrain was ordinarily a thornbush. Remember, according to Genesis 3:17-18, thorns were evidence of sin's curse on the earth.

How was the sacrifice held in the thicket (Gen 22:13)?

_____

Luke 1:68-69 says, "Praise the Lord, the God of Israel, because He has visited and provided redemption for His people. He has raised up a horn of salvation for us in the house of His servant David" (HCSB). Blessed be the horn of our salvation! Jesus Christ was the Ram whose head was wrapped in thorns to secure God's blessing for all who would receive it.

The very heart of the gospel is realizing that God did not simply provide a sacrifice *for* us but *instead of* us. That is the good news. There is only one way to receive it after we have understood it—with profound humility and gratitude. Maybe even on our knees.

♥ **Think of a time you cooperated with God by denying your will and following His leadership. How were you blessed through this experience?**

Day 5
On the Move

"They put slave masters over them to oppress them with forced labor ... But the more they were oppressed, the more they multiplied and spread."

Exodus 1:11-12

Begin your study by reading Today's Treasure and praying that God will speak to you through His Word.

You've made it, Dear One! You persevered through lengthy readings and made it all the way to the final day of our foundational week. One more day of heavy-duty reading, then we'll catch up with the children of Israel in the wilderness. Let's look at it this way. Our heads are always full of something. They may as well be full of Scripture. How I pray our minds are being renewed day by day and things such as bitterness and anger aren't finding enough room to make themselves at home.

Today we finish our bridge connecting the garden to the command to build the tabernacle. I'm so glad to have you along. Let's get started.

In day 4 God's Word invited us to examine Abraham's faithfulness under great testing. Today we begin our study by considering a New Testament commentary on an Old Testament relationship. Romans 4:20-22 says, "[Abraham] did not waver in unbelief at God's promise, but was strengthened in his faith and gave glory to God, because he was fully convinced that what He had promised He was also able to perform. Therefore, 'it was credited to him for righteousness'" (HCSB).

Has someone ever made a big promise to you that wasn't kept? Have you ever made a promise that you didn't keep? I have. The problem usually is not so much the oath giver's lack of desire to keep the promise as a lack of power to do so.

The first six weeks Michael lived with us, I had to snuggle next to him every night so he could sleep. He had often said to me, "I always wanted a mommy just like you." I knew he really meant he had always wanted a mommy like anyone!

I was so inexperienced in the areas of his needs that I felt I was certainly no prize. Every night he would hold my head in an arm lock and repeat the words "Don't leave me, Mommy. Never, never leave me." He would finally fall asleep, the last sentence incomplete. I would whisper softly: "I won't, Darling. Not ever, ever, ever," often with tears streaming down my cheeks.

I had never known a child with such a deep need. And I was the center of that need. The sense of responsibility was overwhelming to me. As I would walk down the stairs utterly drained, Michael's words would ring over and over in my mind, and I would pray to be able to keep my promise to him. I am still haunted by my inability to do so.

I am reminded of another mommy I knew well. During her battle with cancer her children continually asked her, "Mommy, you won't die, will you?" Desperately hoping, she would respond: "Mommy is going to get well. You'll see." At her funeral those precious daughters filed in behind their daddy, one much too young to realize who was in that casket. I sobbed, thinking, "We want to promise our children so much; yet we can truly guarantee so little."

Can you think of a promise you really wanted to keep—meant to keep—but were unable to? Now, what specific promise has God made to you that He tenderly and faithfully kept?

_____

_____

Maybe, like me, you could use a little healing. Maybe, like me, you need to hear God say, "I alone am God, my Child. I am the only One with the power to keep every promise. As they seek Me, I will enable others to forgive you for not being Me."

Thank God, He differs from us! He who promised is also able to perform 100 percent of the time! His every promise is attached to a certified guarantee. Romans 4:20-22 gives us a fresh outlook on Abraham's testimony. Abraham's faithfulness was "credited to him as righteousness" because he had the faith to believe in God's faithfulness! Abraham was freed to be faithful to God on the basis of his belief that God would always be faithful to him. And faithful He was.

To lay further groundwork for our study of the tabernacle, let's briefly build the part of the bridge connecting Abraham's son, Isaac, and Moses. Stay with me here: Isaac's son, Jacob, whom God renamed Israel, had 12 sons, for whom the 12 tribes of Israel were named and from whom all Hebrew people descended. Israel favored his son, Joseph, over the others, resulting in toxic jealousy among Joseph's brothers. They sold him to a caravan and told his father Joseph had been killed by a ferocious animal. By God's design Joseph arrived in Egypt, where, after being falsely accused of a crime, he spent a lengthy time in prison. By interpreting dreams, Joseph found favor with Pharaoh and eventually rose to be his right-hand man, placed over "the whole land of Egypt" (Gen. 41:41).

When severe famine swept the land, Jacob's sons were forced to beg for food from the Egyptian king. Through a dramatic series of events they discovered their brother held authority over all the land of Egypt. In a climactic moment the tables turned, and Joseph held his brothers' lives in his hands. In their humiliation and sorrow Joseph comforted them with the words that still offer solace to many: "Ye thought evil against me; but God meant it unto good" (Gen. 50:20, KJV). Genesis 46:1-7 records that all the nation of Israel moved to Egypt, where God fed and sustained them through the hand of His servant Joseph.

Got that? You make me smile. Well, the overview will be there waiting in case you need to read it again. My mind is a little blown because I'm revising this Bible study not long after writing _The Patriarchs_. Honestly, I can't believe it took me 18 months and 10 chapters to write what I just spit out to you in two paragraphs!

Let's get to the heart of today's lesson as the children of Israel draw toward the moment when God gave Moses instructions for building a divine sanctuary. Yep, you guessed it. Another lengthy reading assignment. Take heart, we're constructing the final pieces in our bridge between the garden and the tabernacle!

I need you to read Exodus 1–3, but at least they're not long chapters! Then, if we are still speaking, answer the following questions.

Why did the Israelites become slaves?
❏ They wanted their own king.　❏ They warred against Egypt.
❏ They were mightier and more in number.

What impact did oppression have on the Israelites?
❏ They multiplied and grew.　❏ They neared extinction.

From which house of Israel did Moses descend?
❏ Judah　❏ Levi　❏ Gad　❏ Joseph

What caused Moses to flee to Midian?
❏ Pharaoh wanted to kill him.　❏ He had killed a man.
❏ He was seeking a wife.

Name every supernatural sight Moses beheld in Exodus 3:2.

_____

By what name did God tell Moses to call Him to the Israelites?
❏ the God of their fathers　❏ the only true God　❏ I AM

I love *Word Biblical Commentary's* explanation of the verbs in the name "I Am that I Am." "The verbs are first person … connoting continuing, unfinished action: 'I am being that I am being,' or 'I am the Is-ing One.'"[4] Take this truth in: whatever your circumstances, your challenges, your doubts, or your pain, if you are in covenant relationship with God through His Son, Jesus Christ, the King of the universe is your Is-ing One and He's presently is-ing in every area of your life.

The chapters that follow are some of the most well known in Scripture. God's words through Moses resound from my earliest Sunday School memories: "Let my people go!" Through 10 plagues, from the river of blood to the harrowing death of the firstborn, Pharaoh relented, and the exodus began. The people of Israel then began their 40-year sojourn through the wilderness to the promised land.

Let's join the Hebrews now as they begin their long journey home. As we catch up with Moses, we find him summoned by God to the top of a mountain and filled with the glory of His presence.

Read Exodus 24. (I saw that look!) God gave instruction about His presence to the following three groups of people (see Ex. 24:1-3). Label the position of each one.

The masses: _____

Aaron, Nadab, Abihu, and the 70 elders: _____

Moses: _____

Do you realize the price humanity paid for a taste of forbidden fruit? God created us to enjoy His fellowship. He walked in our first parents' midst, spoke aloud to them, communed with them, and came down to dwell among them. But as a result of disobedience the masses would not experience the glory of God's presence. Only a few would ascend this holy mountain and truly approach His Holiness.

We will not fully realize sin's cost sin until we finally sit at His feet and know the inexpressible joy of His presence. How can we know what we have lost until we have regained it? Worse than any curse, we lost the right of immediate access to the inner sanctum of God's glory. Yes, there would have to be a ministry of reconciliation.

As we conclude week I, may the magnitude of God's words to Moses burn in your spirit and to result in gratitude: "Have them make a sanctuary for me, and I will dwell among them" (Ex. 25:8). What music these words must have been to the Hebrews' ears! "Amazing grace! How sweet the sound"!

Gathering background information is often tedious. You have done a wonderful job this week.

Number in order these events from this foundational unit.
_____ God revealed His presence through a burning bush.
_____ God provided a substitute for the life of Isaac.
_____ God fellowshipped with Adam and Eve in the garden.
_____ God commanded Noah to build an ark.
_____ God scattered the people over the earth.
_____ God cast Adam and Eve out of the garden.
_____ God gave Abram the gospel.
_____ God told the Israelites to make a sanctuary so that He could
        dwell among them.

As your final exercise, return to the bridge diagram on day 4 and label remaining significant events we've studied together between the call of Abram and the command for the tabernacle.

A+, Dear One! I am so proud of you! After all that, you can't quit now. May God bless you immeasurably for your time in His Word. I'll see you in session I!

I. Spiros Zodhiates, ed. *The Complete Word Study New Testament: King James Version* (Iowa Falls, IA: World Bible Publishers, 1991), 920.

2. Warren Baker, ed. *The Complete Word Study Old Testament: King James Version* (Chattanooga, TN: AMG Publishers, 1994), 2307.

3. Ibid., 2298.

4. John I. Durham, *Word Biblical Commentary*, vol. 3, *Exodus* (Waco, TX: Word Books, 1987), 39.

Viewer Guide

Session 1

Broken Hearts,
Broken Ties

Today we conclude our scriptural overview of events leading up to God's command in Exodus 25:8-9.

God's Heavenly Dwelling

↓

The Garden of Eden ⟶ The Tabernacle

Ties Between God's Heavenly Dwelling, the Garden, and the Tabernacle

1. Compare the settings in Revelation 22:1-2 and Genesis 2:8-10.

a. _____ b. _____ c. _____

2. The consistency of God.

- God told Moses to tell Pharaoh: "Get thee unto Pharaoh in the morning ... And thou shalt say to him, The LORD God of the Hebrews hath sent me unto thee, saying, Let my people go, that they may _____ me in the _____" (Ex. 7:15-16, KJV; recall Gen. 3:18).

- Compare Genesis 3:8 with Leviticus 26:11-12 and Deuteronomy 23:14. According to Dr. G.K. Beale, "The same Hebrew verbal form (stem) *mithallek (hithpael)* used for God's _____ _____ and _____ in the Garden (Gen. 3:8), also describes God's _____ in the _____."[1]

- Man's primary commission was to _____ and take _____ of his garden home (Gen. 2:15). Compare Numbers 3:7-8. "Both terms occur together to describe the charge of the Levites for the tabernacle (Num. 3:7-8; 18:7), thus again suggesting a relationship between _____ and _____."[2] Connect the wording back to Exodus 7:16.

- See the play on words in Genesis 2:24-25 and 3:1. "The term '_____' (pl. *arummim*) is a play on the word '_____' (*arum*), which describes the nature of the serpent."[3]

3. God's determination to connect earth with heaven.

   According to G.K. Beale, the three parts of Israel's temple represented the three parts of the cosmos: the outer court: _____ _____; the holy place: _____ _____; the Holy of Holies: _____ _____ _____.[4]

---

1. Dr. G. K Beale, *The Temple and the Church's Mission: A Biblical Theology of the Dwelling Place of God* (Downer's Grove, IL: InterVarsity Press, 2004), 66.
2. Kenneth A. Matthews, *The New American Commentary: Genesis 1–11:26* (Nashville: Broadman and Holman, 1996), 210.
3. Ibid., 225.
4. Beale, 54.

New Starts and Barren Hearts

DAY 1 • A GLIMPSE OF THE WILDERNESS

DAY 2 • THE BITTERSWEETNESS OF MARAH

DAY 3 • THE TROUBLE WITH OLD APPETITES

DAY 4 • GLORIOUS MORNING

DAY 5 • CLOTHES THAT LAST

WEEK 2

Week I concluded with God's formal invitation for His people to meet Him as the great I AM, the self-existent, sovereign Ruler of all creation. Consistent with His tender heart, God introduced Himself to His people not only as the universal Ruler but also as the personal Provider. Week 2 is dedicated to the study of this concept: God seeks to set His people free from their dependence on themselves so that they depend instead on Him. Throughout this week we will discover that God's supernatural provision for humanity is most recognizable when we find ourselves in a wilderness devoid of self-sufficiency. We will seek answers to the following questions.

Principal Questions

I. How would you describe the physical surroundings of the wilderness?

2. How did God make the bitter water sweet?

3. What did the Israelites long for in the desert?

4. What lesson did the manna demonstrate?

5. How is Christ clothed in Revelation 19:13?

Week 2 will show us that God heard the cries of His children and faithfully met their needs. Our own insufficiencies are only invitations to experience the supernatural sufficiency of a universally powerful, personally responsible God!

Day 1

A Glimpse of the Wilderness

Read Today's Treasure and pray that God will speak to you through His Word.

Before God ever graced the tabernacle with a glimpse of His glory, He manifested Himself to the Hebrew people as Jehovah-Jireh, the Lord their Provider.[1] Before the incarnation of Christ, the generation that sojourned through the wilderness from the exodus to the promised land saw the unmistakable evidence of God as no other people did in all of history.

God Himself attests to this fact in Deuteronomy 4:32-40. Read these verses and complete the following.

Name the many different ways that God uniquely revealed Himself to Israel in the exodus and the wilderness. Be specific.

_____   _____

_____   _____

_____   _____

_____   _____

_____   _____

Why did God reveal Himself by such custom design (v. 35)?

_____

Why did God bless and bring this generation out of Egypt (v. 37)?

_____

Who will reap effects of Israel's obedience or disobedience (v. 40)?

_____

Today's Treasure

"THE LORD WILL FIGHT FOR YOU; YOU NEED ONLY TO BE STILL."

Exodus 14:14

♥ **Have you ever thought of the impact of your faith on your children's future? What difference can this realization make in your daily walk with God and in your parenting?**

What a staggering responsibility the people held for their descendants! The same is true today. Our faithfulness, or lack of it, will have an overwhelming impact on the heritage of our children. If your children's future depends on your obedience to God, how secure do you feel about their future? Surely, "because of the LORD's great love we are not consumed, for his compassions never fail" (Lam. 3:22). Just when we feel that God's righteousness and judgment will consume us, He rushes in as the "Father of compassion and the God of all comfort" (2 Cor. 1:3).

Throughout our study we will see God as the perfect, sovereign Lawgiver, as unapproachable Holiness, as El Elyon, the Most High; but we would be tragically amiss not to arrive at an altogether new appreciation of God as Caregiver. He is El Shaddai, who offers His people His complete sufficiency. You see, that is exactly what the tabernacle is all about—God's provision for His children. We will dedicate this week to studying God's manifestation of Himself to the children of Israel through His unceasing intervention. We will study God's special provisions in the order He revealed them.

To identify with the Hebrew wanderers who experienced God's provision and presence, we must study their habitat and their standard of living through these 40 years. Let's begin by allowing Scripture help us picture the wilderness in which the Israelites dwelled.

El Elyon
The Most High God

El Shaddai
The Caregiver

🔥 **Read Deuteronomy 8:15; Psalm 107:4-5; and Jeremiah 2:6. Check the terms below that best describe the wilderness.**
❑ solitary ❑ vast ❑ lakes ❑ desert ❑ hilly ❑ snakes
❑ scorpions ❑ populated ❑ dry ❑ birds ❑ rocky ❑ cool

The Hebrew word for *wilderness* is *midbar*, meaning *desert*. These Middle Eastern deserts were usually not characterized by sand dunes; rather, the Israelites sojourned through rocky, dry wastelands. Their eyes opened every morning to the inside of a tent or to the expanse of the sky. Either view provided a stark, daily reminder that they were a people without a home.

How often our God seizes a backdrop of darkness to accentuate the light of His presence! Look at the first of several major provisions through which God revealed Himself to His holy nation in the wilderness.

Exodus 13:17–14:31 tells the dramatic story of God's delivering His Hebrew children from slavery in Egypt, guiding them all the way.

Jehovah-Shamma
The Lord is present

How did God manifest His presence to the Israelites (vv. 17-21)?

Day: _____   Night: _____

God's presence was manifested both as a pillar of a cloud by day and a pillar of fire by night. God met the anxious travelers' deepest need in exceeding abundance: they needed to know that He was Jehovah-Shamma, meaning the Lord is present. Our ever-creative God revealed His accompaniment through awesome, multipurpose pillars.

What do the following Scriptures reveal about clouds?

Psalm 104:3 _____

Isaiah 19:1 _____

Nahum 1:3 _____

Luke 21:27 _____

Acts 1:9 _____

I Thessalonians 4:17 _____

Read Exodus 14:19-20.

Jehovah-Jireh provided the pillar of a cloud not only to direct the people but also to protect them. Revel in a God whose business is to come between you and your enemies! Remember when His presence struck Saul of Tarsus to the ground? "'Saul, Saul, why do you persecute me?' 'Who are you, Lord?' Saul asked. 'I am Jesus, whom you are persecuting,' he replied" (Acts 9:4-5).

Because Saul was persecuting followers of Christ, God intervened dramatically. Similarly, as you have seen, God took the Egyptian persecution of His chosen nation quite personally. Therefore, He became personally involved.

What did Moses tell the Israelites as the Egyptian army began to pursue them in Exodus 14:13-14? Check any answers that apply.
- ❏ "Do not be afraid."
- ❏ "The Lord will fight for you."
- ❏ "Stand firm."
- ❏ "Sanctify yourselves."
- ❏ "You need only to be still."
- ❏ "See the Lord's salvation."

Moses told them to "stand still, and see the salvation of the LORD" (v. 13, KJV).

According to Psalm 46:10, what is the purpose of being still?

_____

Psalm 139:1-6 demonstrates exactly the same provision of God described in the wilderness. Verse 5 says, "You hem me in—behind and before; you have laid your hand upon me." He goes before us, follows behind us, and hems us safely inside the realm of His protection. What a precious glimpse at the tender heart of the Father, who went beyond His children's need for direction and protection to fill their emotional need for a perpetual light in the dark of night. The pillar of a cloud was replaced by a pillar of fire at sundown as the loving Parent tucked His children into bed by the glow of a divine night-light.

Jehovah-Jireh
Jehovah will provide

33

Isn't it after the lights go out that the cares of this world seem most overwhelming? Have you ever found it far easier to be strong and full of faith in the clamor of the day than in the quiet of the night? Doesn't the Enemy seem closer? We are soberly aware of how much Satan likes the dark! Remember this foundational truth throughout our study of the Israelites in the wilderness: everything God did with Israel in the realm of the seen, He does with us in the realm of the unseen. God has not ceased actively parenting His children. The same God who made His presence known to the Israelites in their wilderness is just as fully Jehovah-Shamma, "the Lord is present," in ours.

Conclude by writing God's promises that He applies to you.

Psalm 4:8 _____

_____

Hebrews 13:5 _____

_____

How fitting that the same Light that gave security and clarity to the Hebrew people shed calamity and confusion on their enemy. Our God reserves the right to reveal Himself majestically and victoriously only to those who have allowed Him to remove the veil from their eyes. Those who refuse to see are hopelessly blinded to God's awesome and apparent activity.

What enemy are you battling today? First, invite God to come between you and your enemy. Second, invite Him to open "the eyes of your heart" so that you will recognize Him at work (Eph. 1:18). Third, count on Jesus; He never fails.

Day 2
The Bittersweetness of Marah

Today's Treasure

"THEN THEY CAME TO ELIM, WHERE THERE WERE TWELVE SPRINGS AND SEVENTY PALM TREES, AND THEY CAMPED THERE NEAR THE WATER."

Exodus 15:27

Begin your study by reading Today's Treasure and praying that God will speak to you through His Word.

I am simply not a camper. This confession humiliates me because I am convinced it is the one characteristic separating Mother of Excellence from Mediocre Mama. I am certain my deficiency is a sign of weak parenting, because I have attended Girl Scout camp planning meetings when troop captains have asked for volunteer moms. They expressed it like this: "Now you know we can't all go, as much as we'd like to [my eyes start involuntarily shifting back and forth, and my palms grow sweaty], so let's see the hands of all those who would really like to go." I have come to the conclusion that the choice is made on the basis of which mom can wave her hand the wildest and make guttural sounds like a kindergartner wanting to be first for show-and-tell. I have even heard rumors that some moms call the captain in advance and ask to be selected. Not me. I like to do my bonding in the air-conditioning near the microwave. Undoubtedly, camping seems to bring out our worst—especially when we don't get to pick the campsite.

We are studying the living conditions of the Israelites in the wilderness and God's provision for them. On day 1 we studied the pillar of a cloud by day and the pillar of fire by night, which God provided to direct and protect His people. When we concluded our previous lesson, the Israelites had crossed the Red Sea on dry ground, had been guided by a mysterious cloud by day, had been secured by the light of fire at night, and had witnessed a fatal tidal wave engulfing their enemy—a mere day in the life of God's treasured possession!

How did the people respond to God's mighty works (Ex. 14:31)?
❏ **They feared the Lord.**   ❏ **They believed Moses.**
❏ **They believed the Lord.**

In Exodus 15:1-21 we read the words of the song Moses and the Israelites sang. Imagine how they felt. They had been in bondage for four hundred years. Now they were free! God in His awesome power had delivered them. The Israelites basked in the favor of Almighty God. Having witnessed unmistakable evidence of His presence, they had no recourse but praise!

Read Exodus 15:22-27 and check the correct responses.

At what exact location are the Israelites in the wilderness?
❏ **Desert of Shur**   ❏ **Red Sea**   ❏ **Sinai**

How long did they go without water?
❏ **seven days**   ❏ **six days**   ❏ **three days**

Where did they finally discover water?
❏ **Marah**   ❏ **Moriah**   ❏ **Rephidim**

Few of us have ever experienced the kind of thirst the Israelites suffered. Finally, they found water—sparkling, inviting, but horribly undrinkable.

What was wrong with the water? _____

God often meets our needs in unique and unexpected ways. How did He make the bitter water sweet?

_____

♥ **Has God ever led you to taste your own bitterness? If so, what was the occasion, and how have you allowed Him to sweeten your bitter water?**

Remember that God's visible presence in the form of pillars led the Israelites straight to the place of overwhelming thirst only to discover bitter water. The people did not happen there by chance. In Exodus 15:25 God prescribed that a tree be cast into the bitter water to make it sweet. Why a tree?

Read and record what I Peter 2:24 says about a tree.

_____

On a tree at Calvary were cast the bitter waters of all time. Through the death of the One who bore them, the waters were made sweet. Only when we invite the One who hung on that tree to be plunged into our hearts can we begin to know the refreshment of sweet water.

In the New Testament, the Greek word for *baptize* referred to dipping something in dye to change its color. The tree in Exodus 15:25 was baptized by the bitter water, soaking up the bitterness and leaving the water sweet. Likewise, our Savior instantly purified the bitter waters by His perfect sacrifice on a tree when all of humanity's sins were heaped on Him (see 2 Cor. 5:21). He cleansed from the bitterness of sin everyone who would come to the Living Water and drink. Now all who come to Him are baptized into the Living Water by the Holy Spirit. Our spirits are dyed the same color as Christ's—as white as snow.

Notice a crucial factor in these passages: the tree had to be cut down in order to be plunged into the waters, just as Jesus "was cut off out of the land of the living; for the transgression of my people was he stricken" (Isa. 53:8).

Then, on the banks of Marah, God immediately delivered a decree that at first glance seems to have little to do with the miracle He had performed.

In Exodus 15:26 what did God say He would do if His people listened to Him carefully and obeyed? Check the correct answer.
- ❏ "I will lead you always."
- ❏ "I will fight for you."
- ❏ "I will put none of the diseases on you …"
- ❏ "I will show you my glory."

Jehovah-Rapha
God who Heals

If you have never truly, personally, and intimately been introduced to Jehovah-Rapha, allow me to present to you the Lord, your Healer. It is not by accident that God sovereignly chose to introduce Himself as Jehovah-Rapha through the bitter water of Marah. Just think of all the settings He could have used to express Himself as Healer. The people could have come down with diseases, and He could have performed a mass healing. Instead, He introduced Himself as Jehovah-Rapha by demonstrating His power over the most common disease from which His children would suffer—bitterness.

Bitterness is spiritual cancer, a rapidly-growing malignancy that can consume your life. After it consumes the soul, it begins to eat away at the body. It is so contagious that we can pass it to our children, who are often oblivious to the source of their bitterness. No amount of distractions or busywork—not even church work—can treat this spiritual disease. Countless Christians mask their pain with unceasing activity. Bitterness cannot be ignored but must be healed at the very core, and only Christ can heal bitterness. No one can do it for you, and no one can tell you exactly what is required for your healing. Others can direct you to Jesus, but you must show up for your appointments. His ultimate goal is not simply for you to be healed but for you to meet the Healer.

Upon departing from the place of bitter water made sweet, the Israelites came to an entirely different campsite.

According to Exodus 15:27, the Israelites discovered 12

_____ **and 70** _____.

After your Marah comes your Elim—the place of abundance and overflowing refreshment! Whatever you must experience to know His healing is worth it. Elim is also the place of readiness and usefulness. Because numbers in the Bible are often very significant, notice that Elim had 12 springs and 70 palm trees. God specifies these two numbers again jointly only in the Gospels.

Read Luke 9:1; 10:1.

Those 12 went out to represent Christ, His church, and the offer of His healing. From them came 70 laborers ready for the harvest. You will never maximize your gifts and God-given talents until you have camped by the healing springs.

Why wait any longer? We are here for such a brief time. In order to heal, you may need to start by forgiving. Yet you may fear as I did, "If I forgive, that will make it all right, and it's not all right." Let God whisper into your ear what He whispered to me: "No, My child; forgiving will make you all right."

Conclude by finding these Scriptures which will enrich what you have studied today. Then answer the questions that follow.

Read Isaiah 55:1-3,6. What is God's prescription for thirst?

_____

In Psalm 63:1, what did the psalmist do because of his thirsting and longing?

_____

Read Psalm 147:3. What does God do for "the brokenhearted"?

_____

No matter how we resist the process, healing is a cooperative effort. Often, believers let their Healer extract a portion of their spiritual malignancies, then force Him to cease because of their lack of cooperation. Will you allow Him to finish the good work He began in you? Are you ready to trust your life to your Healer? Peace awaits you on the other side of your Marah. Let Him take you there.

Day 3
The Trouble with Old Appetites

Today's Treasure

"THEN THE LORD SAID TO MOSES, 'I WILL RAIN DOWN BREAD FROM HEAVEN FOR YOU. THE PEOPLE ARE TO GO OUT EACH DAY AND GATHER ENOUGH FOR THAT DAY. IN THIS WAY I WILL TEST THEM AND SEE WHETHER THEY WILL FOLLOW MY INSTRUCTIONS.'"

Exodus 16:4

Begin your study by reading Today's Treasure and praying that God will speak to you through His Word. Today we will study the heart of God's supernatural provision for His holy nation in the wilderness.

Exodus 16 continues the fabulous story of God's extraordinary provision. Remember, the children of Israel were moving through a huge wilderness. Different segments of the wilderness are called by different names. So far we have studied the Hebrews' experiences in Shur, Marah, and Elim.

Read Exodus 16:1-4 and answer the following questions.

What is the name of this segment of wilderness? _____

How many grumbled against Moses? _____

What did they say? _____

What was God's solution? _____

What was God's specific instruction? _____

What was God going to do through this provision? _____

_____

Often, our character is at greater risk in prosperity than in adversity.

The Hebrew word translated *test* is *nacah,* which means *to try or prove.* Do you realize that not all of God's tests are hardships? God often tests us through abundance and prosperity! This is one way He proves our character. Often, our character is at greater risk in prosperity than in adversity. You see, somewhere along the way we accept Satan's lie that we had something to do with our provisions.

If it were a simple matter of hard work, the man I observe on a street corner I frequently pass would be the wealthiest man in town. I have never seen anyone work harder to convince people to buy newspapers. He dances, sings, turns cartwheels, and always flashes a toothless grin—all in the hottest climate in Texas. Now that's a hard-working man—but nonetheless a poor one. It is not our effort but God who provides for us. When we have plenty we tend to forget the source of that bounty.

In the wilderness of sin God set a test before His children. In essence He responded to their grumblings like this: "I have shown you My presence again and again. I have intervened on your behalf with signs and wonders. I have healed your bitter water and have led you to the palms. I have also let you go hungry so that you would know that it is I who feeds you. Now I will put you through the hardest test of all: I will let you grow accustomed to My presence. I will feed you from My table daily and prove who you really are. Will you grow in awe, or will you grow cold?"

Chills run down my spine. This is still the most difficult test of all! Have you grown casual with God? Has He become an assumption to you? Do you feel that you know all you need to know about Him? Is it even getting hard to go through the motions? When was the last time you fell on your face before Him and wept over the unfathomable fact that He has chosen to take up residence in your very being? Someone in ministry once said to me about my zeal, "You'll get over it." May God usher me home before I accept an ongoing lifestyle of spiritual mediocrity! As I revise the very first Bible study God ever gave me, I am astonished that 32 years have passed since I experienced the call of God. No, I haven't been covered in nonstop spiritual chill bumps every moment of that time, but, to His great glory, God has sustained a fervent love for Him and His Word throughout. It has been my foremost prayer. Nothing sounds an alarm in my soul like a nagging feeling of distance or cool-heartedness. I run as fast as I can back to the fire of His Presence. The Holy Spirit never runs dry of lighter fluid for a lifeless soul seeking revival. I have glimpsed enough of what Christ has saved me from that I plead never to get over Him.

Are you over it? Do you go to church on Sundays and work tirelessly for your church because it's what you have always done; yet secretly you have lost your fire? Do you serve through boredom or for some future reward? Or do you still expect to learn something new from your encounters with God?

Read aloud Genesis 15:1. What is your reward? _____

If your heart has grown cold, it is because you have moved away from the fire of His presence. He wants your heart back home. Cry out with the psalmist, "Restore unto me the joy of thy salvation" (Ps. 51:12, KJV)! Take the risk of inviting Him to do whatever He must to fan your flame again. "It is God who works in you to will and to act according to his good purpose" (Phil. 2:13). He will rekindle your heart if you will let Him.

Keep these thoughts fresh in your mind as you read Exodus 16:4-8 and answer these questions.

From where did this bread come? _____

What were the instructions for the sixth day? _____

What would the Israelites know in the evening? _____

What would they see in the morning? _____

_____

The quail would specifically remind the Hebrews that God brought them out of Egypt, and the manna would allow them to see the glory of the Lord. The Egyptians specially favored quail.

Twice yearly, huge flocks of quail would migrate across Europe, Asia, and Africa. A quail's wing structure made the bird especially vulnerable to changes in the wind, which at times would force it to fly only a few feet from the ground. A very familiar scene in Egyptian art is an Egyptian catching a quail in his hand. Their sport made the eating that much sweeter.

In Exodus 16 God gave the children of Israel two kinds of food—food from humanity's table and food from God's table. How did they respond? In essence they said, "We want what we had in Egypt." They actually said that they would rather be slaves in Egypt, sitting by their pots of stew, than to be liberated to seek their promised land. How do you suppose God felt about that after all He had done on their behalf?

Does this sound familiar? How often do we stomp our feet at God after He has delivered us from the things of this world and say, "I want some of it back"? He would give us manna from heaven, but we demand to eat from the world's table, too. The sad thing is that we will always have to take on the yoke of slavery to do so. The Israelites wanted both the riches of God and the perks of Egypt.

This subject resurfaced later in the wilderness journey. This story is recorded in Numbers 11:1-20.

What did the Israelites ask for in verse 4?
❑ meat
❑ protection
❑ bread from heaven

What were the Egyptian foods for which they longed?

❑ fish	❑ fowl	❑ manna	❑ leeks
❑ pomegranates	❑ cucumbers	❑ coriander	❑ garlic
❑ legumes	❑ melons	❑ onions	

What did the people do with the manna God supplied (v. 8)?
- ❏ gathered it ❏ beat it in mortar ❏ boiled it
- ❏ hid it ❏ baked it in pans ❏ made cakes of it
- ❏ ground it in mills

How did God respond to the Israelites' weeping (v. 10)?
- ❏ He had mercy on them. ❏ His anger was kindled.

Which of the following best paraphrases Moses' response to God after their weeping (vv. 11-15)?
- ❏ "Please give them something new to eat!"
- ❏ "These people are too heavy a burden for me to carry!"
- ❏ "Get them a new leader. I resign."

Why was God so angry with the children of Israel? Because they wanted the best of both worlds! Haven't we all been there? We want to order the combination platter: the best of the new life and the best of the old. There is only one problem: the mixture invariably causes food poisoning. It just won't work. We must beware of demanding it. He just might give it to us in doses too big to swallow. In week 1 we cited Psalm 106:15 (KJV): "He gave them their request; but sent leanness into their soul." The Israelites experienced this Scripture in living color. First John 2:15-17 warns us about harboring an appetite for the things of the world, which represent the priorities in our lives before we were saved. The Greek words used for *love* in these verses are forms of *agape;* one meaning is *to find one's joy in.*

What must our response be to this world and what it has to offer?
- ❏ Forget it. ❏ Try to change it. ❏ Hate it.

What does Christ call Satan in John 12:31?
- ❏ Prince of darkness ❏ Prince of this world
- ❏ Prince of the power of the air

What impossible situation does 1 Corinthians 10:21 describe?

_____

_____

♥ Whose table do you choose? _____

In conclusion, as you consider the Israelites' craving to have the things of both the old life and the new, is God bringing anything to your mind about your personal life? It is no accident when one particular subject keeps arising in our minds as we study God's Word. The Holy Spirit is at work! Acknowledge ways God seems to be personalizing this lesson for you as you close today's lesson in prayer.

Day 4
Glorious Morning

Manna
a whatness

Begin your study by reading Today's Treasure and praying that God will speak to you through His Word.

In day 3 we discovered why the quail, which God caused to cover the camp in the evening, would remind the Israelites of the Lord's deliverance from Egypt. Because of the Israelites' insatiable appetite for the world from which He saved them, He would let them eat it until they literally choked (see Num. 11). Psalm 78:29 says, "He had given them what they craved." His purpose was to let them discover on their own that they wanted nothing of the old life. Today let's concentrate on Exodus 16:7: "In the morning you will see the glory of the Lord."

What provision of God would the Israelites see in the morning

(Ex. 16:12-15)? _____

Let's discover why the Israelites would see the glory of the Lord through this peculiar "bread from heaven." The Hebrew phrase for *manna* is translated *a whatness.* If I may say it this way, it was Hebrew for our term *whatchamacallit.* They simply had no name for it. These heavenly cornflakes ("corn of heaven," Ps. 78:24, KJV) would come with the dew; and when the dew evaporated, the manna would cover the ground. Why was it coupled with the dew? Any dictionary might define *dew* as *moisture condensed from the atmosphere in small drops on cool surfaces.* Dew originates in the atmosphere, most assuredly as refreshment from God's hand to an earth that groans for the return of the Creator (see Rom. 8:22). Higher still was the origin of the bread for His children—straight from the heavenly kitchens.

Read Psalm 78:23-25. What does God call the manna in verse 25?

_____

What did the manna teach or demonstrate (Deut. 8:3)?
- ❑ reliance on God
- ❑ we don't live by bread only
- ❑ a taste of heaven
- ❑ God's majesty

In what circumstance did Christ quote this passage? (See Matt. 4:4 or Luke 4:4.)

_____

Let's look at Exodus 16 to learn more about manna. First, verse 14 describes a small, thin flake. Isn't it interesting that God let the Israelites see His glory through a small, almost indistinct object? How very much like Him!

What did Isaiah prophesy about Christ's appearance (Isa. 53:2)?

_____

How often we miss God's glory in search of what we think is grandeur!
Second, the manna was white, representing a perfect, pure food (v. 31).

How does Psalm 119:140, KJV, characterize God's Word?

_____

A third characteristic of manna is that it lasted for only one day, except for manna that was gathered the day before the Sabbath.

What happened when the people gathered too much (Ex. 16:20)?
❏ It rotted.   ❏ It was full of maggots.
❏ It disintegrated.   ❏ It began to smell.

Read the familiar words of Matthew 6:11. How far in advance are we to be concerned about God's provision for our lives?

_____

♥ **What do you think God wants to teach us through this crucial portion of the Lord's Prayer?**

_____

_____

How deeply our Provider wants us to recognize that He is our daily provision. Our lives could never be sustained on a once-a-week meal; yet we often expect a hearty Sunday serving to be enough to sustain spiritual growth.

What does Matthew 6:34 tell us about tomorrow?

_____

We need not worry about tomorrow. All we need to know is that God is sufficient for today.

A fourth truth we see through the manna is that it was gathered according to need. Look closely at Exodus 16:18. An omer is a dry measure of a little more than two quarts. That omer was supernaturally adjusted to meet every need!

Today's lesson is very special to me. After a friend lost a five-year-old child to cancer, I fell before God and cried out literally in physical agony: "I could never stand to live if that happened to me! Will my friend ever be all right? Is her life ruined forever? Will she ever smile again?" God led me kicking and screaming to this chapter and taught me through the manna. He repeated the words "in the morning ye shall be filled" (Ex. 16:12, KJV) to me over and over until I understood what He was trying to tell me. He also led me to Lamentations 3:22-23.

Turn to Lamentations 3:22-23. How often are God's mercies new?

_____

Do you see the correlation? He was telling me that a sufficient amount of mercy and grace would be set aside for me every day of my life, enough every morning!

Another characteristic of the manna spoke beautifully of God's mercy: He gives it in perfect supply for the need. Our ratio of mercy matches our present need. When the time arises and the need escalates, so does the grace required for us to make it! God is always sufficient in perfect proportion to our need. Every morning He has already set aside the omer for our daily need.

Although I rejoiced greatly over what God taught me about the manna, one thought kept occurring to me: "Precious Father, I've known a few Christians who did not appear to make it very well through their crises. If Your mercy is always sufficiently given according to need, what happened to them?" In His great tenderness God led me back to the wilderness and instructed me to do exactly what I am going to ask you to do.

In Exodus 16 the word _gather_ appears in verses 4-5, 16-18, 21-22, 26-27. Read those verses.

I finally understood the nature of God's mercy and grace. They are always there, available every day, prior to our need, and in direct proportion to every moment's demand; but we must gather them. That part is completely our responsibility.

What do you think would have happened to the Israelites if they had stayed inside their tents with their stomachs growling? They would have starved to death with the provision right outside the tent! Yet you and I frequently watch Christians do exactly the same thing.

Yes, God's grace is always sufficient, and His arms are always open to give it; but will our arms be open to receive what He so graciously offers? You and I can survive anything, but we must want to. The world offers plenty of quail to satisfy our hunger, but we will stuff ourselves without satisfaction. Only God's provision can satisfy a starving soul.

Only God's provision can satisfy a starving soul.

Read each Scripture and apply it to today's lesson.

John 6:32-35 _____

_____

Matthew 6:33 _____

_____

Psalm 81:10 _____

_____

God desires to teach you His incomparable sufficiency. Will you accept His provisions? They are right outside your tent.

Day 5
Clothes That Last

Begin your study by reading Today's Treasure and praying that God will speak to you through His Word.

Today we will take a final look at the living conditions of the children of Israel in the wilderness. This week we have seen that God manifested His presence to His people through His provision for them. As we continue to build a foundation for understanding how God provides for our deep spiritual need, we will concentrate one more day on God's provision for the Israelites' physical needs.

Much of the Book of Deuteronomy is a sermon Moses delivered to remind the Israelites of the binding, life-giving covenant into which they had entered with Jehovah God. Moses, divinely inspired by the Holy Spirit, recalled before them Jehovah-Jireh's many provisions during their wilderness journey. Today we will turn our attention to one of these wonderful reminders.

What do Deuteronomy 8:4; 29:5 say about God's additional provision for the Israelites in the wilderness?
❑ Their shoes never wore out.
❑ Their supply never ended.
❑ Their clothes never wore out.
❑ Their feet did not swell.
❑ God led them to carry ample clothing from Egypt.

Today's Treasure

"I DELIGHT GREATLY IN THE LORD; MY SOUL REJOICES IN MY GOD. FOR HE HAS CLOTHED ME WITH GARMENTS OF SALVATION AND ARRAYED ME IN A ROBE OF RIGHTEOUSNESS, AS A BRIDEGROOM ADORNS HIS HEAD LIKE A PRIEST, AND AS A BRIDE ADORNS HERSELF WITH HER JEWELS."

Isaiah 61:10

45

God was training His people to depend totally on Him in every area of their lives.

As you can see, God was training His people to depend totally on Him in every area of their lives. He directed them and protected them through pillars of a cloud by day and of fire by night. He fed them with manna and quail. He also clothed them sufficiently for the very long journey.

You might think God cares nothing about clothing but to provide covering; but I think we will discover that God is a very choosy dresser.

What do these verses tell us about how God robes Himself?

Psalm 93:1 _____

Psalm 104:1 _____

I have good news for you. God dresses you just as carefully while you walk this wilderness road as He did the Israelites for those 40 years. Observe that the Lord carefully tends to our clothing.

♥ God revealed Himself to His children through His constant care and provision. He still does. In what ways has He recently shown you His heart by providing for your needs?

Read Matthew 6:28-30. To what does He compare us?

_____

What do you think Christ was teaching in these three verses?

_____

How can He dress us more beautifully than the lilies of the field?

_____

Read Matthew 27:35. What was done with Christ's clothes?

_____

I can more easily tolerate the thought of Jesus' pain on our behalf than His humiliation. I can hardly bear to consider that He not only gave His life for me but also laid down His dignity. My Christ, the King of kings, the Holy One of Israel, was stripped and hung on a cross. Although human eyes may have seen Him naked on that day of all days, His Father saw Him completely clothed. See for yourself.

How is Christ clothed in Revelation 19:13?

_____

A garment of such expense has never existed in all eternity. An unfathomable price was paid for a garment of blood. Why did His robe have to be dipped in blood?

What does Hebrews 9:22 say to this issue? _____

_____

Because our Savior was willing to wear a garment of blood, consider what we are allowed to wear.

Read aloud Today's Treasure.

Garments of salvation! A robe of righteousness! Dressed as a bride awaiting her bridegroom! Celebrate, because that is who you are.

Read Revelation 19:6-8 with rejoicing. What will you wear as a part of the bride of Christ at the marriage supper of the Lamb?

_____

What does this garment represent? _____

You will be adorned with garments of salvation that will never wear out!
    Spend the remainder of your study time today in meditation and praise. Perhaps these words that came to me will lead you to write your own in the margin.

Too much it seems for me You've done
That thieves and liars like me be won,
To stand adorned in righteousness,
Blood bathed from sin's own wretchedness.
Your royal robes you laid aside
That you might dress your blessed bride,
A gift too precious to ignore!
Let me not rest till You're adored!

---

1. God's Covenant Name: You may be confused by the seeing God's name in different translations spelled either as *Jehovah* or *Yahweh*. The two terms are both from Exodus 3:14. They are simply different English renderings of the Hebrew letters. Many words have come to be pronounced differently over time. For example, maps used to show *Peking, China,* and *Bombay, India.* Those cities are now known as *Beijing* and *Mumbai* because linguists determined those pronunciations are closer to an English equivalent. In the same way, scholars recognize that *Yahweh* is a closer English approximation of the Hebrew name of God: YHWH (I Am). However, terms like *Jehovah Jireh* have become too embedded in our culture to change. So in this study we have normally used the current standard spelling of *Yahweh*. In select instances we have used the older spelling *Jehovah*. In either case my desire is to convey the utmost honor and respect to God's self-revealed covenant name.

Viewer Guide

New Starts and Barren Hearts

Today's lesson will draw back to day 4 of our homework as we expound further on the timeless truths represented by the manna in the wilderness.

Read Exodus 16:1-32.

Let's consider the following points from verses 17-18:

1. God is _____ our _____.

   • Read John 6:30-35 then compare 2 Peter 1:3.

2. Daily bread is about _____ _____.

3. Our objections to God's _____ approach are rooted in

_____ and _____.

Conclude with Lamentations 3:19-24.

Amid our objections, God offers compassion.

Video sessions are available for download at *www.lifeway.com/women*.

49

Prepared Hearts

DAY 1 • THE FREEWILL OFFERINGS

DAY 2 • GOLD, SILVER, AND PRECIOUS STONES

DAY 3 • THE COLORS OF LOVE

DAY 4 • A WORKER UNASHAMED

DAY 5 • WAITING ON THE LORD

WEEK 3

Last week we explored God's faithful provisions for His children. We saw proof that when God leads His children, He provides for them. I hope you have a good picture of the Israelites' wilderness environment. We now arrive at a marvelous moment: Moses' invitation to enter God's presence, to hear His intentions. Before God would come down and meet with people, He invited their representative to come up and meet with Him. Week 3 focuses on how God prepared His people for His dwelling. You will witness their hearts' preparation with a painful lesson on grace and His sanctuary's preparation with a glorious lesson on giving.

Principal Questions

1. What happened when the Israelites gave generously?
2. What is the one and only sure foundation?
3. In addition to salvation, with what can we be clothed?
4. With what did God fill Bezalel, and why?
5. Why did God tell Moses to go back down the mountain?

God rarely sheds light on Himself without some of that light spilling on us. The light of His glory invariably sheds light on our intense need for His grace. This week's study will reveal the truth that we rarely discover anything monumental about God without discovering something momentous about ourselves. With every revelation comes an invitation to adjust our lives to what we have seen.

Day 1
The Freewill Offerings

Begin your study by reading Today's Treasure and praying that God will speak to you through His Word.

Congratulations! You have made it to week 3! You are obviously very serious about your commitment and will most likely complete your study. Celebrate in advance the spiritual prosperity God is going to lavish on you because of your obedience to study His Word. Take a good look at His blessed assurance: "His delight is in the law of the LORD, and on his law he meditates day and night. He is like a tree planted by streams of water, which yields its fruit in season and whose leaf does not wither. Whatever he does prospers" (Ps. 1:2-3).

This week we will study the special instructions and preparations God required for His tabernacle, the remarkable structure built for His dwelling.

Exodus 24:9–25:9 tells about a time Moses met with God on Mt. Sinai after Moses had received the Ten Commandments (Ex. 20). The Bible records that Moses, Aaron, Nadab, Abihu, and 70 elders went up on the mountain and saw God, under whose feet they saw a pavement of sapphire. The Lord called Moses to come alone up the mountain, but He told the other men to wait and left Aaron and Hur in charge. After six days God called Moses from within a cloud; the men below saw God's glory like a consuming fire. Moses stayed on the mountain for 40 days and received God's instruction to tell the Israelites to bring Him an offering.

List from Exodus 25:3-7 each specific offering. _____

_____

_____

_____

_____

If we could comprehend this blessed invitation, our hearts would be transformed! Deuteronomy 2:7 says, "The LORD your God has been with you, and you have not lacked anything." As we studied in week 2, Jehovah-Jireh miraculously met the Israelites' every need, using supernatural means to remove all doubt of His complete sufficiency. He manifested His glory before them by providing for them. In fact, since He broke their yoke of slavery, all Jehovah had done was to give. He

"THEY RECEIVED FROM MOSES ALL THE OFFERINGS THE ISRAELITES HAD BROUGHT TO CARRY OUT THE WORK OF CONSTRUCTING THE SANCTUARY. AND THE PEOPLE CONTINUED TO BRING FREEWILL OFFERINGS MORNING AFTER MORNING."
Exodus 36:3

gave when they praised Him. He gave when they murmured. He even gave them the constant request of their hearts at the risk of leanness to their souls. God gave not because of their faithfulness but because of His faithfulness.

In this dramatic turning point in Israel's history, God opened His arms and asked whether anyone would like to give to Him. Through this marvelous invitation God introduced the freewill offering, which He uniquely received only on the basis of a heart's desire. This offering was for all who wanted to give of themselves to Him—just for the simple joy of it. Free of compulsion, devoid of all urging, for those who wanted to give, God extended an opportunity.

Let's take a look at the Israelites' response. Exodus 35:1-29; 36:3-7 records Moses telling the people about offerings and workers needed for God's tabernacle. They responded, bringing offerings morning after morning.

 What happened when the people gave generously (Ex. 36:6-7)?

_____

Imagine your pastor announcing from the pulpit: "Stop that offering plate! And don't offer to fill another leadership position, either! We have far more than enough to do the work God has called us to do!" Allow the response of the children of Israel to provoke a few personal responses: What is the motivation for my personal offering? Is my heart stirred to give? Has my offering become, at best, an act of obedience rather than a festival of opportunity?

This issue is not about checkbooks. It is about hearts—either stirred or stale. Let's analyze why the Israelites gave so abundantly that they had to be restrained.

Exodus 35:22-28 says the people brought silver, gold, jewelry, richly colored yarn and fine linen, ram skins, and acacia wood. Where did they get this wealth? Exodus 12:31-36 says they got it from the Egyptians before they fled.

The Israelites were keenly aware that they were poverty-stricken before God delivered them from bondage. They needed little reminder that everything they owned had been afforded them by God. In fact, they really owned nothing at all. They appeared to be aware of these truths in I Chronicles 29:12-13: "Wealth and honor come from you; you are the ruler of all things. In your hands are strength and power to exalt and give strength to all. Now, our God, we give you thanks, and praise your glorious name."

Remember how often the Israelites brought offerings until they were forced to stop? Morning after morning! They brought offerings morning after morning just as God had provided manna for them morning after morning (Ex. 16).

The children of Israel couldn't even eat breakfast without observing that they would starve to death without their God! Awaking to manna every morning, they had not only keen awareness but also quick appreciation! I believe the Israelites knew the direct correlation between their willingness to prepare for God's presence and His desire to make evident His presence personally. How often we expect big things from God without preparing for big things from Him!

Has my offering become, at best, an act of obedience rather than a festival of opportunity?

Perhaps most of all, the Israelites gave because their hearts were stirred by a desire to participate in God's work. Perhaps they were overwhelmed as they realized that gifts from their hearts would be woven into the fabric of the place God had chosen to manifest His presence. By giving of themselves toward building God's tabernacle, it somehow became theirs as well. If you faithfully attend one church for 20 years and never miss an obedient tithe yet don't give the freewill offering of your heart to God's work there, it will still not seem like your church. Service under compulsion or from a sense of obligation is not a freewill offering. The only motivation for an earnest freewill offering is the joy of giving.

Just as surely as God was building His tabernacle through the Israelites thousands of years ago, Christ is building His kingdom through us today.

The motivation for an earnest freewill offering is the joy of giving.

♥ What is your freewill offering to the construction of Christ's kingdom? Turn your answer into a written prayer of response to God.

Complete the following statements that apply to you.
Dear Father, You know my thoughts before I do. Please shed Your light over every part of my personal offerings and give me insight as I take an inventory of my heart. I recognize You are building Your kingdom and deeply desire the freewill offerings of my heart as available materials for that structure. I ask You, through the Holy Spirit's power, to help me distinguish between what I offer from obligation, compulsion, or compensation and what I offer from the sheer joy of having something to place on Your altar.

Without a doubt, one of my freewill offerings is _____.

I persistently try to act as if I cannot hear You ask me to give You

my _____ freely.

I recognize that You are completely able to transform my heart, but I have been unwilling to allow You to change my heart about

_____

_____

(Hear His response. Will you now let Him change your heart?)
Right now I am not lifting up a freewill offering to You at all.

The reason I am most aware of is _____

_____.

Could there also be some other reasons, Lord? (Meditate on this question a moment. Is He bringing anything to mind?)

_____

I presently give my freewill offering at my local church by:

_____

Complete the following statements that apply to you:
Lord, I believe that You have led me to my congregation, because—

_____

I am not sure that You have led me here, because—

_____

I feel great joy when I am able to give of my _____.

I feel no joy when _____.

Help me listen directly to You now, Lord, as You tell me what You desire my freewill offerings to be. Give me the strength to risk allowing You to make the changes in my heart that joyfully giving these offerings would require. Amen.

Today's Treasure

"If any man builds on this foundation using gold, silver, costly stones, wood, hay or straw, his work will be shown for what it is, because the Day will bring it to light. It will be revealed with fire, and the fire will test the quality of each man's work. If what he has built survives, he will receive his reward. If it is burned up, he will suffer loss; he himself will be saved, but only as one escaping through the flames."

1 Corinthians 3:12-15

Day 2
Gold, Silver, and Precious Stones

Begin your study by reading Today's Treasure and praying that God will speak to you through His Word.

Consider how few chapters in God's Word are devoted to the creation of all the universe. Yet the Pentateuch (the first five books of the Bible) and the Book of Hebrews dedicate 50 chapters to information about the tabernacle. What might be the reason? Because the universe was created to be the habitation of people; the tabernacle, the habitation of God! God needed no instructions when He built our habitation. On the other hand, He gave very detailed instructions for building His tabernacle. When He agreed to receive a freewill offering from His people, whether they gave was a personal choice; what they gave was not.

Exodus 25:3-7 lists materials people brought as offerings for the tabernacle including gold, silver, bronze, and precious stones. Today we will survey the significance of several of these materials, most of which we will study in greater detail in another lesson. We will consider the offerings later in our study.

Valued because of its rarity, gold is mentioned in God's Word more often than any other metal. Scholars agree that gold in its rarity and purity seems to represent God's deity in both Moses' tabernacle and Solomon's temple. The heavenly city is replete with gold (see Rev. 21:21-22).

Read Matthew 2:11 and record what it says about gold.

_____

Silver was a visual aid by which God introduced and taught the concept of redemption and atonement through ransom money.

What do you learn about ransom and about silver from each of the following Scriptures?

Exodus 30:11-16 _____

Zechariah 11:12-13 _____

Matthew 26:14-16 _____

Matthew 27:3-10 _____

Bronze appears to symbolize strength and judgment.

What do the following Scriptures say about bronze?

Numbers 21:5-9 _____

Job 40:18 _____

Revelation 1:12-15 _____

Precious stones, or jewels, appear to represent God's saints—His treasured possession, His children—complete with the gifts of the Holy Spirit! These also appear in the temple and in the heavenly Jerusalem.

How are precious stones used in Revelation 21:18-21 to describe the heavenly city?

_____

Gold, signifying rarity and purity, represents God's deity.

Silver represents redemption and atonement.

Bronze suggests strength and judgment.

Precious stones represent God's children.

The elements God chose to build the tabernacle were very important.

Read Hebrews 8:5. These elements were a pattern of _____

Let's look at the specific meanings several of these symbols of heaven possess for believers in Christ. We will discover similarities between the materials used to build the tabernacle and the elements mentioned in New Testament passages.

Read I Corinthians 3:9-15 and answer the following questions.

What is the basic message of this New Testament passage?

_____

In Old Testament times God sought a dwelling place among His people through the tabernacle. The tabernacle thus came to represent the foundation of the Israelites' faith. The New Testament teaches that the one and only sure foundation is—

_____

From what six materials can we choose to build on this foundation?

_____ _____

_____ _____

_____ _____

Divide the materials into two groups of three. How do these categories differ?

_____

How will our works be revealed and the quality of each tested?

_____

List the main ways you expend your energy during a typical week.

_____

_____

_____

♥ Now go back and circle your activities that will stand the test of the fire. Cross out the activities you think will burn up.

How did the Israelites describe the glory of the Lord (Ex. 24:17)?

_____

According to 1 Corinthians 3:9-15 who is being judged?

_____

How does 2 Corinthians 5:9-10 describe this believers' judgment?

_____

Many believers in Christ are shocked and disappointed to realize that we will first be judged by fire. But after we understand the process of our judgment and the purpose of the fire, we should no longer have cause for surprise or dismay.

Hebrews 12:29 says: "For our 'God is a consuming fire.'" You can see that it would be impossible to be judged by God without being judged by fire. In fact, understanding the role of the fire in our judgment is crucial.

What is the first purpose of the fire (1 Cor. 3:13)?
❑ to try everyone's work by burning away the temporal
❑ to determine appropriate crowns
❑ to burn away everything unclean

What is the second purpose of the fire (vv. 14-15)?
❑ to prepare each person for eternity
❑ to see what abides so that God can give rewards
❑ to consume all pride

God judges us with fire for two reasons:
1. To cast a revealing light over all of our works and the motivations that bore them and to burn away all works of temporal value: the hay, wood, and straw
2. To reward what is left after the fire consumes everything temporal: the imperishable, eternal works of gold, silver, and precious stones
   • Works of gold acknowledge that He alone is worthy, that He alone is God.
   • Works of silver proceed from a heart that responds with inexpressible gratitude for our redemption and the inestimable price paid for our atonement.
   • Works of precious stones result when children of the royal priesthood, serve and minister as we are fully equipped with the gifts of the Holy Spirit.

If you are a believer, your judgment will not determine your eternal destiny. Christ's finished work on Calvary was applied to you the moment you accepted Christ as Savior. There is no condemnation for those who are in Christ Jesus (see Rom. 8:1)! Your judgment simply establishes rewards, some of which we will receive and some of which we will miss. But one sure reward is promised to every true believer, and you do not have to wait until you reach heaven to obtain it.

By now you should be able to paraphrase Genesis 15:1 from

memory. What is your chief reward? _____

Also consider an important role of fiery trials in a believer's earthly life: to reveal the quality of our character.

What do these verses say about fiery trials?

Job 23:10 _____

1 Peter 1:6-7 _____

Yesterday you learned gold was named first in God's list of freewill offerings. Today it was listed first among works of eternal significance. Why? Because we offer God something more precious than gold when we joyfully lay our sufferings on His altar and agree to be purified by the flames that threaten to consume us.

Think about this: "Those who suffer according to God's will should commit themselves to their faithful Creator and continue to do good" (1 Pet. 4:19).

Write 1 Peter 4:19 in the margin and meditate on it for a moment.

You are looking at a classic freewill offering. No one can make you surrender your sufferings to God. Only you can decide how your fires will affect you. Will you be sanctified or scarred? Listen as He says to you, "My precious child, I bore My scars so that you would not have to!" He has suffered enough for both of you.

Once in a while, God reminds me of His presence in an almost overwhelming way. As I concluded this lesson and wrote the previous paragraph, it was late. My children were asleep, and Keith was attending a discipleship group. It was a perfect study moment. The children did not have a clue what I was writing about because I try not to work in their presence. I had just described the significance of the gold, silver, and precious stones for you when Melissa, 10 years old at the time, got out of bed, came downstairs, and said, "I want to sing a song for you before I go to sleep." Happy to have the break, I leaned back, closed my eyes, and said, "Sing on, child!" With deepest earnest she began to sing:

Lord, You are more precious than silver.
Lord, You are more costly than gold.
Lord, You are more beautiful than diamonds,
And nothing I desire compares with You.[1]

How precious the praises of children must be to Him. Why not praise Him right now? He is real, my friend, and present with you. He is worthy of your heart's dearest offerings.

Day 3
The Colors of Love

Begin your study by reading Today's Treasure and praying that God will speak to you through His Word.

Today we will continue studying the freewill offerings. On day 2 we saw the significance of gold, silver, bronze, and precious stones. Today we focus on the colors God commanded to be used in the tabernacle's materials. Exodus 25:3-4 named three colors of yarn appropriate for offerings—blue, purple, and scarlet.

On a clear day only a glance upward would reveal the significance of blue. This color would constantly remind the Israelites that the tabernacle was of heavenly descent: "Make this tabernacle and all its furnishings exactly like the pattern I will show you" (Ex. 25:9), "a copy and shadow of what is in heaven" (Heb. 8:5). Sapphire, or the Hebrew *sappir*, is a breathtaking color of blue.

Research the following verses and list specific locations of the heavenly shade of sapphire.

Isaiah 54:11 _____

Ezekiel 1:26 _____

Purple, the most valued color among ancient cultures, represented royalty, kingship, and elegance. Find the locations of this color.

Judges 8:26 _____

Mark 15:17-18 _____

Luke 16:19 _____

Scarlet readily denotes bloodshed, pain, and sacrifice. What did

God consider scarlet in Isaiah 1:18? _____

In addition to specifying colors to be used in the tabernacle, God repeatedly emphasized the use of fine linen.

Today's Treasure

"GOD MADE HIM WHO HAD NO SIN TO BE SIN FOR US, SO THAT IN HIM WE MIGHT BECOME THE RIGHTEOUSNESS OF GOD."

2 Corinthians 5:21

To identify the symbolic nature of fine linen, read the following Scriptures and describe the use of fine linen in each one.

Genesis 41:41-42 _____

I Chronicles 15:25-27 _____

Proverbs 31:24 _____

Luke 23:52-53 _____

Luke 24:12 _____

Read Revelation 19:6-8,11-16 and check three facts you discover about fine linen.
❑ Christ is arrayed in fine linen.
❑ The bride of Christ is arrayed in fine linen.
❑ The angels are arrayed in fine linen.
❑ The armies in heaven are arrayed in fine linen.
❑ Fine linen represents the purity of saints.
❑ Fine linen is the righteousness of saints.

Week 2 reminded us that Christ has clothed us with His salvation. In addition to salvation, with what can we be clothed? Read Job 29:14 and Psalm 132:9 and check each correct answer:
❑ peace   ❑ love   ❑ joy   ❑ righteousness   ❑ grace

Turn to I Samuel 18, a wonderful Old Testament account through which we can begin to comprehend what it means to put on Christ's righteousness as He puts on our sin. Read verses 1-4. Although only Jonathan's gift to David is recorded, these verses probably portray the covenant of exchange, a practice in which two persons sealed a binding covenant by exchanging attire. This covenant represented a basic precept: "I will become what you are, and you will become what I am, with the result that our souls are knit together as one." Because Jonathan was the royal son, the offspring of the first king of Israel, he was dressed in the finest royal robes. The riches of the kingdom were at his disposal, and his wishes were another's commands. But he desired one thing: for David to have everything he had. Jonathan was so intent that he was willing to change places with him and to become what David was.

David, on the other hand, was only a shepherd boy. He came from a meager home and was a servant to King Saul. He wore a simple cloak, which likely still reeked of sweat and sheep. Can you imagine how he must have felt when Jonathan began to remove David's worn, rugged cloak and to place his own on David's back? This passage attests only to the love Jonathan had for David. This covenant was based on Jonathan's love, not on David's. David's love is never mentioned.

Supply the missing phrase from 1 John 4:10 in the blank.

"This is love, _____,
but that he loved us and sent his Son as an atoning sacrifice for
our sins."

Having put on Jonathan's robe, David rose as a king's son, dressed in splendid regalia, with the king's emblem pressed on him. He might have experienced a moment of pride until he looked at Jonathan standing before him, probably having put on David's worn-out robe, suddenly a servant. Perhaps as long as David looked at himself, he could almost believe that he deserved this destiny, but he could only feel humble when he looked steadfastly into the eyes of his covenant partner.

♥ Reread Today's Treasure. What clothing did your Savior put on so that you could become righteous?

_____

May we never forget that in the "great exchange" Christ also put on our robe: "God made him who had no sin to be sin for us, so that in him we might become the righteousness of God" (2 Cor. 5:21).

God addresses three kinds of righteousness in His Word: (1) Self-righteousness—a narrow-minded belief that we are superior to others (see Matt. 5:20). (2) Imputed righteousness—righteousness given to us on the basis of our salvation when we became "the righteousness of God" (2 Cor. 5:21). After we are born again, the state of our imputed righteousness does not change. (3) Imparted righteousness—the fleshing out or expression of the righteousness we have received in Christ, the Holy Spirit's righteousness applied to the soul. This is the difference between owning the royal robe and actually wearing it! How do we live out God's righteousness? Let's examine two significant passages.

List each action phrase in the verses below. The first one is provided.

Romans 13:12-14   Ephesians 4:22-24

Put aside the deeds of darkness   Put off the old self

_____   _____

_____   _____

_____   _____

_____   _____

The key to wearing our new self, rather than allowing our robes of righteousness to hang in the closet, is found in Ephesians 4:23. Are you storing anything of the old self in the new mind? We are new creatures in Christ; but if we still think like the old creature, we will find it impossible to personify the new. Most of our wars are fought on the battlefield of the mind.

How does Romans 12:2 say we can personally experience the transformation Christ afforded us on Calvary?
❑ Think with the mind of Christ.   ❑ Renew your mind.
❑ Meditate on the Word of God.

Complete the missing phrase, according to Mark 12:30, KJV:

"Thou shalt love the Lord thy God with all thy heart, and with all

thy soul, _____, and
with all thy strength: this is the first commandment."

We will never experience the rich righteousness that Christ exchanged for our sins until we learn to love God with our minds. Meditate on this truth today.

Day 4
A Worker Unashamed

"IF YOU THEN, THOUGH YOU ARE EVIL, KNOW HOW TO GIVE GOOD GIFTS TO YOUR CHILDREN, HOW MUCH MORE WILL YOUR FATHER IN HEAVEN GIVE THE HOLY SPIRIT TO THOSE WHO ASK HIM!"

Luke 11:13

Begin your study by reading Today's Treasure and praying that God will speak to you through His Word.

We studied this week about God's directing the nation of Israel to follow certain preparations and instructions for the structure He would indwell. We learned that He sought a specified combination of freewill offerings from desiring participants, and we witnessed their overwhelming response. Though their enthusiasm was unleashed, their obedience was precise. They never deviated from the proposed offerings list. Today we will meet those appointed to use the offerings.

Exodus 36:1-7 tells about two very important contractors, Bezalel and Oholiab. These two men are worthy of study because God handpicked them by nonnegotiable and perfect design as His servants to furnish His dwelling place.

Read Exodus 31:1-11 and answer the following questions.

Who chose Bezalel? _____

From what tribe was he? _____

Who else was from this tribe (see Rev. 5:5)? _____

With what did God fill Bezalel? _____

Why? _____

What was Oholiab's role? _____

Of the tens of thousands of able-bodied men in Israel, God chose Bezalel for this divinely unusual task. Although we cannot know with certainty the reason for God's choice, we can surmise that Bezalel was chosen because of his availability to God and his obedience.

Did you know that prior to the Day of Pentecost, the Holy Spirit descended on only a handful of persons? Of God's chosen leaders, we read of only Moses, Joshua, Othniel, Gideon, Jephthah, Samson, Saul, and David being touched by the Holy Spirit's presence. Of His prophets the 70 elders of Israel had the Spirit of God on them, as well as Balaam, a few messengers of Saul, Amasa, Azariah, Zechariah, Isaiah, and Ezekiel. These were members of an elite group!

Fewer still were the number in which the Holy Spirit chose to remain. Prior to Acts 2 the Holy Spirit came and went as God pleased, falling on His subjects for a temporary task. Recall King David's words after he was confronted about his sin with Bathsheba: "Do not banish me from Your presence or take Your Holy Spirit from me" (Ps. 51:11, HCSB). David knew firsthand that God could remove the Holy Spirit just as quickly as He introduced Him. David witnessed in Saul the tragedy of a life devoid of God's Spirit. It is no wonder that David basically said, "You can say what You want and judge me as You choose. I have sinned against You only. But whatever You do, I beg You not to take Your Holy Spirit from me!" (see Ps. 51:4,11).

One of the most tragic lives in the Old Testament is Samson, who grew so far from the Lord that he was not even aware when the Holy Spirit left him. When he needed his strength, he experienced the sobering realization that it had never been his strength but God's presence (see Judg. 16:20). What a rare privilege he had enjoyed to be literally energized by the Holy Spirit to lead God's people!

In the list of those important few who were filled by the Spirit, Bezalel was the only one who was not a leader or a prophet. He was a wage earner—a blue-collar worker. Yet he is the only one in Old Testament history to be filled and empowered by the Holy Spirit to construct a building by a heavenly pattern!

Several life applications can be drawn from Bezalel's experience. First, he was God's laborer.

What does 1 Corinthians 3:9 say about being laborers together with God?

_____

You and I are not leaders, kings, and prophets over God's chosen Israel. We are laborers just like Bezalel. Names were very important to the Hebrew people, often expressing character and destiny. The name Bezalel means *in the shadow of God*. He was not taking a power hike or craving recognition. He was happy to dwell in the shadow of the Almighty. God's name was enough for him. He considered it a privilege just to work on God's team. God wants willing laborers!

Read Matthew 9:37. Does He have enough workers?

_____

Second, Bezalel's job was also out of his league. If he had already possessed everything he needed for the task, God would not have bothered to empower him with His Holy Spirit. God is far too practical for that! He purposely assigned Bezalel a task beyond his capability so that He could fill him with His power.

God has rarely given me an assignment that I considered to be in my league. Anything of priority in the Kingdom is out of our league. When we serve in our church, we must never forget that we are dealing with people's lives—their internal struggles and eternal destinies. Sincerity and sweat do not always suffice. God places us in positions beyond our capabilities so that we will be at His absolute mercy, realizing that only He can succeed.

Because God has a perfect plan for His kingdom, He gives great attention to detail, no matter how uncomfortable that makes us. In Acts 1:4,8 Jesus commanded the disciples not to take one more step in their ministries without the Holy Spirit's power. If they had, the results would have been disastrous. Jesus' message? "Stay where you are until My Holy Spirit empowers you to move." When we step outside of God's will, we step outside the guarantee of His power.

Third, God empowered Bezalel to perform his assignment, apparently viewing the situation like this: "I have a job that needs to be done, and I want it done right the first time. That means I will have to do it Myself." So He did—through Bezalel. God searches for laborers who will simply let Him do His job through them as His vessels. When you work for God, with your assignment comes the guarantee that you will be equipped for the job.

Record the equipping promises you find in the following verses.

I Corinthians 12:7 _____

Ephesians 4:7,11-12 _____

2 Timothy 3:16-17 _____

♥ Name a job God gave you that was out of your league. How did you respond? In what ways did God empower you for this task?

Finally, Bezalel worked well under authority. Notice in Exodus 36:1-7 that Bezalel not only worked well under God's instruction but also submitted himself to the earthly authority God had designated—Moses. Authority is an important issue to God and one we struggle with deeply. We may not mind being under God's authority at times, but we often resist human authorities God places over us. Remember, God is sovereign. If you are where God has placed you—whether at home, on the job, or at church—He has established the authority over you to work His glory in you. And while He expects us to submit to our authorities, He also empowers us for the difficult task.

Examine the following verses and answer the questions.

Read Romans 13:1-6. Who is addressed? _____

To whom must they submit? _____

Why? _____

Read 2 Corinthians 10:8; 13:10. Who is addressed? _____

To whom must they submit? _____

Why? _____

Read Ephesians 6:1-3. Who is addressed? _____

To whom must they submit? _____

Why? _____

Read Ephesians 6:5-8. Who is addressed? _____

To whom must they submit? _____

Why? _____

Read I Peter 3:1-2. Who is addressed? _____

To whom must they submit? _____

Why? _____

First Timothy 2:1-2 provides a crucial component of submitting to authority. What does God command us to do? Check one:
- ❑ Pray for a submissive spirit.
- ❑ Submit only to those in Christ.
- ❑ Pray for those in authority.

I'm glad we got to know Bezalel, our fellow laborer and good example of excellence on the job. He was pretty special, wasn't he? But so are you, for the Holy Spirit dwells in you! See for yourself.

Match each reference below with its paraphrased assurance that you are God's colaborer and that the Holy Spirit is your enabler.

_____ 1. Luke 11:13   a. In due time we will reap the results of our efforts for the sake of Christ.

_____ 2. John 14:16-18   b. God has established, anointed, and sealed us for our callings.

_____ 3. Galatians 6:9-10   c. We need only ask to receive the Holy Spirit.

_____ 4. 2 Corinthians 1:20-22   d. The Holy Spirit sent by Christ dwells in us.

Day 5
Waiting on the Lord

Today's Treasure

"I LOOKED FOR A MAN AMONG THEM WHO WOULD BUILD UP THE WALL AND STAND BEFORE ME IN THE GAP ON BEHALF OF THE LAND SO I WOULD NOT HAVE TO DESTROY IT, BUT I FOUND NONE."

Ezekiel 22:30

Read Today's Treasure and ask God to speak to you through His Word.

Today we will pour the last bit of cement for the foundation of our study. On day 1 of week 4 we will begin researching every section of the tabernacle in the wilderness, God's dwelling place among His Chosen People.

Two major sections in Exodus focus specifically on the tabernacle. Chapters 25–31 record God's construction commands to Moses. Chapters 35–40 record the construction that fulfilled God's commands. The three chapters between God's revelation and the people's response contain a significant amount of information and function as a parenthesis in which "these things happened to them as examples and were written down as warnings for us" (1 Cor. 10:11). While Moses was on the mountain with God, the people asked Aaron to build them a god. And Aaron did. When Moses came down from the mountain and saw the people dancing around the golden calf, he threw down the stone tablets containing the Ten Commandments and broke them.

Read Exodus 24:15-18. How long was Moses away?
❑ 7 days   ❑ 40 days and nights   ❑ Many days

When God detained Moses, whom did the people approach (32:1)?
❑ The elders   ❑ Bezalel   ❑ Aaron   ❑ Oholiab

What did they ask him to do?
❑ Go to the mountain and find Moses.
❑ Lead them to the promised land.
❑ Make them gods who would lead them.

What was Aaron's response (Ex. 32:2-4)?
❑ He rebuked their advances.   ❑ He did what they asked.
❑ He prayed for God's intervention.

What had Aaron experienced in Exodus 24:9-10?
❑ He saw Moses talking with God.
❑ He saw the God of Israel.
❑ He saw the people's disobedience.

Although Moses was out of sight, God as Jehovah-Jireh was not. He revealed Himself daily through manna. Isn't it interesting that the Israelites wanted something tangible to worship, though evidence of the one true God surrounded them?

Why might they have been so vulnerable to such disobedience?

_____

What did Aaron tell the people to do in Exodus 32:2-4?
❑ Give him their jewelry
❑ Give him their cooperation.
❑ Give him their allegiance.

As slaves the Israelites had no jewelry. Where did they get these gold earrings (see Ex. 12:35-36)?
❑ from their forefathers   ❑ from God's own hand
❑ from the Egyptians at God's command

What had God told Moses He wanted done with their riches, according to Exodus 25:1-8?
❑ He wanted them taken into the promised land.
❑ He wanted them offered as redemption money.
❑ He wanted them offered to Him as a gift for His dwelling.

How typical of Satan to steal the riches God has given us, melt them into golden calves, and beckon us to worship them. God had other plans for those riches! Divine plans! Eternal plans! As we so often do, the Israelites yielded to the temptation to worship the gift instead of the Giver.

What did Aaron build in front of the calf (Ex. 32:5)? _____

What announcement did Aaron make in Exodus 32:5?
❑ "Hear O Israel, the LORD our God is one God!"
❑ "Tomorrow there will be a festival to the LORD."

Notice that Aaron attempted to pull God into their actions: "Let's make this a festival to the Lord!" Have you ever witnessed an individual or a group do something totally without God, then turn around and try to figure Him into it?

Why did God tell Moses to go back down the mountain (32:7-8)?
❑ "Aaron has lost control of the people."
❑ "The people are overtaken with wickedness."
❑ "The people have corrupted themselves."

Notice the Israelites and God used different words to describe the time since Moses had been on the mountain. In Exodus 32:1 the Israelites considered Moses to have been "delayed" (KJV) or "so long" (NIV) in returning to His people. In verse 8 God labeled the same passage of time as quick. Convicting, isn't it?

How did the Lord describe these people in Exodus 32:9?
❑ stiff-necked   ❑ adulterous   ❑ sin-sick

A stiff neck hinders our looking far to the right or left and makes looking up nearly impossible. Have you ever had a spiritual stiff neck and refused to look up?

What did God tell Moses He wanted to do in Exodus 32:10?
❑ Send them on without Him.   ❑ Cast a plague on them.
❑ Consume them.

By what petitions did God allow Moses to talk Him out of such judgment (vv. 11-14)? Choose two answers.
❑ "The Egyptians will say that You took the Israelites out to harm them."
❑ "These people will repent if You give them a chance."
❑ "Take my life instead of their lives."
❑ "Remember Your promises to our forefathers."

What does Ezekiel 22:30 say about the importance of intercessors?

_____

What did Moses do in Exodus 32:20?
❑ He made the people hide their faces from God.
❑ He had the people cast the calf's ashes on the water.
❑ He made the people drink the water with ashes in it.

How did Aaron explain his behavior (see 32:22-24)?

_____

What did Moses instruct those "on the Lord's side" (vv. 26-27)?
  ❏ "Come with me and enter the promised land."
  ❏ "Separate yourselves from the wicked and be sanctified before the Lord."
  ❏ "Kill the offenders with the sword."

How many were slain (v. 28)?
  ❏ 10,000 ❏ The entire tribe of Benjamin ❏ 3,000

So this is what the people were doing while God was planning their participation in a divine assignment. What untimely disobedience! Or was it? With their sin fresh on the people's minds, what a great time for God to teach them a firsthand lesson on the costly sacrifice of reconciliation. Humility tends to make our hearts more teachable.

Let's conclude our lesson by taking a New Testament "when all was said and done" approach to the events we have studied today.

♥ Read 1 Corinthians 10:1-13 and answer the following questions.

Why were "these things" recorded for us, according to verse 6?

_____

Before we judge the Israelites' sins, what does verse 12 tell us?

_____

What is our assurance when temptation strikes?

_____

Viewer Guide

Prepared Hearts

In today's session, we will pick up the narrative portion of Exodus 32–34 exactly where it ended on day 5 of our homework. As Exodus 33 opens, the Israelites have sinned so grievously against God that the entire relationship seems at risk. Ironically, right here in the aftermath of Israel's great offense, Exodus 33 records "the most elevated glimpse of God Moses has ever had and will have."[1]

Our specific goal today is that God would use Exodus 33 to give us ...

An Elevated Glimpse of God

1. His stunning _____

2. His willing _____

3. His priority _____

"My Presence will go and, thus I will dispel your _____."[2]

God's Distinguishing Presence

• Our "_____" need

• Our "_____" need

4. His incomparable _____.

1. Peter Enns, *NIV Application Commentary: Exodus* (Grand Rapids: Zondervan, 200), 583.
2. John I. Durham, *Word Biblical Commentary*, vol. 3 (Nashville: Nelson Reference, 1987), 444.

Video sessions are available for download at *www.lifeway.com/women*.

Hearts Approaching the Altar

DAY 1 • BREAKING GROUND FOR CONSTRUCTION

DAY 2 • THE ALTAR OF SACRIFICE

DAY 3 • ACCEPTABLE OFFERINGS

DAY 4 • CLEAN HANDS AND A PURE HEART

DAY 5 • CONTENTMENT IN THE CALLING

WEEK 4

This week we will begin our actual construction of the Old Testament tabernacle and will begin examining each blessed component. Our approach to the tabernacle's contents will take place from the outside in. Over the next seven weeks you will be escorted through this divine sanctuary step-by-step from outside its walls into its innermost room. This week we will study the gate and the contents of the court: the altar of burnt offering and the basin. We will seek answers to the following questions.

Principal Questions

1. What place designed for God to fellowship with His people also had an eastern entrance?
2. What did Aaron do with the blood of the sacrifice?
3. What are the distinctions between the different offerings?
4. Why was the priests' washing so important?
5. What was to be a reminder to the Israelites that God was sovereign in how He had chosen to make Himself approachable?

Join me as the walls are raised and the gates are opened to the living God's most remarkable Old Testament dwelling place.

Day 1
Breaking Ground for Construction

Begin your study by reading Today's Treasure and praying that God will speak to you through His Word.

What an exciting day! Today we begin to penetrate the very heart of our study of the tabernacle. Grab your hard hat because it's time to start construction!

Open your Bible and scan Exodus 25–31. If your Bible has section headings, pay special attention to the order of God's instructions to Moses for building the tabernacle.

What is the first piece of furniture God instructed Moses to make (Ex. 25:10)?

_____

As you skim over these chapters in Exodus, you see that God gave Moses instructions for the tabernacle virtually from the inside out. Why? Because this sacred dwelling place reflected God's approach to humans: built from the origin of the holy of holies and pointing outward beyond the veil. Because God has since completed His approach to us in the finished work of Christ Jesus, we will study the tabernacle from our perspective: from the outside in. Today we will construct the perimeters of the outer court.

Read Exodus 27:9-19, paying attention to details. At the top of the next page draw a diagram of the tabernacle according to the following directions.

How long are the north and south sides to be? _____

How long are the east and west sides to be? _____

As you discovered, the east and west sides of the structure are half as long as the north and south sides. Therefore, you should draw a rectangle that is twice as wide as it is tall. Make the diagram small enough in the middle of the space provided to add details around it.

A cubit is between 18 and 20 inches long. Therefore, the tabernacle was approximately 150 feet from the east gate to the west wall and around 75 feet from the south wall to the north wall.

Today's Treasure

"THE LORD YOUR GOD MOVES ABOUT IN YOUR CAMP TO PROTECT YOU AND TO DELIVER YOUR ENEMIES TO YOU. YOUR CAMP MUST BE HOLY, SO THAT HE WILL NOT SEE AMONG YOU ANYTHING INDECENT AND TURN AWAY FROM YOU."

Deuteronomy 23:14

Label 100 cubits on the north and south walls and 50 cubits on the east and west walls.

From how many pillars were the linen curtains to be hung on the north and south sides (Ex. 27:10-11)? _____

How many pillars or posts were to be on the west side (v. 12)? ____

On the lines you drew, place bold, black dots to represent pillars.

Exodus 27:12-16 describes the tabernacle's gate. There was only one entrance to the accessible presence of God. Regardless of age, gender, or status, all persons entered God's sanctuary the same way, and God gave specific instructions for the gate's location (v. 13).

Draw a wide gate on the east side of your drawing.

Let's discover why God chose the east for His one entrance to the tabernacle. Read Genesis 3:24. What place designed for God to fellowship with His people also had an eastern entrance?

_____

Read Matthew 2:2,9. Where did the eastern star lead the wise men?

_____

At the break of every new day, light shone on the gate to the tabernacle, beckoning the people to find refuge in God.

God may have had countless reasons for choosing the east as the entrance to His presence; but surely, not the least is the fact that His perfect light interrupts the darkness every morning from the east. At the break of every new day, light shone on the gate to the tabernacle, beckoning the people to find refuge in God.

Psalm 30:5 says "His anger lasts only a moment, but his favor lasts a lifetime; weeping may remain for a night, but rejoicing comes in the morning." Picture the pure, white linen curtains hung from hook to hook and from pillar to pillar, forming the walls of the blessed tabernacle.

Read Exodus 27:16 and check the special requirement for the gate.
❏ **colored hangings or curtains** ❏ **pure gold overlay**

The gate was to be embroidered with blue, purple, and scarlet yarns. The beautifully expressive hues we studied in week 3 provided a breathtaking contrast to the stark, white linen curtains that surrounded it.

How high did the wall and the gate stand (see v. 18)? _____
Make a notation of that measurement on your diagram.

Before we take our first step inside the divine dwelling, let's study the special instructions for an important addition to the outside of the tabernacle. The second chapter of Numbers describes the order in which God commanded the children of Israel to camp on the four sides of the tabernacle.

Carefully read Numbers 2 and list each tribe according to God's instruction on the east, south, west, and north of your diagram. Specify the total number in each tribe, then the sum of all three tribes on each side. Don't be discouraged if you have to redraw your diagram to make room for the tribes. We will draw the tabernacle several times until we feel that we have been there. Be sure to complete your diagram. Building this structure is vastly important for your absorption of the study. You will often refer to this diagram during the next seven weeks.

Take another look at your diagram. You have drawn what God called the camp. The Hebrew word for *camp* is *machaneh,* meaning *army, band, company, station.* This military term was given to the children of Israel, the army of the living God! Several decades would pass before the Israelites faced a human foe. But long before they took the promised land by storm, God gathered them as an army, stationed in the wilderness, and led them as Commander in chief. Why would God position them in the wilderness as a battalion on the battlefield, with the conspicuous absence of an enemy? No reference supports an unseen war with Satan, although he could have chosen no more important place to be. We will discover quickly that the children of Israel were on the toughest battlefield of their nation's history, facing the most vicious enemy of all: themselves.

Henry Blackaby has well said: "In every generation there seem to exist certain clichés used by members of the body of Christ. No doubt, on the top of the list for this generation are the words 'I'm under attack!' Every difficulty seems to be labeled 'spiritual warfare.' Without question we fight wars in the heavenlies; but before we can be sure it's spiritual warfare, we must be able to answer three questions negatively: (1) Am I living outside the will of God? (2) Do I have any unconfessed sin? (3) Is God simply working His completion in me? Far more often, our difficulties originate from one of these three realms."

MACHANEH
army, band, company, station

♥ Think of a difficulty you are dealing with. Test it according to Henry Blackaby's three questions.

Are you under attack from Satan or from your flesh?

If you are fighting your flesh, how can you be victorious?

What can you do to ensure that you are camped close to your Commander?

I responded to those words with a very heartfelt "Amen!" I cannot number the times people have asked me if I am under Satan's continual attack. I have often responded, "My own flesh is twice the enemy to me that Satan is." You see, once we know how, we do not hesitate rebuking Satan, because we despise him. On the other hand, we dearly love our own flesh. We have far more difficulty rebuking it.

Romans 7:14-25 describes our battling ourselves. Read the verses and mark the following statements *T* (true) or *F* (false).

_____ Often I do what I hate.
_____ Even when I do good, evil is present with me.
_____ In my flesh dwells no good thing.
_____ My inward person delights in God's law.
_____ Another law wars with my mind.
_____ Christ is the only One who can deliver me from sin.

Each statement above is true. As you can see, we could fight quite a battle with sin without ever leaving our homes or seeing another person! One of our greatest battles is within ourselves, warring with our minds. But although a continual war is waged against us internally, we must never accept defeat!

Consider the prescription for our internal problem. What does 2 Corinthians 10:3-5 say about the weapons of our warfare?
❑ 1. We war after the flesh.
❑ 2. We walk in the flesh.
❑ 3. Our weapons are not carnal.
❑ 4. Our weapons are found deep within.
❑ 5. Our weapons can pull down strongholds.
❑ 6. Our weapons are only as effective as our ministries.
❑ 7. Our wars with the flesh are successful when we bring every thought captive to the obedience of Christ.

Statements 2, 3, 5, and 7 all apply to 2 Corinthians 10:3-5. In week 3, day 3 we discussed loving God with our whole minds. Now we discover another reason to surrender our minds to Christ. Clearly, the mind is the largest battlefield of our struggles with the flesh.

We have looked at our problem with ourselves and the prescription for the problem. Let's conclude with a promise found in Deuteronomy 23:14.

What is God's promise if we choose to camp and walk with Him?

_____

_____

You accomplished a lot today! Great work! Don't forget this week: the weapons of your warfare are mighty as long as you camp beside your Commander.

Day 2
The Altar of Sacrifice

Begin your study by reading Today's Treasure and praying that God will speak to you through His Word.

Today we take our first step through the tabernacle gate with its blue, purple, and scarlet tapestry inviting us to discover the wonderful mysteries within. Listen closely and you can almost hear our Savior's invitation: "Come, you who are blessed by my Father" (Matt. 25:34). As you walk through the eastern gate, your attention is immediately compelled by a most imposing structure ablaze with passion.

Carefully read about God's commandment and the construction of this crucial piece of furniture in Exodus 27:1-8; 38:1-7. Fill in the blanks beside the following questions with the letters that correspond to the correct answers.

_____ 1. What was the altar made of?

_____ 2. What shape was the altar?

_____ 3. What was on the corners network of the altar?

_____ 4. What overlaid the acacia wood?

_____ 5. What was under the altar?

_____ 6. What utensils were necessary to perform the priestly duties at the bronze altar?

_____ 7. How was the altar to be transported when God, through the movement of the pillar of a cloud, so led?

a. brass or bronze

b. 5 by 5 by 3 cubits

c. brass or bronze

d. pots, shovels, bowls, meat forks

e. poles in brass or bronze rings

f. 5 by 5 by 5 cubits

g. wood

h. horns

Today's Treasure

"THE FIRE ON THE ALTAR MUST BE KEPT BURNING; IT MUST NOT GO OUT. EVERY MORNING THE PRIEST IS TO ADD FIREWOOD AND ARRANGE THE BURNT OFFERING ON THE FIRE AND BURN THE FAT OF THE FELLOWSHIP OFFERINGS ON IT."

Leviticus 6:12-13

Let's try to visualize this vital piece of equipment, the altar of sacrifice, which occupied front-and-center priority in the tabernacle courtyard. The moment we stepped through the embroidered gate, we would have faced it. Elevated off the ground, the five-cubit-square altar was constructed of acacia wood. God's choice of wood was extremely significant. Acacia wood was well known for its incorruptibility because it resisted decay. Scholars believe that this unique wood represented Christ's humanity. In Isaiah 53:2 He is called "a root out of dry ground." John 15:1 calls Him "the true vine." Like the acacia wood, although He was "cut off from the land of the living" (Isa. 53:8), His body never decayed (see Ps. 16:10). One of the most remarkable similarities between the acacia wood and our Savior was that it bore heavy, sharp thorns—a likeness that deserves our attention.

The primary role of the horns was to secure the sacrifice.

A horn at each corner of the square bronze altar served as the means by which the innocent sacrifice was tied down. Can you remember from the Book of Genesis the first animal caught by its horns in a thicket, providing a substitutionary sacrifice (22:13)? The primary role of the horns in both Abraham's offering and the tabernacle's offerings was to secure the sacrifice.

By what names does David call God in Psalm 18:2?

_____

Christ is the horn of our salvation, the One who was secured on a cross so that we could be secured in the Lamb's book of life. The horn has three major uses in Scripture. We have already discussed the first example.

Name the other two uses of horn in Scripture.

Genesis 22:13 __to secure substitution_____

Joshua 6:13,20 (the trumpet was a ram's horn) _____

_____

I Samuel 16:13 _____

Christ secured Himself as our sacrifice, anointed us with His Holy Spirit, and leads us to victory.

What a perfect picture of Christ, the horn of our salvation! He secured Himself as our sacrifice, anointed us with His Holy Spirit, and leads us to victory!

Just how important was the altar on which the horns rested? Our Lord, Christ, testified to the altar's extreme significance in Matthew 23:16-19. Jesus was outraged by the Pharisees' self-centered, religious perspectives.

What did Jesus say in Matthew 23:19? _____

_____

The obvious answer to His question was the altar. If the altar, representing the vehicle or the means by which we bring an offering, is unacceptable, how can the sacrifice placed on it be acceptable? Thus, the acceptability of the altar itself was necessary for the acceptability of everything placed on it. God commanded that three major preparations be made before He could deem the bronze altar acceptable. First, the altar had to be built to perfection from a heavenly blueprint. Bezalel accomplished such a task through the empowerment of the Holy Spirit.

According to Exodus 30:22-29; 40:9-10, what was the second special preparation for the altar of burnt offering?
❑ Bless the altar. ❑ Anoint the altar. ❑ Light the altar.

The third preparation is described in Leviticus 8. Although we will study the tabernacle priests in a future week, it is important that you have in place the next preparation now. In Leviticus 8, Aaron and his sons and even their garments were ordained, set apart or consecrated—actions which prepared them to minister before the Lord in the tabernacle.

How long did the priests "stay at the entrance to the Tent of

Meeting" (Lev. 8:35)? _____

What might have happened if they had been disobedient to God in the details of their consecration?
❏ They would be replaced.   ❏ They would become leprous.
❏ They would die.

The altar had been built according to God's design and anointed according to His command. The priests had been ordained for service at the blessed place of sacrifice. All preparations had been completed. Now only one question remained: was the altar acceptable to God?

What would be the outcome of their obedience to God's command

(Lev. 9:6)? _____

Read John 15:10-11. What is the purpose of obedience?

_____

Our obedience does not make God bigger or better than He already is. His essence is unchanged by our obedience or lack of it. Anything God commands of us is so that our joy may be full—the joy of seeing His glory revealed to us and in us! Two major reasons for obedience are that we may become targets of blessing and that He may have the pleasure of bestowing it. Either way, obedience benefits us!

For whom were the offerings made and in what order (Lev. 9:7)?

_____

What did Aaron do with the blood of the sacrifice (Lev. 9:9,12)?

_____

_____

What happened when Moses and Aaron came out of the tabernacle and blessed all of the people (Lev. 9:23-24)?

_____

_____

I am covered with chills as I witness this divine display. God christened the altar with fire from heaven, bathing it in purification and consuming its blessed contents in glorious approval! We must not miss the perpetual significance of this heavenly fire. Read Leviticus 6:12-13. God had lit the fire from His own holy hand. Only fire originating from Himself could truly purify and consume, or approve, an offering. Therefore, the fire must never be allowed to go out. Wood had to be added continually so that the original, divine flame would never be exhausted. God lit the fire, but humans had to fuel it.

Second Timothy 1:6 says, "For this reason I remind you to fan into flame the gift of God, which is in you." The Greek word for _gift_ in 2 Timothy 1:6 is _charisma_, which means _a gift of grace, an undeserved benefit from God_. It refers not only to salvation but also to the gifts of the Holy Spirit distributed as God deems necessary to every believer. Even your talents were not earned but given by God.

If you have accepted Christ as Savior, in that moment He lit a flame in you.

♥ **What is your responsibility after God lights the fire in you**

(2 Tim. 1:6-8)? _____

Again we see God's sovereign desire to interact with His children. Power is up to God. Participation is up to us. It is our right to participate and interact with God. Such interaction would never have been possible without the ultimate altar of sacrifice—the cross.

CHARISMA

a gift of grace, an undeserved benefit from God

Today's Treasure

"Let him offer a male without blemish: he shall offer it of his own voluntary will at the door of the tabernacle of the congregation before the Lord."

Leviticus 1:3, KJV

Day 3
Acceptable Offerings

Read Today's Treasure and ask God to speak to you through His Word.

In day 2 we studied four elements that readied the bronze altar for service: the construction of the altar, the anointing of the altar, the ordination of the priests to serve at the altar, and God's approval of the altar. At this point the bronze altar was ready for service.

Recall Leviticus 9:7: "Moses said to Aaron, 'Come to the altar and sacrifice your sin offering and your burnt offering and make atonement for yourself and the people; sacrifice the offering that is for the people and make atonement for them, as the LORD has commanded.' "

All salvation rests on this precept: Acceptance is always based on atonement. Do not allow this fact to escape your mind for a moment throughout our study.

In the time prior to Calvary each Israelite's salvation was based on faith in God's acceptance of the type, or picture, of atonement He had revealed to them. Just as we are saved by faith as we look back at Christ's atoning work on Calvary, the Israelites were saved by faith as they looked toward it. They placed their faith in the disclosure of Christ given to them through the atoning sacrifices. They were asked to be faithful in accepting the part of Christ that God had made recognizable to them.

Although many Hebrews died in the wilderness and most did not enter the promised land, do not assume that all of them were unsaved. Moses was also forbidden to enter the promised land because of disobedience; yet Scripture vividly pictures him on the mount of transfiguration with Christ (see Matt. 17). We must not begrudge the Israelites the same grace that has saved us. May we be filled with holy fear when we presume to judge another's soul.

Let's look at atonement as the Israelites understood it. Leviticus 1–7 offers the best compact description of Israel's sacrificial system. This passage describes five types of sacrifices, which will be listed and briefly defined.

 As you study each of the following offerings, underline or highlight the distinctions that will help you remember it.

The burnt offering. This was offered in the evening and the morning, as well as on the Sabbath, at annual feasts, and other special days. The offering could be a young bull, goat, lamb, pigeon, or dove; but it must be a perfect specimen. The entire animal was burned on the altar. The offering apparently differed according to the giver's capability.

The grain offering. This was the only offering that did not involve bloodshed. Rather, it was offered from the harvest of the land and was composed of fine flour combined with oil, frankincense, and salt. It could also be baked into cakes, although leaven could not be used. A portion of this offering was burned on the altar, and the remainder was given to the priests.

The peace offering. The instructions for this offering were very similar to that of the burnt offering, the major difference being that only certain parts of the internal organs were burned. The priest received the breast and right thigh, and the giver received a quantity of meat for a meal of celebration. Thanksgiving was the heart of the peace offering.

The sin offering. This offering was designed to atone for sin that was committed unintentionally. Many of the same instructions for the other animal sacrifices applied here as well. One major difference was the distinctive instruction if the offender happened to be the priest or the congregation as a whole. In these cases the blood was sprinkled seven times before the veil in the sanctuary, then

♥ You may be surprised and even disappointed to learn that sacrifice was acceptable only on the basis of the graphic procedures examined in this week's study. What was God trying to teach by demanding such sacrifices?

sprinkled on the horns of the incense altar. Only certain internal organs were offered, and the remainder of the animal was disposed of outside the camp.

The guilt offering. This is sometimes referred to interchangeably with the sin offering and is therefore difficult to distinguish from it. The most outstanding difference between the two is that the guilt offering was chiefly concerned with restitution. That is, the sacrifice was accompanied by some kind of repayment or restitution offered to the one who was offended.

All five of these sacrifices could be carried out on an individual or a corporate basis. The sacrificial system God demanded of the Israelites had two obvious purposes: there must be payment for sin, and God had a payment plan.

We will observe the actual procedure of sacrifice by examining Leviticus 1. Although we might be tempted to omit the details of the sacrifice, in doing so we would overlook the perfect picture of our precious Lamb of God. Although Israel was called to experience sacrifice literally, we are called to experience it spiritually and typically.

Read Leviticus 1:3-6. Number the following procedures for the person offering the sacrifice in the order they were to occur.
_____ Lay hands on the animal's head.
_____ Slaughter the animal.
_____ Present the animal voluntarily at the door.
_____ Cut the animal into pieces.
_____ Choose a male animal without defect.
_____ Skin the animal.

Number the following procedures for the priests in the order they were to occur, according to Leviticus 1:5,7-9.
_____ Arrange the wood on the fire.
_____ Burn the offering.
_____ Arrange the carcass pieces on the fire.
_____ Sprinkle blood on the sides of the altar.

I once assumed that the priests performed all of the slaughtering, but I was incorrect. Each person desiring atonement made a personal sacrifice. Can you imagine laying one hand on the animal's head and slaughtering the animal with the other? We cringe at the thought; yet as the sinner held the animal's head while its life fled, God's purpose was clearly stated in living, crimson color: an innocent victim lost its life because of the sin of its killer. God desired that humans comprehend to some degree what price would later be paid on a wooden altar mounted at Golgotha. However, a significant difference would exist: He never asked one of them to slaughter an only child on an altar (see Gen. 22:2; Mark 1:11). Guilt was the emotional tie between the Israelite and the animal. Unspeakable love was the emotional tie between God and His Son. Oh, how He must have longed to hold the head of His precious Son until the life fled from Him, but all humanity would have remained lost. Sins could be atoned for on the cross only by heaping them on Christ Jesus, the unblemished Lamb. Think how many were yours and mine. His Father had no choice but to muster every degree of His omnipotence and to turn His head: "This is the will of Him who sent Me: that I should lose none of those He has given Me" (John 6:39, HCSB).

Read Leviticus 6:8-13. Number the following procedures for the priests' handling of the burnt offering in the order they were to occur, according to verses 8-11.

_____ Put on linen garments and undergarments.
_____ Keep the fire burning on the offering throughout the night.
_____ Carry the ashes outside the camp.
_____ Change clothes again.
_____ Place the ashes at the side of the altar.

At nightfall Aaron and his sons were to slay and burn an evening sacrifice that God commanded to be left burning on the altar all night. They were to rise early in the morning and wait for the last of the ashes to fall through the bronze grate of the altar. The ashes invariably fell at dawn. Ancient Hebrew history records that the moment the last ash fell, the priests blew the trumpets in celebration, shouting, "It is finished!" "When he had received the drink, Jesus said, 'It is finished.' With that, he bowed his head and gave up his spirit" (John 19:30).

This has been a hard lesson for us. As I first came to this point in the lesson, I felt an overwhelming need to talk to my Father. My guess is that you feel that need, too. Spend time expressing your gratitude for His amazing provision for our sins through the sacrifice of His beloved Son.

Day 4
Clean Hands and a Pure Heart

Begin your study by reading Today's Treasure and praying that God will speak to you through His Word.

Today we will take a step beyond the bronze altar to examine the other piece of furniture in the outer court: the bronze basin or laver.

Read Exodus 30:17-21 and answer the following questions.

What is the exact location of the bronze basin?
❑ beside the bronze altar   ❑ at the entrance of the tabernacle
❑ between the altar and the tabernacle

Today's Treasure

"WHO MAY ASCEND THE HILL OF THE LORD? WHO MAY STAND IN HIS HOLY PLACE? HE WHO HAS CLEAN HANDS AND A PURE HEART."
Psalm 24:3-4

What was the only material used to make the bronze basin?
❑ gold   ❑ brass   ❑ silver

What is the exact purpose of the basin?
❑ washing   ❑ cleaning sacrifices   ❑ purifying the water

Who was to use the bronze basin?
❑ Aaron   ❑ Aaron, his sons, and Moses
❑ Aaron and his descendants
❑ No one. It was to remain untouched.

What were they to do at the basin?
❑ wash their faces   ❑ wash their hands and feet
❑ sprinkle water on the sacrifices

Why was washing their hands and feet so important?
❑ They would otherwise die.
❑ They would set an example for the people.
❑ They would otherwise be cursed.

God sovereignly chose to tell us little about the wonderful bronze basin, but the brief insight in Exodus 38:8 is memorable.

From what was the basin made, according to Exodus 38:8?

_____

The basin was filled with water for cleansing the priests' hands and feet.

Based on the information we've already acquired, three questions arise that must be answered for us to comprehend the bronze basin's special significance.

What was the purpose of the bronze basin? Exodus 30:17-21 told us the basin was filled with water for cleansing the priests' hands and feet. The question remains, Why just the hands and feet?

What exact instructions do these verses give for priests' cleansing?

Exodus 29:4 _____

Exodus 30:19 _____

Notice that Exodus 29:4 implies washing of the entire man, while Exodus 30:19 speaks of the need to wash only the hands and feet.

What was the purpose of the cleansing? Exodus 29:1 says, "This is what you are to do to consecrate them, so they may serve me as priests." God was consecrating the priests for service in a one-time experience in which they were sanctified and deemed acceptable. On the other hand, Exodus 30:19-20 describes an ongoing act of cleansing the priests performed before entering the holy place. The first act of cleansing was initiated *for* them. The second was initiated *by* them.

The holy place was the sanctuary of fellowship. Priests could enter God's court based on a complete cleansing performed only once; however, to enter the place of fellowship with God, ongoing cleansing had to occur. That's why priests had to pass by the bronze altar before they could wash in the bronze basin. Without passing by the place of sacrifice, there was no cleansing from ongoing sin.

Why did the priests specifically wash their hands and feet? Note what the following Scriptures teach about hands and feet.

Exodus 3:1-5 _____

Psalm 24:3-6 _____

What was the significance of the bronze basin's being formed from mirrors? The gracious women likely chose their offering from riches received from Egyptian women in the exodus. These mirrors were flattened pieces of highly-polished brass—luxuries in any home. Common women had to catch their reflections in the nearest pond.

How fitting that the basin of cleansing was from mirrors! The women contributed these costly mirrors to offer something that represented vanity. It was a beautiful Old Testament expression of dying to self. The mirrored basin also provided a sharp reflection of the priest as he stood before it for cleansing. The purpose is clear: before we can truly come before God for cleansing, we must examine ourselves to discover how we have erred. Several years ago I ceased the repetitious prayer "Forgive me of all my sins" because I realized that I could not turn away from a sin I had not first confronted.

"Godly sorrow brings repentance that leads to salvation and leaves no regret, but worldly sorrow brings death" (2 Cor. 7:10). God has used this verse to help me understand the definition of true repentance. Real repentance is always accompanied by godly sorrow. Asking God to forgive us for a sin we are not yet sorry we committed is a waste of time. If that is the case, we must begin by asking Him to give us godly sorrow for our sin so that we can know true repentance, which guarantees forgiveness (see 1 John 1:9).

No doubt you realize that every detail of the Old Testament tabernacle reflects a deep New Testament truth we can apply. The bronze basin is no exception. What acts as our basin as Christians today? What is our mirror?

Record the information each Scripture offers about cleansing.

Ephesians 5:25-26 _____

Hebrews 10:22 _____

1 Peter 1:22 _____

The perfect sacrifice was offered for us on Calvary.

The outer court had only two fixtures, but how vital they were! You must pass by the blood and the water to enter the place where the fellowship is sweet. Just as the bronze basin offered the Israelites the right to be cleansed from daily sin, the perfect sacrifice was offered for us on Calvary. "One of the soldiers pierced Jesus' side with a spear, bringing a sudden flow of blood and water" (John 19:34).

In the upper room Christ retaught this same divine lesson to the disciples in an unforgettable way.

John 13 records the Passover Feast where Jesus washed His disciples' feet. What was Peter's response to Christ in verse 8?

_____

What was Christ's rebuttal to Peter in that same verse?

_____

Notice that Christ did not say, "You have no part of me" but, "You have no part with me." Again, the crucial message is that the full cleansing they had received on accepting Him concerned regeneration. The partial cleansing of their feet concerned relationship.

Why did Christ wash only their feet? Obviously, to enable them to walk with Him, which would be possible only through an ongoing cleansing, and to teach them servanthood.

When we witness the disciples being forced to confront their egos, we may be strangely moved to confront our own.

What was Jesus' command in John 13:14?

_____

Consider seven reasons we have difficulty following Jesus' command.
1. We lack the assurance of who we are. Look at John 13:3. Jesus knew what the Father had given Him. He knew His position with His Father. He had nothing to prove; therefore, He was not humiliated by humility. We are coheirs with Christ (see Rom. 8). If you know who you are in Christ, your personal ego is not an issue. Sadly, most Christians do not have the confidence in Christ to humble themselves.
2. We don't want to leave the table to do it. John 13:4 says Christ got up from the table. We fear leaving the comfort of the familiar. But remember what we learned in week 1: if we are never able to get outside that which is *comfortable*, we will often forfeit the very thing that is *conformable* to Christ.
3. We would have to lay aside the outer garments. It is difficult to hide when washing another's feet. True servants are only those who are willing to be vulnerable.

4. All too often, our pitchers are empty. Look at John 13:5. We might wash a few feet if we had something in our pitchers. When we fail to be filled, we have nothing to pour out. Be encouraged: the first miracle Christ performed was filling up empty pitchers. He is a master at it!

5. We do not like feet. They are smelly and dirty, and we could minister to persons far more easily if they would just stay behind their sparkling facades. Facing the worn, calloused areas of others' lives might remind us of our own. Much too risky indeed.

6. We'd have to get on our knees to do it. John the Baptist said of Christ, "He must increase, but I must decrease" (John 3:30, HCSB). Now that's servanthood. You may think, *I can gladly humble myself before Christ.* But He said, "Whatever you did for one of the least of these brothers of mine, you did for me" (Matt. 25:40).

7. Perhaps the most important reason we somehow cannot bring ourselves to wash another's feet is that we refuse to let Christ wash our own. Notice that not until He washed their feet were they enabled to go and wash one another's. Have you learned how to let Christ minister to you? Let me make this assignment: let Christ love you today. Curl up in His arms and tell Him you need Him. Until you learn to let Him serve you at the point of your need, you will never be truly free to serve others.

Let's end today's study with the assurance found in Zephaniah 3:17: "The LORD your God is with you, he is mighty to save. He will take great delight in you, he will quiet you with his love, he will rejoice over you with singing."

♥ Recall a time when your "pitcher" was empty. How did you feel when others asked you for something during this period of time?

How was your pitcher finally refilled?

Day 5
Contentment in the Calling

Begin your study by reading Today's Treasure and praying that God will speak to you through His Word.

We cannot leave the perimeters of the outer court to enter the holy place without rejoicing over the privilege of having been there! You see, to the masses of people, the outer court was as close as they would ever come to God. The outer court was not just the means by which people could get to the holy place. To many it was as holy a place as they would ever get to experience. Only the priests could enter farther.

God has divinely inspired a beautiful testimony of what it was like to dwell in the court of His tabernacle.

Read aloud Psalm 84. Feel the flow of the psalm and rejoice as you read it.

Today's Treasure

"LOOK UPON OUR SHIELD, O GOD; LOOK WITH FAVOR ON YOUR ANOINTED ONE. BETTER IS ONE DAY IN YOUR COURTS THAN A THOUSAND ELSEWHERE; I WOULD RATHER BE A DOORKEEPER IN THE HOUSE OF MY GOD THAN DWELL IN THE TENTS OF THE WICKED."
Psalm 84:9-10

87

Many Bible versions have headings above each psalm stating who wrote it and for whom it was written. If your Bible has this information, you can see that the sons of Korah were to sing this psalm. Likely, the Korahites' music director wrote it specifically for them. Let's learn some of their history so we can appreciate their ability to rejoice over the courts of the Lord. According to *Holman Illustrated Bible Dictionary*, the Korahites were "descendants of Korah who belonged to the Kohathite Levites." *Kohathite* is an "alternate spelling of Korahites," inviting us to often view the terms interchangeably.[1] Your reading in today's lesson will be important to our comprehension of the Old Testament tabernacle's outer court.

Read Numbers 4:1-33 and answer the following questions.

Of what tribal descent were the sons of Korah? _____

Glance at verse 20. What was God's warning to the Kohathites?

_____

Aaron and his sons, the chosen priesthood, had the awesome responsibility of collecting and covering the divine articles of the holy place and the holy of holies, when it was time for them to be moved. The Korahites were Levi's descendants, so God assigned them the crucial task of transporting through the wilderness the articles that had first been carefully covered by Aaron and his sons. Scripture teaches if they looked at these holy articles for even a moment, they would die.

Numbers 16 tells about a rebellion against Moses. Read the verses noted and answer the following questions.

What was the basis for the Korahite rebellion (v. 3)?

_____

Who, in His sovereignty, had set apart the leaders of this

wilderness generation (vv. 8-9)? _____

What questions did Moses ask Korah in verses 9-11?

_____

_____

What was God's judgment on the Korahites (vv. 31-33)? _____

_____

What was to be a reminder to the Israelites that God was sovereign in how He chose to make Himself approachable (vv. 39-40)?

_____

God must have either spared or appointed a godly remnant of Korahites to take their place and assume their name. We know this because *sons of Korah* in Psalms refers to the descendants who became temple musicians in the days of the monarchy under Kings David and Solomon. Many generations may have passed between the wilderness and the kingdom, but the sons of Korah never forgot their fathers' sins. We should have the same response to our fathers' sins that the sons of Korah had to theirs. They did not accept the shame or the blame for their fathers' sins, nor did they bask in the bitterness of their unfortunate heritage. Yet they readily accepted and learned the lesson that was taught through their fathers' judgment. This is the perfect balance God teaches us in Ezekiel 18. "O house of Israel, I will judge you, each one according to his ways, declares the Sovereign LORD" (v. 30).

Now reread Psalm 84 with understanding as the sons of Korah sing a new song!

After you have read the psalm again, ponder the words of verses 2,9-10, meditating on the significance of the word courts. Allow me to paraphrase these verses: "O God our Shield, You may turn Your face to look on us once more. We are the anointed servants You assigned to a task. We are not guilty of our fathers' sins, for we have found complete satisfaction in Your courts! Hear from our hearts, O God! We are a people humbled to accept any form of servitude You would grant us. I would rather be a doorkeeper in the house of my God than to take up residence in the finest abodes this world could boast. For a day in Your courts is better than a thousand elsewhere."

If you struggle with your importance in God's kingdom, realize that one day at the task God has personally assigned only you is better than a thousand days at someone else's. Just as demanding a greater position of service meant literal death for the Korahites, craving what God did not choose us to do would mean death for our ministries. Only God's chosen task for you will ultimately satisfy. Do not wait until it is too late to realize the privilege of serving Him in His chosen position for you.

Let's close this week with these special verses from Psalms: "Blessed are those you choose and bring near to live in your courts! We are filled with the good things of your house, of your holy temple" (65:4). "Enter his gates with thanksgiving and his courts with praise; give thanks to him and praise his name. For the LORD is good and his love endures forever; his faithfulness continues through all generations" (100:4-5).

♥ Read Psalm 84. What does it mean to enjoy God's presence and worship Him intimately?

Only God's chosen task for you will ultimately satisfy.

---

1. *Holman Illustrated Bible Dictionary* (Nashville: Holman Bible Publishers, 2003), 1001.

Viewer Guide

Hearts Approaching the Altar

Today we will review our construction site thus far and then set our gaze on the imposing vessel positioned between the gate and the door of the Tabernacle. Outside the holy of holies, no vessel had greater significance than the altar of sacrifice. We will recap some of the details we learned in day 2 of our homework, add to them, and picture ourselves within them.

Recap Exodus 27:1-8 then read Exodus 29:42-46.
May God choose to meet us at the altar today, take us to its four corners, and show us the altar from four perspectives.

I. A place of _____

Read Isaiah 6:1-8.

2. A place of _____

See the words "atoned for" in Isaiah 6:7. The Hebrew transliteration *kapar* means "to _____ … make _____ … It is often used with reference to 'covering' sin with the blood of a _____."

Compare Psalm 32:1-7.

3. A place of _____
Read I Kings 1:50-53 (drawing back to Ex. 21:13-14).

4. A place of _____

Read Leviticus 9:22-24 and compare Exodus 29:35-37.

Consider Psalm 32:1 again. The Hebrew word translated "blessed" in this verse means *happy.*

Hearts in Fellowship

DAY 1 • THE HOLY PLACE

DAY 2 • THE GOLDEN LAMPSTAND

DAY 3 • FILLING THE LAMPS

DAY 4 • A TABLE SET BEFORE HIM

DAY 5 • THE BREAD OF THE PRESENCE

WEEK 5

This week we are invited to behold and go beyond the first curtain concealing the sanctuary—what we will sometimes call the tabernacle proper. We now have the opportunity to enter the holy place, the center of service and fellowship. We will determine the perimeters of the tabernacle proper and will distinguish the holy place from the holy of holies. We will relish the appearances of the lampstand and the table of bread of the Presence and will discover their apparent representations. We will seek answers to the following questions.

Principal Questions

1. What was woven in the fine linen ceiling?
2. What happened to Aaron's rod?
3. Whom did Christ send to fuel us so we can be His light in a dark world?
4. How often was the bread to appear on the table?
5. By what name did Christ refer to Himself in John 6:32?

Enter the holy place and discover the privilege of service and joy of fellowship in God's presence.

Day 1
The Holy Place

Read Today's Treasure and pray that God will speak to you through His Word.

What a joyous privilege we will experience today as we enter the tabernacle proper, the home of the holy place and the holy of holies. Holy indeed is the outer room of the tabernacle. Only priests may enter its perfectly-ordained perimeters. Do you meet this important qualification?

Write the phrase in which the word *priest* or *priesthood* appears.

I Peter 2:9 _____

Revelation 1:5-6 _____

Today's Treasure

"HE WILL COVER YOU WITH HIS FEATH-ERS, AND UNDER HIS WINGS YOU WILL FIND REFUGE; HIS FAITHFUL-NESS WILL BE YOUR SHIELD AND RAMPART."

Psalm 91:4

If you have accepted Christ's gift of salvation, you are a part of the royal priesthood of His present kingdom. You have permission to enter the holy place!

I hope that daily you prepare for your study with prayer. Without the personal supplication of the Holy Spirit, your text today will seem confusing and impossible to picture. John 16:13 says that the Holy Spirit "will guide you into all truth." If you have not done so, pause and ask God for the understanding that only His Spirit can bring.

We will follow the same approach to the holy place that we practiced with the outer court: we will study the structure from the outside in. Exodus 26 tells about the materials used and the instructions of how the tabernacle curtains were to be designed. Exodus 36 then tells how the workmen carried out the instructions just as they had been given.

Read the verses indicated and fill in the blanks.

The boards or frames were made of _____ wood and

overlaid with _____ (see Ex. 36:20,34). Each board or

frame was _____ cubits long and _____ cubits wide (v. 21).

These boards stood upright, making the tabernacle proper 10 cubits tall. Examine the diagram you completed in week 4 (p. 74).

_____ frames were on the north and south sides (36:23,25).

Six frames were on the west or back wall, with an extra frame or board on each end to provide for the corners.

> The boards or frames were placed in _____ silver sockets or bases (v. 26). These boards were connected, forming three solid walls on the north, west, and south sides and leaving a space for
>
> the entrance on the _____ side. Verses 31-32 tell us that
>
> _____ bars or crossbars connected the boards on the three walls of the tabernacle.

Four of these crossbars ran through perfectly aligned gold rings on the outside of the three walls. The fifth was inserted through a hole that ran through the insides of the boards, connecting them with one common link.

> Draw a replica of the outer court you drew in week 4 (p. 74), including only the tribe of Judah at this time. Mark the perimeters 100 cubits in length and 50 cubits in width. Next you will draw the actual tabernacle in the court.

The tabernacle proper was also rectangular in length but much smaller. Because each board or frame was 1½ cubits and 20 of them were on the north and south walls (in other words, running the length of the tabernacle from the front entrance to the back wall), the tabernacle proper measured 30 cubits from front to back. The west or back wall, excluding the corners, consisted of 6 boards 1½ cubits long, so it measured 10 cubits.

Place your pencil at the center of the courtyard in your diagram. This is the approximate position of the entrance to the tabernacle proper, with the remainder of the structure aligned behind it. Draw the tabernacle proper inside the outer court. Your drawing should include an outer court, with the tabernacle proper in its back half and ample space around it. Both structures are rectangular, with the length running east to west.

Divide the tabernacle proper into thirds. The front two-thirds of the tabernacle proper make up the holy place. The back third is the holy of holies.

You know what crucial articles are placed in the space between the outer court gate and the tabernacle proper's entrance: the bronze altar and the bronze basin. Draw the altar and the basin in their appropriate places. Now label every part of your diagram.

Glancing back over Exodus 26 and 36, you will undoubtedly notice that the tabernacle proper was covered by a series of carefully-specified curtains—custom draperies, you might say. Let's attempt to picture the curtains.

The tabernacle did not have a solid ceiling; rather, four large canopies were draped over the top and hung down the north, west, and south sides in perfect order. Again, let's proceed from the outside to the inside of the tabernacle proper's curtained "ceiling." Visible from the outside were the hides of what the New International Version calls sea cows (see Ex. 26:14). Most scholars agree that they were the hides of the sea cow or dugong, a herbivorous mammal native to the Red Sea often used to make sandals. Doesn't sound like a lovely sight, does it? But only those who dared to enter could behold the beauty hidden within. How like our Savior's incarnate presence: "He had no beauty or majesty to attract us to him" (Isa. 53:2). Yet within Him "all the fullness of the Deity lives in bodily form" (Col. 2:9).

Exodus 26:14 mentions a second curtain. Just inside the outer curtain was a garment of rams' skins dyed _____.

The ram was the sacrificial offering accepted as a substitution for Abram's beloved son, Isaac. The ram was also the acceptable sacrifice for the consecration of the tabernacle priests. How beautifully the red rams' skins picture our risen Savior, Jesus Christ! He is the Sacrifice: "He has appeared one time, at the end of the ages, for the removal of sin by the sacrifice of Himself" (Heb. 9:26, HCSB). He is the Substitute "who gave himself for our sins" (Gal. 1:4). He is the Consecration: "The law appoints as high priests men who are weak; but the oath, which came after the law, appointed the Son, who has been made perfect forever" (Heb. 7:28). When we are covered by the Ram's skin baptized in blood, we have redemption from sin.

The third curtain serving as the ceiling for the tabernacle proper is named in Exodus 26:7: the curtain of goats' hair. Certainly, the goat was the preeminent sacrifice for the sin offering, but let's not miss an additional application.

Christ is the Sacrifice, the Substitution, and the Consecration.

What two men wore "garments of hair"?

2 Kings 1:8 _____   Matthew 3:4 _____

Christ Himself proclaimed that Elijah was a type, or picture, of John the Baptist (see Matt. 11:7-15). These two were forerunners of the first and second comings, of Christ (see Mal. 4:5; John 1:23). These garments of hair distinguished them as God's chosen prophets. Within the two curtains made from the skins of sacrificial animals was draped a promise of the Messiah's coming.

The colors woven into the fine linen ceiling were the same as the ones embroidered into the outer court gate we studied previously—blue, scarlet, and purple (see Ex. 26:1-6).

The entrance to the holy place was also beautifully designed with the same colors as those hung from the five golden posts (see Ex. 26:36).

Despite the similarities of fabric and colors in the outer court's gate, the holy place's door, and the holy place's ceiling, one remarkable difference existed.

What was to be woven in the fine linen ceiling (see Ex. 26:1)?

_____

Prior to study I had assumed that the blue, purple, and scarlet cherubim woven into the white linen symbolized the heavenly hosts that surround God's throne; however, Psalm 61:4 tells us something entirely different!

In what structure will the psalmist abide forever according to Psalm 61:4?
❏ the house of the Lord   ❏ the heavenlies
❏ His tabernacle or tent

Under whose wings will the psalmist find cover?
❏ the wings of God   ❏ the wings of the cherubim
❏ the wings of the wind

What do the following verses say about God's wings?

Psalm 17:8 _____

Psalm 63:7 _____

Psalm 91:4 _____

What did Christ want to do for the nation of Israel (Matt. 23:37)?

_____

How perfectly Christ portrays the nurturing wings of El Shaddai, the Caregiver. God's wings covered His children with safety, security, joy, and affection. In His perfect parenting God is both paternal and maternal, both the loving disciplinarian and the nurturing protector who covers His children with His life.

Let Me Illustrate provides a penetrating illustration that represents God's protection. In pioneer days, wood-burning locomotives frequently sparked fires. Wheat ripens enough to burn 10 to 15 days before it is ripe enough to cut, and sometimes the fires swept wheat fields for 10 miles. A farmer saw billows of smoke in the distance and knew his house, barn, and surrounding buildings were in danger. He set backfires and burned his own wheat fields in a circle so that when the great fire met the place he had burned, it passed around and went on. With that backfire the farmer saved his buildings but lost his crop. As he walked the burned field grieving, he saw the charred body of a hen. He tipped the hen over with the toe of his boot, and out ran a dozen little chicks. Because the mother's burned body was over them, the chicks lived. Because she had been willing to die, those under the cover of her wings would live.[1]

"He will cover you with his feathers, and under his wings you will find refuge" (Ps. 91:4). Learn to experience the warmth and protection of life beneath the wings of the Almighty.

♥ **Write a prayer acknowledging God as your caregiver and thanking Him for covering you with His wings.**

The Golden Lampstand

Read Today's Treasure and pray that God will speak to you through His Word.

We now stand at the entrance to the tabernacle proper. We have passed the place of sacrifice and cleansing. We await our entrance into the holy place. Picture the scene: five golden columns reflect the blue, purple, and scarlet embroidery on the white linen curtains hung behind them. Go ahead. Lift the heavy curtain and enter as His guest. Undoubtedly, your eyes are first drawn to the light, just as He planned it. The lampstand is the only source of illumination in the tabernacle.

Exodus 25:31-40 gives the instructions for making the lampstand. Verse 31 tells that the lampstand was made of only one type of material. What was it?

_____

What kinds of flowers were to be emulated in the lampstand's design (v. 33)?

_____

Today's Treasure

"THE SPIRIT OF THE LORD WILL REST ON HIM— THE SPIRIT OF WISDOM AND OF UNDERSTANDING, THE SPIRIT OF COUNSEL AND OF POWER, THE SPIRIT OF KNOWLEDGE AND OF THE FEAR OF THE LORD."

Isaiah 11:2

How many lamps were to be on the single stand (v. 37)? _____

What other accessories had to be made of pure gold (v. 38)?

_____

The lampstand
was the only
means for seeing
evidence of God
in His holy place.

Imagine how the light from the lampstand danced off the golden walls. What indescribably rich hues must have filled the holy room! There were no windows and no other sources of light, only a single stand with seven lamps. Just to gaze on the lampstand would have been a heavenly sight for earthly eyes. Made from a talent of gold, about 75 pounds, this fixture would have been worth well over $500,000 by today's standards. The lampstand's spiritual worth was infinite, for it was the only means for seeing evidence of God in His holy place. In darkness the other articles would have been impossible to see.

In contrast to the exact perimeters of the holy place we studied in day 1, measurements for the golden lampstand were not given.

How did the craftsmen know how large to make the lampstand?

_____

To whom were instructions provided so that the lampstand could be made according to the heavenly pattern given to Moses? Review Exodus 31:1-3. _____

God, in His infinite wisdom, did not desire for those measurements to be recorded. You see, His illumination cannot be measured.

How was the lampstand to be constructed (Ex. 25:31)? Check one of the following.
❑ beaten or hammered
❑ twisted and shaped
❑ poured into molds

This process must have been more than tedious. Very likely, it was painful as well. Notice that the lampstand had to be hammered or beaten from one large piece of gold into its heavenly form. It continually had to bear the purifying fires to make it pliable for shaping. The result, however, was a work of incomparable beauty!

The lampstand had a single shaft with three branches proceeding from each side, for a total of seven lampstands. Importantly, it was built from a heavenly pattern, reminding us again that each part of the structure represented the true Lampstand that existed in heaven. Let's get a glimpse of that heavenly pattern as we seek to learn more about the tabernacle's lampstand.

Read Revelation 4:1-5, the Apostle John's divinely inspired description of the throne room of God. Give special attention to verse 5, in which the seven lamps burn before the throne. God interprets these lampstands to us immediately. They are

_____

At first this explanation seems confusing. Isn't there only one Holy Spirit of God? Yes. Seven is the number of perfection and completion in God's Word. The lampstands represent the seven perfections of the one Holy Spirit, or the sevenfold Spirit of God.

In the space below draw a lampstand with one middle shaft, three branches to its right, and three branches to its left.

Read Isaiah 11:1-2.

God used the prophet Isaiah to define the sevenfold attributes of the Spirit of God. Of those seven, one stands by itself: the Spirit of the Lord. On the diagram of the lampstand you drew in the margin, label the middle shaft with the all-encompassing title *The Spirit of the Lord* because it proceeds directly from the "root" of the lampstand. Now fill in the other six attributes (wisdom, understanding, counsel, might, knowledge, fear) in proper Hebrew form: from right to left.

♥ How has the Holy Spirit recently made Himself known in your life through one of these six attributes?

Look again at Isaiah 11:1. Who was the rod or the shoot to come from the stem of Jesse (see Rom. 15:8-9,12-13)?

_____

Read John 15:2,4-6, and complete the selected sentences.

"He _____ every branch in me that bears no fruit, while every branch that does bear fruit he prunes so that

it will be even more _____. ...

99

No branch can bear fruit by itself; it must remain in the vine.

Neither can you _____

unless you remain in me. I am the vine; you are the _____.

If a man remains in me and I in him, he will _____

_____. ... If anyone does not remain in me, he is like a

branch that is _____ and _____;
such branches are picked up, thrown into the fire and burned."

These branches also refer to Christ's bride. Just as Eve, Adam's bride, was formed from his side, we, Christ's bride, are formed from the side of the Vine: "I in them, and thou in me, that they may be made perfect in one" (John 17:23, KJV).

What is the significance of the almond flowers with buds and branches? In the passage you just studied, the comparison is that we are pruned to bear more fruit "to my Father's glory" (John 15:8). The branches attached to the tabernacle lampstand's "vine" all bear "fruit" to God's glory. On day 3 we will discover further why Christ might have been glorified in the lampstand.

Let's draw another comparison by reading Numbers 17:1-11. What happened to Aaron's rod?

_____

What was the purpose of the budding rod? Check one.
❏ to reveal God's glory ❏ to guide the children of Israel
❏ to identify God's chosen servant

What does Matthew 12:33 say about fruit?
❏ The deeds of darkness are fruitless.
❏ A tree is known by its fruit.
❏ Fruit is the outcome of obedience.

The fruit of Aaron's rod and the fruit from our own branches have the same purpose: to authenticate the fruit bearer.

Of what will our fruit consist? Record every quality you discover in Galatians 5:22-23.

_____

_____

What kind of fruit is this?
- ❑ the fruit of the Spirit ❑ the fruit of believers
- ❑ the fruit of good works

Recall what the seven lamps of fire burning before the throne are in Revelation 4:5.
- ❑ the children of God ❑ the light of God
- ❑ the seven attributes of the Holy Spirit of God

Obviously, the branch's ability to bud, blossom, and produce fruit has everything to do with the Holy Spirit. We will dedicate day 3 to the discovery of this relationship. I pray that you are delighting in the discovery of God's truth, beautifully portrayed in the Old Testament tabernacle. Stay attached to the Vine, for without Him we can do nothing!

Day 3
Filling the Lamps

Read Today's Treasure and pray that God will speak to you through His Word.

Today we will continue our study of the golden lampstand in the tabernacle of testimony.

In Exodus 25:31-40, the King James Version uses the word *candlestick* rather than *lampstand*. Understand that no traditional candles were involved. One major difference exists between the way a candle burns and the way a lamp burns: a candle burns by consuming itself, while a lamp burns by consuming a continuous supply of oil from another source. The seven lamps on the one golden lampstand were fueled by oil.

Read Leviticus 24:2,4 and answer the following questions:

Who was to bring the oil for the lamps? _____

What kind of oil did it have to be? _____

How often was the lampstand to burn? _____

Romans 11 reminds readers that the Israelites were the original olive branches.

Look back at Leviticus 24:2. To reinforce an important point, answer this question one more time: Who was to bring the oil?
- ❑ the Israelites ❑ sons of Aaron ❑ priests

"YOU ARE THE LIGHT OF THE WORLD."

Matthew 5:14

101

Read Romans 11:17. Who are the "wild olive shoots" who have been grafted in?

❏ believing Gentiles   ❏ believing Jews

❏ the righteous remnant

Who do you think is the Olive Tree into whom all believers, Jews and Gentiles, will be grafted (see Rom. 11:24)?

_____

Matthew 5:14-16 speaks of a lampstand that thrives on oil rather than a candle that consumes its own wax. What does Christ call us

in these verses? _____

How did Christ's body respond to His deep anguish and fervent prayer according to Luke 22:39-46?

_____

Now read Mark 14:32. What was the name of the garden where Christ agonized on the Mount of Olives?

_____

Who was pressed or beaten to make the pure, clear olive oil so that we could continue to burn as the light of the world?

_____

Why did Christ tell His disciples that it was good for them that

He was departing (John 16:7)? _____

In the margin, list every fact about the Holy Spirit you find in John 14:16-17.

From what you read in John 14:16-17; 16:7, whom did Christ send to fuel us so that we can be His light in a dark world?

_____

According to John 14:16, how long will that heavenly "fuel" remain with believers in Christ?

❏ as long as we obey   ❏ until Christ returns   ❏ forever

We are the heavenly lampstands of this age to show Jesus to a dark world. He is no less present when we hide our lamp, but, when we do this, we make it harder for those walking in darkness to see. Christ was the Olive Tree pressed to make available the pure oil of the Holy Spirit to fuel our lamps continually.

When we receive Christ as our personal Savior, the fuel of the Holy Spirit sparks the life of Christ in our hearts. Although that light can never be extinguished, the brightness of our flame entirely depends on how much oil (the Holy Spirit) we allow Christ to pour on us. God's entire being unites to produce in you the brightest possible flame. The Father offered the Light (John 1) and created every human with a wick to receive it (2 Pet. 3:9). The Son came bearing the light to any who will receive it. The Holy Spirit came to fuel it perpetually. If we do not burn with a passionate flame, it is because we have limited God, who prepared us for victory. Paul warns us: "Do not put out the Spirit's fire" (I Thess. 5:19).

Which does Paul command us to be in Ephesians 5:18?
❑ baptized
❑ led by the Holy Spirit
❑ filled

God's entire being unites to produce in you the brightest possible flame.

If we invite God to pour on His Holy Spirit and if we allow that perpetual light to burn unhindered and uncovered, an amazing phenomenon takes place: we are filled with the Spirit. When we are filled with the Spirit, another chain reaction takes place. We produce the fruit of the Spirit (see Gal. 5:22-23)!

♥ **Can you identify the fruit of the Spirit in your life? If not, what do you need to change for your life to exhibit this fruit?**

_____

_____

_____

Now we have arrived at the answer to today's final question: What is the relationship between the Holy Spirit and the fruit depicted on our holy lampstands?

Just as the gifts of the Spirit represent Christ's ministry, the fruit of the Spirit represents Christ's personality. When we allow the Holy Spirit to flow freely through our purified vessels, His personality takes over and we display love, joy, peace, patience, kindness, goodness, faithfulness, gentleness, and self-control. How often we wear ourselves out praying for more patience, faith, joy, or peace. All of these are the supernatural response of a Spirit-filled believer! A more appropriate prayer is "Lord, purify me and make me a fit vessel for Your presence. Then fill me to overflowing with Your precious Holy Spirit." The fruit will supernaturally and automatically be produced.

Number in order the following activities that link the Father's gift of Light to the believer's production of fruit.

___ a. Christ sends His Spirit to all who receive Him.

___ b. The oil (Spirit) fills all lamps (believers) who surrender to become the light of the world in Christ's visible absence.

___ c. The Father sent His gift of Light, Jesus Christ, who ministered on earth as the Light of the world.

___ d. Through His agony Christ went through the olive press, making the oil of the Holy Spirit available as He promised.

___ e. The filling of the Holy Spirit produces light for the world to see and fruit for the believer to bear.

___ f. The Father is glorified.

You will find the answers at the end of today's lesson. Do you see this process as a blessed chain reaction that is beautifully portrayed in the lampstand bearing almond blossoms? Perhaps you are frustrated and low on fuel because you are the only lampstand in your home or workplace. You wonder how much light you can be in your dark surroundings.

What happens if you place your lamp on a stand? (Matt. 5:14-16)

"It gives light for _____ "

Persevere. Your light may be the one God uses to illuminate Himself in the midst of your dark surroundings. One morning I removed the ashes from our fireplace and set them in a paper bag on the back porch. Because we had not built a fire since the afternoon before, I could handle the ashes with my hands. That night one of my daughters began screaming, "Fire!" I turned to see my entire back porch illuminated by a fire from the blazing paper bag! Once a tiny ember neared something flammable, the flame spread wildly. In addition, the fire seemed much brighter against the backdrop of darkness.

Conclude today's study by reading Genesis 1:1-3. What were God's first recorded words?

_____

Hear Him whisper those same words to you every morning when you open your eyes: "Today, My precious child, let there be light."

And at the end of the day, when He tucks you tenderly into your bed, may He delight to say, "There was light."

Answers to the activity on page 103: a. 3, b. 4, c. 1, d. 2, e. 5, f. 6.

Day 4
A Table Set Before Him

Read Today's Treasure and pray that God will speak to you through His Word.

On days 2 and 3 the golden lampstand illuminated its own architecture. Today as we glance to the right and behold what the light illuminates directly across from it, the first thing we see in the tabernacle is the table. Its description appears in Exodus 25:23-30; 37:10-16. Like the lampstand, the first passage gives God's instructions for making the table, and the second passage records the making of the table to the exact specifications given.

Today's Treasure

"YOU PREPARE A TABLE BEFORE ME IN THE PRESENCE OF MY ENEMIES. YOU ANOINT MY HEAD WITH OIL; MY CUP OVERFLOWS."

Psalm 23:5

What materials were used to construct the table (Ex. 25:23)?

_____

What were its measurements (25:23)?

_____

What was the purpose of the rings (25:26-27)?

_____

What vessels were made as accessories for the table (25:28-29)?

_____

What was to be placed on the table (25:30)? _____

How often was the bread to appear on the table (25:30)?

_____

Cite all uses of gold (25:25-26,28-29).

_____

_____

Today we search the Scriptures for the interpretation of the table; day 5, for the truths of the bread of the Presence (NIV) or shewbread (KJV) on the table.

This is the first time from the first word of creation to the wilderness wanderings that God mentions the word *table*. Our word *table* is a translation of the Hebrew word *shulchan*, which means *a meal* or *spread*, most often implying *on a table*.

The table was undoubtedly a place of communion and fellowship. Being asked to sit at another's table was both a privilege and a sign of acceptance. The table was a center of fellowship, just as it is today. Rarely do we accept an invitation to someone's home without a table of some kind being prepared. Whether we share a meal or a simple dessert, fellowship is the goal.

Christian psychologists have stated that one of the greatest losses of communication in the modern family is the near extinction of the family meal. A well-known psychologist said we cannot estimate the far-reaching negative repercussions the family, the church, and ultimately the nation will reap for trading a half hour of family unity around the dinner table for other activities.

Read each Scripture reference; then draw a line to match it with the corresponding occasion in the opposite column. Look for a common thread that weaves together every mention of a table.

2 Samuel 9:1,6-7,10	• celebrating the presence of the Bridegroom
1 Kings 2:7	• those appointed to the kingdom
Psalm 23:5	a show of kindness to Barzillai's sons
Luke 5:27-35	• prepared in the presence of his enemies
Luke 22:27	• a remembrance of Jesus
John 12:1-3	• the acceptance of Jonathan's son as his own
1 Corinthians 10:21	• the inability to sit at both the Lord's table and the table of devils
1 Corinthians 11:24-26	• to honor Jesus after He raised Lazarus from the dead

All of these events did not occur coincidentally at a table. What is the common thread weaving together these experiences?
❑ **Christ, the Head of every table**
❑ **believers' avoiding unbelievers**
❑ **the fellowship and acceptance that occur at the table**

I can testify the table does not have to be of traditional stature to provide opportunities for fellowship. We do not have a study in our home; therefore, when I began to write full-time, my computer and books took up residence on our dining table. Another result of my commitment to full-time writing (from school bell to school bell) is that the maid got behind, and clean clothes began to stack up on our breakfast table. (If you see her, please direct her our way. She looks a lot like me.) The Moores learned to share many happy meals on a blanket spread on the den floor. We found ourselves reclining to eat "just like Jesus did," as Michael once said.

> **Certainly, the table of the bread of the Presence represented communion. Of what two materials was the table constructed?**
> ❏ bronze   ❏ gold   ❏ wood   ❏ silver

Remember that the wood represents humanity and the gold represents deity. God and persons communed at the table of the bread of the Presence. Thus, the marvelous ministry of reconciliation is evident once again in the tabernacle. Notice several other unique attributes of God's table.

> **According to Exodus 25:25, what surrounded the table of the bread of the Presence?**
> ❏ golden almond blossoms   ❏ the lampstand   ❏ a border or rim
>
> **What might you assume was the purpose of this golden rim?**

_____

The table's rim was to secure the articles so that none of them would be lost. Even the measurement of the rim supports this interpretation: "a handbreadth wide."

> **What assurance do you find in John 10:27-29?**
> ❏ No one can pluck His sheep from His hand.
> ❏ God has the future in His hands.
> ❏ They pierced His feet and His hands.

> ♥ Read one of God's perfect promises, Isaiah 49:14-16. What phrase tells you something about God's hands?

_____

Luke 13 records three of Jesus' parables—the lost sheep, the lost coin, and the lost son. In the first two the owner searched for a single lost sheep and a single lost coin until they were found. The third story, the story of the prodigal son, tells about forgiveness and restored relationship. Note that all three stories end with a celebration because that which was lost has now been found. When the lost son returned home, the father celebrated with a feast.

Our hearts are prone to wander and tempted to squander our Father's inheritance on the world's cheap amusements. But when our eyes awaken to reality, when we lift our heads above the compromise, and when our stomachs ache for the food of home, a certain Father will always be standing at the gate, ready to prepare a feast for us, waiting anxiously for His prodigal to come home.

Day 5
The Bread
of the Presence

Today's Treasure

"THE BREAD OF GOD IS
HE WHO COMES DOWN
FROM HEAVEN AND GIVES
LIFE TO THE WORLD."

John 6:33

Read Today's Treasure and ask God to speak to you through His Word.

In day 4 we studied the glorious table, which was positioned across from the golden lampstand. Today will be dedicated to the study of the offering on the table: the bread of the Presence.

Read Exodus 25:30 and Leviticus 24:5-9. Then read the following statements and determine whether they are true or false, writing *T* or *F* in the space provided. If the answer is false, cross out the incorrect word and write the correct word above it.

_____ I. The main ingredient of the bread of was yeast.

_____ 2. Twelve cakes or loaves were to be prepared and placed on the table.

_____ 3. The cakes were positioned in three rows of four on the table.

_____ 4. Incense was also placed along the rows of the bread.

_____ 5. The stated purpose of the incense was for a memorial.

_____ 6. Fresh bread was placed on the table every Sunday.

_____ 7. The bread was placed on the table on the basis of an everlasting covenant.

_____ 8. The bread had to be set before God every morning.

Answers appear at the end of today's lesson. The Hebrew word used for *bread* in these passages is *lechem,* which means *bread* or *grain.* The Hebrew word for *presence* is *peneh,* which means *countenance, presence,* or *face.*

Bread of the Presence was prepared by crushing whole kernels of wheat into fine powder. Some moisture must have been added to it; then it was baked. Recall that the ancient ovens were heated by fire, so this holy bread clearly qualified as an offering made by fire. We learned from the Scriptures we read that this bread was offered on behalf of the children of Israel as an everlasting covenant.

All twelve tribes of Israel were represented on the table. All 12 loaves came from the same original piece of dough. Paul may have been thinking about this as he wrote to the people in the church at Corinth: "Because there is one loaf, we, who are many, are one body, for we all partake of the one loaf" (I Cor. 10:17).

The amount of flour in each loaf is very significant.

Look back in Leviticus 24:5. How much flour was in each loaf?

An ephah is about half a bushel. Two-tenths of an ephah is about four quarts.

Look back at the manna in Exodus 16:16,36. How much manna equaled an individual, daily portion on any given weekday?

_____

How much manna was gathered on the Sabbath (Ex. 16:5,22)?

_____

According to Leviticus 24:8, how often were fresh loaves of the bread to be placed on the table?

_____

The loaves represented the double portion God offers His covenant children: one portion to suffice for the daily demands of our wilderness experience and another portion to receive freely the refreshment of our Sabbath rest. According to Deuteronomy 21:17, the double portion is also the heritage of the firstborn.

What is Christ called in Romans 8:29? _____

The manna in Exodus 16:7 was to remind the Hebrews of the glory of the Lord. We saw that the Hebrew word *presence* means *countenance, presence, or face.*

Read John 6:32-35. How did God ultimately show His glory?

_____

By what name did Christ refer to Himself in the above reference?

_____

By what name did God refer to the bread of the Presence in Leviticus 21:21-22, KJV (see margin)?

_____

Marvel at the emerging heavenly pattern. The bread of God was devoid of leaven or yeast, just as the Bread of life was devoid of spot or blemish. He was the Manna from heaven offered to all who partake of the Lord's table.

No man that hath a blemish of the seed of Aaron the priest shall come nigh to offer the offerings of the LORD made by fire: he hath a blemish; he shall not come nigh to offer the bread of his God. He shall eat the bread of his God, both of the most holy, and of the holy.

Leviticus 21:21-22, KJV

109

♥ **Do you find the bread of Christ's presence satisfying in your life? Why or why not?**

_____

Let's look briefly at the significance of the incense on the table.

What does Matthew 2:11 tell you about incense?

_____

Sometimes referred to as frankincense, this was a very aromatic incense that came from the gum resin of a Boswellia tree. Considering the worth of frankincense was in its aroma, enjoy a glorious application to us in 2 Corinthians 2:14-15: "Thanks be to God, who always leads us in triumphal procession in Christ and through us spreads everywhere the fragrance of the knowledge of him. For we are to God the aroma of Christ." Just as we are the light of the world, we are also the aroma or the incense of Christ! We will have far more to learn about incense next week, but I wanted you to enjoy one application of the incense now.

Notice the bread with the frankincense was to be offered as a memorial of the covenant. As believers in Christ, we should have no difficulty understanding this aspect of the bread.

> Just as we are the light of the world, we are also the aroma or the incense of Christ!

Read Luke 22:14-20 and notice the parallel between the two memorials, one perfectly fulfilling the other.

Our communion table reminds us of our deliverance from sin and the costly redemption of our release, which allowed us to enter a new covenant. The Hebrews' communion table reminded them of God's atonement and deliverance through His covenant with Abram. The psalmist prophetically spoke of our new-covenant communion in Psalm 16:5: "The Lord is the portion of mine inheritance and of my cup" (KJV). He did not say, "The Lord _gives me_ the portion" but, "The Lord _is_ the portion." Abram's words to his beloved son, Isaac, ring once again in my memory: "God will provide _for Himself_ the lamb for the burnt offering" (Gen. 22:8, NASB, emphasis added).

Soon and very soon all representations and shadows of things to come would cease; He would have to become the "Lamb that was slain" (Rev. 5:12), the broken Bread (see 1 Cor. 11:24), and the spilled-out wine (see Matt. 26:28).

The fact is significant that the priests could eat of the holy bread on the seventh day, when freshly baked loaves took their place. The bread had to remain on the table before God's presence until He was satisfied. God's rest, which represented His satisfaction, was commemorated every Sabbath. Remember God's response after six days of creation?

Read Genesis 1:31; 2:1-2. What was God's verdict of all creation?

_____

Then what did He do? _____

In the same way, the bread of the Presence had to appear before Him until He was satisfied. Not until He was satisfied with the portion offered before Him could the priests then partake of the holy bread.

When the unleavened Bread was set before God on Golgotha, this tabernacle shadow, the bread of the Presence, found its fulfillment. As the sun ceased to shine that Friday afternoon, the Sabbath abruptly pressed in. The sun set early for a while that fateful afternoon, almost as if God wished to hasten the end of His Son's agony. "He shall see of the travail of his soul, and shall be satisfied" (Isa. 53:11, KJV).

From that moment forward He spread a feast across His table, inviting His royal priesthood to partake of the Manna from heaven. "He is able" (Heb. 7:25) invites you to His table. In 1926 B. B. McKinney wrote a hymn that poses a penetrating question:

> _I am satisfied with Jesus,_
> _But the question comes to me,_
> _As I think of Calvary,_
> _Is my Master satisfied with me?_[2]

He was satisfied with Jesus. And that is enough to cover me.

My father was in the battalion that broke open the gates and announced freedom to prisoners in Dachau, a Nazi concentration camp. The emaciated prisoners kissed the soldiers' feet and repeatedly cried out their thanksgiving. In that moment the soldiers were forever changed. The liberation, however, posed an immediate problem: the children. Either they had been separated from their parents, or their parents were dead. Either way, they had nowhere to go. An army hospital was set up at once to care for them, where they were bathed, fed, and warmed. However, it was not enough. Every night brought horrifying nightmares, making rest impossible for the children and the personnel.

Finally, one man lined up the children one night at bedtime, gathered loaves from the kitchen, and tore off a piece of bread for each child. The children curled up in their beds, nestled the bread against their breasts, and slept with the angels.

The Bread of the Presence. Partake and be satisfied.

Answers to the activity on page 108: 1. F, flour; 2. T; 3. F, two rows of six; 4. T; 5. T; 6. F, Sabbath, which was Saturday; 7. T; 8. F, always.

---

1. Donald Barnhouse, _Let Me Illustrate_ (Grand Rapids: Fleming H. Revell, 1967), 261.
2. B. B. McKinney, "Satisfied with Jesus," © 1926 Broadman Press. All rights reserved. International copyright secured. Used by permission.

Viewer Guide

Hearts in Fellowship

This week in our study we joyfully entered the holy place. This large room constituting the first two-thirds of the tabernacle housed three holy vessels. Each symbolized the privilege of serving God and fellowshipping with Him in some unique way. Two of them—the golden lampstand and the table of the bread of Presence—preoccupied our thoughts throughout week 5 while the altar of incense awaits us. Today we will return to the golden lampstand and see what additional light God may grant us. Review Exodus 25:31-40.

More Insights on the Lampstand

I. The _____ of _____. Compare Exodus 25:40 to Numbers 8:1-4. Hear from Vern S. Poythress in *The Shadow of Christ in the Law of Moses*: "The tabernacle is a renewed version of the _____ _____ _____. But curtains with _____ on them still _____ the way into _____ _____, just as cherubim barred the way into the original Garden of Eden after the Fall (Gen. 3:24)."[1]

2. The suggestion of the _____, _____, and _____ (v. 33). "It is a message about _____, the familiar cycle of growth of plants, _____, _____, and _____." He goes on to say, "This strange tree has buds, blossoms, almond flowers, and fruit _____ _____

_____, because it must be a static picture of the whole cycle

of _____ that God has created and sustains."[2]

3. The significance of the _____ _____ (v. 33).

Compare Jeremiah 1:11-12. The Hebrew word for *almond (shaqed)* "is related

to the Hebrew word for '_____' *(shaqad).*" According to the *JPS Torah*

Commentary on Exodus, The stem sh-q-d means "to be _____

wakeful, _____."

• The almond tree is "the _____ spring-flowering plant in

the land of Israel, often even before the end of February."

• The NEB conveys the overtone: "I am early on the watch *(soqed)* to carry

out my purpose" (Jer. 1:12).

4. The continued _____ _____ of the tree and

the lampstand. This is a great time for a reminder of the kind of oil used

in the lampstand. (See Lev. 24:1-4.) Now compare Zechariah 4:1-14 and

Revelation 11:1-4.

5. Reread Leviticus 24:4. The exhortation to _____ the lampstand

_____. Compare this to John 15:1-3.

_____

1. Vern S. Poythress, *The Shadow of Christ in the Law of Moses* (Phillipsburg, NJ: P&R Publishing, 1995), 19.
2. Ibid.

The Heart of a Servant

DAY 1 • THE ALTAR OF INCENSE

DAY 2 • A HARD LESSON IN HOLINESS

DAY 3 • THE INHERITANCE OF A SERVANT

DAY 4 • THE GIFT OF SUPPORT

DAY 5 • THE GARMENTS OF THE PRIESTS

WEEK 6

Having entered His courts with praise in week 4 and having found light and fellowship in His holy place in week 5, we are invited to take another step deeper into God's tabernacle. In week 6 we will discover the altar of incense. At this point in our study we will consider the holy calling of God's priesthood. Here at the second altar God taught Israel a lesson about serving Him with reverence that the nation might someday ignore but would never forget. We will seek answers to the following questions.

Principal Questions

1. What duty was performed once a year at the altar of incense?
2. What did Nadab and Abihu offer before the Lord?
3. How did God respond to the actions of the Levites?
4. What did God call the Levites in regard to the priests?
5. What garments were made for Aaron?

As God's royal priesthood today, we can learn many life lessons from the priesthood God ordained hundreds of years ago. This week we will consider the meaning of a holy calling in today's world.

Day 1
The Altar of Incense

Begin your study by reading Today's Treasure and praying that God will speak to you through His Word.

Enter farther into God's sanctuary and let Him reveal some of His marvelous mysteries to you. The holy place invites you to partake of God's presence with all of your senses. See the glorious reflection of the lampstand dancing on the golden walls. Feel the warmth of its glow. Touch the ornately crowned rim outlining the communion table and taste the bread of the Presence, which satisfies the starving soul. The overwhelming response of another sense draws you still nearer to the holy of holies. Smell the unmistakable fragrance billowing from an object just before the veil; then hear the faint crackle of the glowing embers below it. What is this structure that activates our senses?

"BECAUSE JESUS LIVES FOREVER, HE HAS A PERMANENT PRIESTHOOD. THEREFORE HE IS ABLE TO SAVE COMPLETELY THOSE WHO COME TO GOD THROUGH HIM, BECAUSE HE ALWAYS LIVES TO INTERCEDE FOR THEM."

Hebrews 7:24-25

Read Exodus 30:1-10 and answer the following questions.

What is this structure's name and purpose? _____

_____

What is the shape of this altar? _____

What directions did God give Moses in Exodus 30:3?

_____

What other object in the tabernacle had horns on its corners

(see Ex. 27:1-2)? _____

What other object in the tabernacle had gold molding or rimming around it (see Ex. 25:23-24)?

_____

Where is the altar of incense positioned in the tabernacle?

_____

Who was to tend the altar of incense, and how often was the duty performed?

_____

What duty was to be performed only once a year at the altar

of incense? _____

Read Exodus 30:34-38. These verses contain the instructions for the fragrant blend of incense to be placed "in front of the Testimony." This altar of incense stood just before the veil that concealed the holy of holies.

Read the sentences below and mark them *T* or *F* to indicate whether they are true or false instructions given for the incense.

_____ 1. The incense was to consist of equal amounts of several spices.
_____ 2. The incense was to be prepared like a perfume.
_____ 3. The incense was to be pure and holy.
_____ 4. The incense was to be sprinkled on the table.
_____ 5. The incense was to be placed before the testimony in the tabernacle.
_____ 6. Only the high priest could obtain this perfume for personal use.
_____ 7. No one could use this perfume for himself.
_____ 8. Anyone who made this perfume for himself would have to be killed.
_____ 9. Anyone who made this perfume for himself would be cut off from his people.

Answers appear at the end of today's lesson.

A sacrifice burned on the bronze altar. Incense burned on the golden altar.

To keep the two essential altars distinct from each other, read Exodus 39:33-40. By what names did God refer to the two tabernacle altars?

_____

To distinguish between the two altars, remember them this way: the bronze altar was the one on which a sacrifice perpetually burned, and the golden altar was the one on which incense perpetually burned.

We have already noted that one major difference between the two

altars was the material that overlaid them: _____

_____ covered the altar of sacrifice, and _____ covered the altar of incense.

Now compare their two positions in the tent of meeting. Read Exodus 40:5-6. You may need to review your diagram in week 5. Where was each altar positioned?

The altar of sacrifice, or the bronze altar: _____

The altar of incense, or the golden altar: _____

Today we will discover the distinction of the golden altar, and tomorrow we will highlight the link between it and the bronze altar. Let's explore the magnificence of God's sovereign command to have fragrance continually offered to Him. The altar of incense was positioned as deep in the sanctuary as the priest could go on a daily basis. Only the high priest could go beyond the veil, and even he could dare take that step only once a year.

Let each of these Scriptures help you interpret the meaning of the golden altar of fragrance. Record how each Scripture uses the word *incense.*

Psalm 141:2 _____

Revelation 5:8 _____

Revelation 8:3 _____

Obviously, the incense on the altar represents _____.

Who kindles the coals and releases the fragrance of saints' prayers toward heaven? You may already know this answer by faith, but God's Word also states the answer as fact. Read Romans 8:34.

From all you have been taught through the Word of God, what did Christ die to do (see Rom. 5:8)?
❑ make us perfect   ❑ make us happy   ❑ save us from our sins

According to Hebrews 7:25, what does Christ live to do?
❑ intercede for us   ❑ keep us from sinning   ❑ give us peace

Only the high priest could go beyond the veil, and even he could dare take that step only once a year.

117

The altar of incense speaks to us of intercession. Our great Intercessor is Christ Jesus. Several years ago God began convicting me of the sin of prayerlessness. I was certainly aware that the times I failed to pray were great losses to me, but I had never confronted the fact that they were truly sins.

What does each Scripture say about spending time in prayer or neglecting to pray?

Isaiah 50:4-5 _____

Mark 14:38 _____

Philippians 4:6-7 _____

James 4:2 _____

Prayerlessness is a sin because: (1) it causes us to forfeit some of God's precious gifts to us, (2) it makes us much weaker when tempted, (3) it causes us anxiety, and (4) it closes our ears to God.

Look again at Isaiah 50:5. What does God call turning our ear

from Him? _____

You see, praying is not just God's hearing from me. Perhaps more importantly, it is my hearing from God!

♥ Name any results of prayerlessness in your own life. What do you need to do to make prayer a greater priority in your life each day?

Add the fifth and most important reason prayerlessness is a sin.

Hebrews 7:25 _____

Prayerlessness is a sin because Jesus Christ our Savior lives to intercede for us! Understanding that Christ sat down at God's right hand to intercede not only with our petitions but also with our praise is imperative. What could be sweeter to God's senses than the sweet fragrance of our worship?

We have much to learn in day 2 about true worship, but for the remainder of today let's bask in the lovely portrayal of fragrant worship in Luke 7:36-50. After you complete your reading, consider the following points.

1. Fragrant worship is costly. It comes only when what is deep inside is lavished on Christ.
2. Often, the fragrance of worship cannot truly be released until the vessel is broken.
3. Fragrant worship is not hindered by others. Notice the company this precious woman in Luke 7 shared! Read Galatians 1:10.

4. Fragrant worship places us in a right relationship with God. Tears do not always accompany fragrant worship, nor are they synonymous with fragrant worship; but an awareness of who He is, which caused the woman's tears, is indeed a necessity in fragrant worship.

5. We cannot out-sin God's ability to forgive. Let me remind you as many times as it takes—no one has ever out-sinned me. After we have truly repented and reveled in God's sure forgiveness, our worship becomes the fragrance of purest nectar. In fact, we who have faced the depths of our own depravity may find worship to be the privilege it really is. The tragedy is that the same persons who have the deepest capacity for worship are sometimes those who feel the least right to worship. I am convinced the greatest cause of a believer's inability to offer fragrant worship is a feeling of worthlessness, whether self- or environmentally imposed. Please realize your past sins may forfeit respect or position; but after you have truly repented, past sins cannot annul your right to the deepest invitations of the Christian experience: to know God and to worship Him. If your feelings of worthlessness have been environmentally imposed, you have only one solution: allow God to lavish His love on you. Lavish worship comes from lavish love. If you receive God's love, you can then return it. Many believers can accept Christ's gift of salvation but not the love that enabled it.

Ask Him to show you your great worth to Him! He may say it in many ways, but it will always stem from the same basic truth He has revealed to you through this lesson: "I love you so much that I died for you, and I love you so much that I live for you." What more can He do? Right now He sits at the right hand of the Father, living to intercede in your behalf. Can you resist? You must give Him the opportunity to continually present your prayers and praises as acceptable before the throne of grace. He waits for you.

Answers to the activity on page 116: 1. T, 2. T, 3. T, 4. F, 5. T, 6. F, 7. T, 8. F, 9. T.

Day 2
A Hard Lesson in Holiness

Today's Treasure

"A TIME IS COMING AND HAS NOW COME WHEN THE TRUE WORSHIPERS WILL WORSHIP THE FATHER IN SPIRIT AND TRUTH, FOR THEY ARE THE KIND OF WORSHIPERS THE FATHER SEEKS."

John 4:23

Reading Today's Treasure and ask God to speak to you through His Word.

In day 1 we learned that the altar of incense represented the intercession made on our behalf by our Advocate, who sits at God's right hand. Through Hebrews 7:25 God shared with us that Christ literally lives to make intercession for us! He intercedes not only with our petitions but also with our praise. We also viewed the altar of incense from the perspective of privilege. Today we will gaze at the altar of incense from the perspective of reverence.

Read Leviticus 10:1-3,10 and check the correct answers.

Who were the two sons of Aaron mentioned in the passage?
❏ Nadab   ❏ Mishael   ❏ Elzaphan   ❏ Abihu

What did they offer before the Lord that He had forbidden?
❏ a blemished sacrifice
❏ an inappropriate grain offering
❏ incense on unauthorized fire

What happened to these two men?
❏ They were cut off from their people.
❏ They were swallowed by the earth.
❏ They were consumed by fire from God.

What was Moses' explanation to Aaron for God's action in verse 3?
❏ His sons were victims of generational sin.
❏ His sons were unacceptable priests.
❏ God will be worshiped only in holiness.

What conclusion can you draw from verse 3 about Nadab

and Abihu? _____

_____

Accounts like this really shake us up. God owes us no explanations for His righteous judgments. After all, "as for God, his way is perfect" (Ps. 18:30). However, He often allows us to peek inside a rebellious heart so that we can learn from this example. Let's consider Nadab and Abihu's grave sin.

 Again, what does Leviticus 10:1 say they offered before the Lord?

_____

What could have made the fire they used strange, unholy, or unauthorized? The only coals that could be used to keep the altar of incense perpetually burning were those taken from the altar of sacrifice. Priests used authorized censers to scoop coals from the altar of sacrifice and to place them underneath the altar of incense to keep it burning.

Nadab and Abihu made the fatal mistake of placing fire underneath the altar of incense from some other source. So unacceptable was the offering that they were consumed. This judgment seems harsh to us, but we must understand that God was using this generation of priests to teach all subsequent generations how to approach Almighty Yahweh. Moses' explanation was clear: those who share the privilege of being nearest to God must also bear the awesome responsibility of exemplifying His holiness through obedience: "Unto whomsoever much is given, of him shall be much required" (Luke 12:48, KJV).

Now we can see the perfect link between the two altars in the tabernacle of testimony: the only coals that could heat the incense to make it a fragrant offering were those on which the blood of sacrifice had been spilled. Any other fuel for petition and worship made it unacceptable. Remember, God lit the altar of sacrifice when He accepted the offerings at the tabernacle's dedication. Any other fire was strange fire. Any other coals except those stained in blood were unacceptable.

You now understand why the two altars were positioned as they were. Fragrant offering was possible only on the basis of sacrifice. Until someone had experienced atonement at the first altar, he could not offer the fragrant incense of prayer, praise, and worship at the second because there would be no intercessor!

You see, we never have the right simply to chat with God. No matter how spiritual we become, we will never have the right to lift even the most pious prayers to God. Only Christ has that right. He must intercede with our every word before the throne of grace. Only after we have met Him at the altar of sacrifice are we eligible for petition, praise, and worship at the altar of incense.

What is the only form of true worship according to John 4:19-26?

_____

What is worshiping in spirit and in truth? When God created humans, He gave them something no other creature had received: a spirit. This spirit makes us in God's image because, as you have just read, "God is spirit" (v. 24). Our spirit gives us the capacity to know and experience God. Our soul, on the other hand, is the source of our emotions and personality—that which represents our conscious selves. The third component of the triune human is the physical body.

When God says that we must worship Him in spirit, He means that the only acceptable worship is that which is motivated and controlled by our spirits. The body and soul may accompany the spirit in worship, but they can never acceptably overthrow it. Our bodies and souls may express praise as long as they only accompany a deep spiritual longing to know and reverence God. Only the spirit can provoke and control worship for it to be acceptable. We can clap our hands or lift our hands as an accompaniment to worship if we are so led by the Holy Spirit, but the body can never acceptably take the lead. We can weep, laugh, or shout hallelujah from our souls as an accompaniment to spiritual worship, but the emotion and personality can never acceptably take the lead. Any variance from this balance would be "strange incense" (Ex. 30:9, KJV).

Spiritual worship comes from our very core and is fueled by an awesome reverence and desire for God. Spiritual worship is focusing all we are on all He is, both personally and universally. It is the incomparable expression of both awe and affection for God. And it is one of the highest privileges we can experience on this earth.

Those who share the privilege of being nearest to God must also bear the awesome responsibility of exemplifying His holiness through obedience.

♥ What fuels your personal expression of worship?

Can you sense when God is pleased with your worship, and if so, how?

Now let's consider the meaning of worshiping in truth. One of the first rules of Bible study is to examine the context. If you have trouble understanding a writer's terminology, look at his other uses of those exact words. Always look for a repetition of the same word in the same book of the Bible before you travel outside it. The Book of John uses the same word for truth several times. Every verse you are about to read translates the word *truth* from exactly the same Greek word, *aletheia*. This word means *unveiled reality*.

Keeping this definition in mind, look up each verse and record the information you derive about truth.

John 1:14 _____

John 1:17 _____

John 8:32 _____

John 14:6 _____

John 16:13 _____

Who is the Truth? _____

Remember the act of fragrant worship we studied in the Gospel of Luke yesterday? The only reason that offering was a sweet savor to God was that it was lavished on Christ, His Son. Fragrant worship is only that which rises to God after it is poured on Christ. Christ is the Truth through whom we must worship! He is our only access to the throne of grace.

How do we ensure that our worship combines both spirit and truth? Acceptable worship proceeds from the Holy Spirit inside us only on the basis of the Savior who died for us. That is what it means to worship in spirit and truth.

To place our incense before the throne of grace on any other basis except the blood atonement of Jesus Christ is to offer "unauthorized fire" (Lev. 10:1). Thus, the incense of our prayer and worship is the Holy Spirit, and the fire that enables the fragrance to rise is Jesus Christ.

The One who deems the fire and incense acceptable or unacceptable is Father God. All three members of the holy Trinity act on our behalf. All of the Divine Nature combines to offer us the privilege of true worship. God the Father invites us to worship, God the Son ignites us to worship, and God the Spirit incites us to worship. To worship inappropriately will not likely cause our physical deaths because we enjoy the grace of Calvary, but it can indeed cause the momentary death of communication with the Almighty.

All of the Divine Nature combines to offer us the privilege of true worship.

Now that we have talked about it, let's spend time in worship.
Write your own words of worship, knowing that Christ is carrying
them to the Father, who delights in them.

_____

_____

_____

_____

_____

Day 3
The Inheritance of a Servant

Reading Today's Treasure and ask God to speak to you through His Word.

Throughout our study we have gained glimpses into the lives of several members of Israel's holy priesthood, those God ordained to minister in His tabernacle. Now that we have pictured the structure where their daily duties took place, we will devote the remainder of this week to a more detailed look at the significance of their holy calling. We will step back in time before the grave sin of Nadab and Abihu, and we will see the error of their ways more clearly.

Let's begin our study by considering the tribe from which the priests came.

The son of Jacob for whom the whole tribe was named is

introduced to us in Genesis 29:34. His name was _____.

He was born of Jacob's wife, Leah. Interestingly, his name means *a joining.* Two very significant persons in Israel's rich history descended from the tribe of Levi.

Read Exodus 4:10-14. Aaron and Moses were: _____

What far more important task came to these Levites (Ex. 28:1)?

_____

Today's Treasure

"THE LORD SAID TO AARON, 'YOU WILL HAVE NO INHERITANCE IN THEIR LAND, NOR WILL YOU HAVE ANY SHARE AMONG THEM; I AM YOUR SHARE AND YOUR INHERITANCE AMONG THE ISRAELITES.'"

Numbers 18:20

You could have noted that Aaron and Moses were both brothers and Levites. From the tribe of Levi God drew Aaron and his sons to be the priests who would minister in the presence of God. As long as an earthly dwelling place made with hands existed, only Aaron's direct descendants were to fill the office of priesthood. However, God did not forget the remainder of the tribe of Levi, because they had responded favorably to Him in a time of crisis. Do you remember the three chapters we noted between the commandments for the tabernacle and the actual construction of the tabernacle (Ex. 32–34)? Do you remember the sin that took place in the camp while Moses was on the holy mount?

Refresh your memory about the Levites. Read Exodus 32:25-29.

How did the Levites honor the Lord? _____

_____

What was God's response to their actions? _____

_____

The Levites were called out from among all other tribes and awarded a place of service before God in conjunction with the Aaronic priesthood. References to the priests and the Levites appear throughout the Old and New Testaments. Remember that the Levites were all of the descendants of the tribe of Levi, the son of Jacob and Leah, while the priesthood was the direct family line of Aaron within the tribe of Levi. The priests and the Levites shared a relationship not only on the basis of kinship but also on the basis of calling.

Study Numbers 3:1-10; 18:1-7 and list the responsibilities God commanded for the priesthood (Aaron and his sons) and the Levites (the tribe of Levi).

The Priesthood	The Levites
_____	_____
_____	_____
_____	_____
_____	_____
_____	_____

Now look closely at Numbers 18:20,23. One of these verses is a message to the priesthood, and one is a message to the Levites. What is the message?

They would have no _____ among the

_____.

What was their inheritance? _____

The priests and the Levites shared a great burden of responsibility. Even though their holy calling carried great privilege, it also involved difficult and dangerous work. God ordained that neither the priests nor the Levites would receive an inheritance in the promised land. Rather, He would be their inheritance! Because of their faithfulness to devote their entire lives to His service, He had a very special way of caring for the priests and the Levites.

Carefully search Numbers 18:8-9,21,25-26,29-32 and record every provision of God for the priests' and Levites' care. You will find the priesthood's list much longer.

The Priesthood	The Levites

Now look closely at God's special provision for His ministers. By God's sovereign design He provided for those who served Him full-time. As you can see, the priests were supported by a portion of the tabernacle offering, and the Levites were supported by tithes.

> **Read I Timothy 5:17-18. In one statement what is God saying through Paul to the New Testament church?**

_____

♥ **When have you ministered recently as an act of obedience to God? What were the results?**

Sometimes we hear the opinion that ministers of the gospel should not be paid for doing God's work. That is not God's way. He meant, unequivocally, for the community of believers in both Israel and the New Testament church to support their ministers. In fact, the Apostle Paul was so convicted to preach this message that he held two jobs, ministering and tent making, so that he could openly proclaim God's will on this matter without suspicion.

Cases have been well publicized in which pastors extorted great wealth from their flocks, but these situations are infrequent in the entire scope of vocational ministry. In the reciprocal method God has ordained, His minister should neither experience need nor accumulate vast wealth. Cases will always exist in which that balance is offset. Nevertheless, as the body of Christ whom God holds responsible, we are to continue steadfastly doing what Scripture clearly teaches: we must support our ministers. Those God has called to focus on special ministries should not also have to labor outside the church to support their families. This principle does not contradict God's delight over freewill offerings. Few churches could afford to pay their ministers what they are worth. The work can be difficult, draining, thankless, and unending.

How beautifully God balanced His community and ministers! The priests and Levites totally depended on the community's generosity. God provided a wonderful, workable safeguard against pride. The community was also allowed the privilege of expressing its support and appreciation for God's ministers.

> **What specific instruction did God give about the Levites in Deuteronomy 12:10-12; 16:9-12?**
> ❑ Pay the Levites tithes at your celebrations.
> ❑ Take food to the Levites after your celebrations.
> ❑ Make the Levites part of your celebrations.

God instructed the Israelites to set extra places at their tables during celebrations and feasts for His servants in ministry. How wonderful to see the precious provisions God made for those who were called to give their entire lives in concentrated service to Him! A few weary saints in your church might need to know that their service is not going unnoticed by God or by you.

Day 4
The Gift of Support

Begin your study by reading Today's Treasure and praying that God will speak to you through His Word.

Today we will continue our study of the serving relationship that existed between the priesthood and the Levites.

Look again at Numbers 18:1-7 and answer the following questions.

To whom was the Lord speaking? _____

What did God call the Levites in regard to the priests?

The Levites were given to the priests as a _____

What did God call the office of priesthood in verse 7?

_____

The ministry God gave Aaron and his sons was a gift. Likewise, God gave the Levites' support ministry to Aaron and his sons as a gift. They did not earn it. Certainly, Aaron's actions while Moses was on Mount Sinai with God indicate that he had done little to deserve such an honor. God literally called out the Levites as a support ministry to the priesthood and offered them to Aaron and his sons as a present.

Today we will meditate on the support ministry God presented to His people as a gift. In day 3 God revealed to us in Exodus 4:14-17 that Aaron was called to support Moses. Today we have seen that the Levites were called to support Aaron. What a fascinating idea: a ministry within a ministry! Look at the chain reaction of God's chosen design:

- God called Moses to lead the children of Israel.
- God called Aaron to be Moses' helper.
- God called the Levites to minister to Aaron and the priests.
- God called the Israelites to support the priests and the Levites.

In our previous lesson we also had the privilege of seeing some ways this support system worked. Today let's look at another example of support ministry.

Read Exodus 17:8-16 and meet another of the Hebrew greats placed in God's Word for our example. His name is Hur. What other information can you derive from Exodus 24:13-14; 31:1-2 about this workman of God? Check all correct answers.

❏ He and Aaron settled matters while Moses was on Mt. Sinai.
❏ He was Miriam's son.
❏ He was great in the sight of Israel.
❏ He was the father of Uri and the grandfather of Bezalel.
❏ He was from the tribe of Levi.
❏ He was from the tribe of Judah.

Now return to Exodus 17:8-16. What action by Moses did God require for the Israelites to be victorious?

_____

Was Moses able to cause the army of Israel to be victorious by himself? ❏ yes ❏ no

What action did they take to ensure victory? _____

_____

Could God have supernaturally made Moses' arms strong enough to stay up on their own? ❏ yes ❏ no

What lesson do you think God was trying to teach?

_____

Don't forget! Another group was intricately involved in the victory that day. What was Joshua's responsibility in verses 9-10?

_____

What was the outcome of Joshua's efforts in verse 13? _____

_____

Look at the chain through which God brought victory. Israel could be victorious only if Moses held up his staff. Moses could hold up his staff only if Aaron and Hur helped him. Joshua and his army could experience victory only as long as Aaron and Hur held up Moses' arms. Joshua could lead Israel's armies only as long as they followed him. And the armies of Israel could slay the Amalekites only as long as God empowered them. Because God ordained compulsory participation, many experienced glorious victory that day—Moses, Aaron, Hur, Joshua, and the entire army of the living God!

God delights in allowing us the privilege of experiencing spiritual victories. When we refuse to allow anyone to share our personal battles, we risk two negative consequences: (1) We often lengthen the battle. Can you imagine how many days the Israelites would have needed to slay the Amalekites if they were victorious only when Moses could muster the energy to lift his staff? Without a doubt, teamwork hastened the victory. (2) When we do not ask for support, we cheat others of the joy of victory. Some of the greatest moments of ecstasy I have experienced in my Christian journey have been others' victories.

Some years ago Connie, a young married woman in my Sunday School class, visited me and, in near hysteria, told me that a sonogram of her unborn child strongly indicated Down's syndrome. Tears poured down her cheeks as she cried: "Beth, I can't bear this. How could God let this happen to us? It can't be true!"

The diagnosis was not true. It was far worse. Within a few short weeks her unborn baby was diagnosed with a form of anencephalia. She was missing a great portion of her brain. The next months passed painfully, and I sat on the end of her hospital bed the morning Connie delivered Grace Ann. The final diagnosis had been correct.

"Have you seen her?" she asked me.

I responded: "Yes, I have, Connie. I love her already."

She said, "I guess God thinks we can do this."

"I guess He does, Connie."

"Well, then," she continued, a touch of resolve emerging from beneath her exhaustion, "I guess we will." The next months were excruciating. Sleep was rare; care was constant; her medical condition was precarious; and, in the midst of it all, a big brother, just a baby himself, vied for attention. Six months after God gave us Grace Ann, He took her home. Her life on earth was temporal, but the gift she left was eternal. All of us were changed but none of us so completely transformed as that beautiful young mother.

Several years later Connie stopped me at church. She was expecting again. I will never forget the words she said to me: "Beth, the doctor said this baby may have Down's syndrome. When he said those words to me, I looked at him and said: 'Down's syndrome? Is that all? Piece o' cake!'"

I got in my car, my emotions somewhere between hysterical laughter and hysterical tears. I was standing right there when Almighty God stretched out His righteous right arm and handed down the victory! Because Connie had allowed me the privilege of standing close by through her battle, when God poured on her victory, it splashed all over me.

God gave that faithful family a completely normal little boy at the end of that pregnancy and another one after that. They have since moved to another city, but a friend called not long ago to say they are expecting yet another. Any sign of Down's syndrome? No. But I have no doubt that Connie could have handled it.

♥ Do you have a support system within your ministry? in your personal life? If so, who are they and how do they support you?

As much as you may wish you were, you are not autonomous. God has chosen that our victories are sweetest when shared. You are a gift to the body of Christ. The body of Christ is a gift to you.

Conclude by reading Ecclesiastes 4:9-10; I Corinthians 12:7; and Hebrews 10:24-25.

The Garments of the Priests

"MAKE HOLY GARMENTS FOR YOUR BROTHER AARON, FOR GLORY AND BEAUTY."

Exodus 28:2,HCSB

Read Today's Treasure and pray that God will speak to you through His Word.

We have had an opportunity to discuss the Hebrew priesthood in rather general terms this week. Now it is time for us to approach some specific commands God delivered about those honored recipients of His gift of service. Be prepared for a lesson dedicated almost entirely to revelation and painfully little to application. In week 7 we will draw application from the work you will do today.

Read all of Exodus 28:1-5 and complete the following.

List the names of God's priests.

_____

_____

What was to be made for Aaron (v. 2)? _____

What was the purpose of these sacred garments?

_____

Name each garment to be made for Aaron.

_____

_____

What qualifications did the seamstresses and craftsmen have to

possess to make the proper garments? _____

What colors were the craftsmen to use? From memory, can you also list the representation of each metal and color?

_____

_____

_____

_____

_____

_____

In what locations in the tabernacle were blue, purple, and scarlet previously employed? (Hint: we've already seen them three times.)

_____

_____

_____

What does fine linen represent (see Rev. 19:8)?

_____

Exodus 28:6-14 describes a garment called the *ephod.* Apparently, the ephod was a sleeveless vest worn as an outer garment. It seemed to be two pieces attached together at the shoulder. A girdle or a belt was also worn around the ephod, embroidered with the same colors.

EPHOD
a sleeveless vest worn as an outer garment

What kinds of stones were to be attached at the ephod's shoulder?

_____

What was to be engraved on these stones? _____

_____

How was the order of these names determined? _____

_____

According to verse 11, how were these gems to be handled? Check the two correct answers.

❑ They were to be cut according to the pattern shown on the mount.

❑ They were to be cut the way a jeweler or engraver engraves a signet.

❑ They were never to be touched by unclean hands.

❑ They were to be set in gold mountings.

What purpose did these stones serve as they were fashioned to the shoulders of the ephod? Check the correct answer.

❑ They served as a memorial.

❑ They represented God's brilliance.

❑ They symbolized that Israel was God's chosen treasure.

What was attached to the onyx settings on the ephod?

❑ golden rings   ❑ golden clasps   ❑ golden chains

The high priest's breastplate was to be made with materials identical to those of the ephod. It was shaped in a perfect square, measured about nine inches in diameter, and had four rows of precious stones.

Read Exodus 28:21,29-30,34-37.

What was to be engraved on the 12 stones? _____

_____

You may want to turn back to your diagram of the outer court in week 4 (p. 74) and list the names of the 12 tribes in order on the stones above. Although we cannot be certain, the order probably proceeded from the east, where the door was positioned.

Where was the breastplate to be worn (see v. 29)? _____

_____

What two other objects were to be placed in the breastplate (v. 30)?

_____

What was the purpose of these two objects?

_____

What was to be placed on the hem of the high priest (v. 34)?

_____

What was the bell's purpose (v. 35)? _____

_____

What words were written on the plate of pure gold (v. 36)?

_____

To what garment was this gold plate attached (v. 37)?

_____

♥ What attributes of God show Him as a God of individuality?

Aaron, the high priest of Israel, had to wear these custom-designed garments every time he entered the sanctuary. To fail to wear them properly could easily incur death (see vv. 35,38). As a representative of the Hebrew people, he bore their guilt as he presented their gifts to the Lord. The gold plate on his forehead constantly reminded Aaron and all who saw him that Israel had been called out to purity. What a holy God He is! And how flippantly we often confront the words "Be holy, because I am the LORD your God" (Lev. 20:7). My heart stands convicted when considering that I could dress in all of the holy robes designed by a divinely-inspired seamstress yet underneath would remain a sin-prone woman in desperate need of grace.

As you can see, God is detailed. He is not a God of generality. He is a God of individuality. Do not let Satan convince you that God is not actively involved in the intricate design of your life. God has not missed a single stitch or left a stone unturned on your behalf; furthermore, His activity in the details of your life most often displays His glory and beauty.

Do you avoid sharing the details of your life with God? Do you avoid asking certain things of Him because they seem too trivial? Intimate relationships are defined by the intimate experiences shared. Look for Him in the details!

You have done good work today. In week 7 we will learn the purposes of the priests' garments.

God is actively involved in the intricate design of your life.

Viewer Guide

The Heart
of a Servant

In our sixth week of homework we moved as close to the veil as the holy place allowed us. There we studied the altar of incense and began our more in-depth look at the Old Testament priesthood. In today's lesson we will stand at the altar of incense again, seeing new insights as well as further developing several segments of Scripture you've considered this week.

Let's review and build on the following segments from your homework:

- Exodus 30:1-10. Consider the original meaning of the word translated "altar" both here and in reference to the bronze altar. The Hebrew transliteration *mizbeah* means "an altar, a place of _____."

- Psalm 141:1-2. The altar of incense symbolizes _____.

Compare Revelation 5:6-9; 8:3-5; and 6:9-11.

Not coincidentally, the Gospel of Luke unfolds with a wonderful account involving the altar of incense. We'll read Luke 1:5-25 and consider the following for those of us who help comprise the New Testament "royal priesthood" (1 Pet. 2:9).

Parallels with New Testament Priesthood

1. The _____ of Zechariah and Elizabeth
   (v. 6; compare Ps. 19:13).

How might you complete the following about you and/or others you love?
"But (I, we, they) _____ _____ _____."

2. The specification of the angel _____
(v. 19; compare Dan. 9:20-23).

3. The initial words of Gabriel: "Do not be _____ … your
   _____ has been _____" (v. 13; compare John 11:41-42).

4. God never receives more glory than when we can say beyond question,
   "The _____ has _____ _____ _____ _____"
   (v. 25).

A Heart That Intercedes

DAY 1 • THE HOLY CALLING OF THE PRIESTHOOD

DAY 2 • A PECULIAR PRIEST

DAY 3 • THE OPEN DOOR

DAY 4 • THE RIGHT HAND OF GOD

DAY 5 • HEAVEN, THE BLESSED ADOPTION AGENCY

WEEK 7

This week we will continue to study the priesthood God ordained to minister before Him in His sanctuary. Week 6 concentrated on the relationship between the original priesthood and today's priesthood, believers in Christ. Although this week's study will shed additional light on this relationship, it will concentrate less on our priesthood and more on Christ's. We will study both the frailty of Aaron's position and the finality of Christ's. We will seek answers to the following questions.

Principal Questions

1. Why did God impose concrete qualifications on His priests?
2. What was the basis on which the next "Melchizedek" would be named?
3. How was Christ's priesthood superior to Aaron's?
4. What will be different about the new covenant?
5. What is one major way God reveals sonship to us?

This week's study will guide us to a fresh understanding of how our relationship with God has been transformed through the great high priesthood of Jesus Christ.

Day 1
The Holy Calling of the Priesthood

Begin today's study by reading Today's Treasure and praying that God will speak to you through His Word.

Last week we searched Exodus 28 for specific descriptions of the garments worn by Aaron, Israel's high priest. Today's study will expound on the priesthood's role, which, in turn, will further explain many of the garments and sacred accessories we have already examined.

God's ordination of strict qualifications was foundational to the priesthood. You have already received just a glimpse of the priests' separateness as defined by their dress.

Find the other qualifications God demanded of His priesthood.

The age of the tabernacle ministers (see Num. 8:24-26):

_____

The appearance of the priests (see Lev. 21:5,10):

_____

_____

The marriage of the priests (see Lev. 21:13-14):

_____

The personal life of the priests (see Lev. 10:8-10):

_____

Read Leviticus 22:31-33. Why did God impose such concrete qualifications for His priesthood?

_____

_____

"I AM SENDING YOU OUT LIKE SHEEP AMONG WOLVES. THEREFORE BE AS SHREWD AS SNAKES AND AS INNOCENT AS DOVES."

Matthew 10:16

137

According to Leviticus 22:9, what might happen if God's instructions were disregarded?

_____

In the last phrase of Leviticus 22:9 God states the reason for His rigid qualifications. What has God done for the priests?

_____

Sanctification appears as a continuing theme in the lives of Noah, Abraham, Isaac, Joseph, and countless other patriarchs, judges, prophets, priests, and kings. The words *holy, consecrated,* and *sanctified* in the Old Testament find their roots in a common Hebrew word: *qodesh.* The term denotes something separate that contrasts with the profane. This thesis is perpetuated throughout God's Word. God essentially says: "I, the Lord, have set you apart."

Not only had the Israelites been called out as a people, but also those God specified to serve them were singled out further. Earlier we identified this principle: what God desired of Israel in the tangible realm, He desires of Christians in the spiritual realm.

One of the best examples of this principle is God's attitude toward sacrifices. God demanded blood sacrifices from His chosen nation as a means of recognizing atonement and substitutionary death. Because of the death of our risen Lord and Savior, the unblemished Lamb, "no sacrifice for sins is left" (Heb. 10:26). Yet Christians are told in I Peter 2:4-5, "As you come to him, the living Stone—rejected by men but chosen by God and precious to him—you also, like living stones, are being built into a spiritual house ... offering spiritual sacrifices acceptable to God through Jesus Christ."

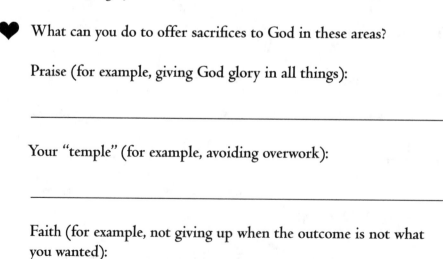 What can you do to offer sacrifices to God in these areas?

Praise (for example, giving God glory in all things):

_____

Your "temple" (for example, avoiding overwork):

_____

Faith (for example, not giving up when the outcome is not what you wanted):

_____

Tangible sacrifices offered for atonement have ceased; but our God delights in the spiritual sacrifices of our praise (see Heb. 13:15), our "temples" (see Rom. 12:1), and our faith (see Phil. 2:17). Likewise, God applies to believers in Christ the principle of separateness.

In John 17:13-21 Christ perfectly expressed His earnest desire for our separateness as He intercedes for us. Carefully read these verses and answer each question by writing the letter representing the correct answer.

_____ 1. For whom does Christ offer this intercession (see v. 20)?

_____ 2. Why has the world hated them?

_____ 3. By what tool does Christ ask God to sanctify His own?

_____ 4. To what mission field is Christ sending His own?

_____ 5. What is Christ's specific prayer in verse 15?

a. the world
b. protect them from the evil one
c. believers
d. truth
e. they aren't of the world

In this utterly divine intercession, Jesus prayed that we might have the perfect balance in our sanctification or separateness, a balance He lived every day of His earthly ministry. What kind of relationship are we to have with the world? In the world, not of the world, and protected from the world.

God calls us to be sanctified servants, ministering in the world yet untainted by the world. Embedded in the Book of Numbers is a chapter appropriated just for individual Israelites desiring to be sanctified servants.

> We are to be in the world, not of the world, and protected from the world.

Read Numbers 6:1-5 and answer the following questions.

Who could take this vow, according to verse 2? _____

From what must he or she abstain, according to verses 3-4?

_____

What must he or she do during his or her separation (v. 5)?

_____

_____

Notice the words in verse 2: "If a man or woman wants to make a special vow, a vow of separation. ..." This was a _voluntary_ vow taken by a man or a woman who desired total devotion to God for a length of time.

The word *Nazirite* means *consecration, devotion, separation.* Sound familiar? It was a vow of complete focus. One of the Nazirite's most interesting characteristics is that the vow was one of complete consecration in the midst of service. The vow could be taken by anyone who desired to be totally separate to God yet unable to be totally separate from the world—in other words, separated to God without being separated from people.

Very likely, you are familiar with several biblical Nazirites. In several cases God set aside entire lives as Nazirites. Other times parents vowed that their children would be set apart to God as Nazirites. Samson, Samuel, and John the Baptist were lifetime Nazirites—internally (spiritually) without the world, externally (physically) within the world.

Deuteronomy 29:6 expresses why at times God allowed no wine or fermented drink. What reason did He give?

_____

You see, total devotion meant being under only one influence: the single-minded person as opposed to the double-minded person of James 1:8, who is unstable in all her ways. Uncut hair reminded not only Nazirites but also others that they were set apart. It fulfilled in a literal sense the instruction to "let your moderation be known unto all men" (Phil. 4:5 KJV).

Look at someone else who took such a vow. Read Acts 18:18. To whom does this verse refer, and what did he do in Cenchrea?

_____

I will never forget stumbling on this verse when I was teaching the Book of Acts. I stared at the verse and kept thinking, *God uses comparatively few words. Why would He think it was important for us to know that Paul stopped by the barbershop?* Studying the question led me to the Nazirite vow. Why did Paul take such a vow? Certainly, he above all others knew that he was free from the law! Remember, this was a *voluntary* vow. Paul was not tying himself back to the law from which he had been freed; he simply recognized a wise move in the midst of worldly service.

Review Acts 18:18 (NIV). From where had Paul departed?

_____

Corinth was famous for carnality. Morality was rare, and unabashed immorality was rampant. Paul knew when God sent him to Corinth that he would likely be exposed to things he had never witnessed. Temple orgies were part of the pagan worship. "Religion" was filled with perversion. To minister to this lost city, Paul would have to walk inside this world. He wisely knew that he must do everything he could to ensure that this world did not walk inside him! Thus, he took the Nazirite vow of total consecration to God as a constant reminder of his calling as he ministered to the people of Corinth. Surely, Paul was thinking with the mind of Christ.

Jesus' words that we read earlier in John 17:13-21 reflect the spirit of the Nazirite—separated to God yet not separated from the people. We are the light of the world! We cannot hide our lampstands under the bushels of spiritual monasteries. Yet we cannot let the darkness rub off on us. How do we accomplish such a balance? The answer is found in Matthew 10:16: "I am sending you out like sheep among wolves. Therefore be as shrewd as snakes and as innocent as doves."

God never called us to naïveté. He called us to integrity. There is a very big difference between the two. The biblical concept of integrity emphasizes mature innocence, not childlike ignorance. Like Paul, we must be aware of what is out there before we walk into the middle of it. Like Paul, we must recognize situations that demand an extra degree of consecration, preparation, and protection.

Sanctification is not about long hair and abstinence. It is about purity—purity maintained in the midst of an impure world. Understand this vital precept: Maintaining purity in ministry is the result of nothing less than deliberate devotion. For those really fulfilling their calling of evangelism and ministry, purity is neither easy nor accidental. We must guard our minds and put on our armor. A war rages out there. And we are Satan's favorite prisoners.

What do you deliberately avoid for the sake of purity?

_____

How do others know you are set apart to God?

_____

_____

If you have children, what habits toward purity are you helping instill in them?

_____

_____

_____

In the world but not of the world. As shrewd as snakes but as innocent as doves. Are you up to it?

The power to live this way was made available the moment Christ prayed that prayer in your behalf. You see, God's precious Son gets anything He wants.

> We cannot hide our lampstands under the bushels of spiritual monasteries.

Day 2
A Peculiar Priest

"NOW THERE HAVE BEEN MANY OF THOSE PRIESTS, SINCE DEATH PREVENTED THEM FROM CONTINUING IN OFFICE; BUT BECAUSE JESUS LIVES FOREVER, HE HAS A PERMANENT PRIESTHOOD."

Hebrews 7:23-24

Begin today's study by reading Today's Treasure and praying that God will speak to you through His Word.

Yesterday we examined the strict qualifications of God's chosen priesthood: called out of the world but called *into* the world for service. The priests' calling was much like our own: internal devotion in the midst of external commotion. After the priests met the qualifications we studied, they were ready to assume their responsibilities.

Look at the diversity in the ministry of the priests' holy calling. Read Exodus 28:30; Numbers 6:22-26; and Deuteronomy 33:9-10 and check each priestly responsibility you discover.

❑ Care for their families.
❑ Guard the covenant.
❑ Sing before the Lord.
❑ Make decisions for Israel.
❑ Minister in the sanctuary.
❑ Offer incense and burnt offerings.
❑ Bless the Israelites.
❑ Teach precepts and laws.
❑ Govern the people.
❑ Watch over the Word.
❑ Determine God's will.

The priests ministered in the sanctuary, offered intercession at the altar of incense, instructed the people, blessed the people, determined God's will for the people, and offered sacrifices for the people. And we think we are busy!

Keeping these responsibilities in mind, read the following verses and identify the responsibilities of another man of God.

Mark 10:16 _____

Mark 12:35 _____

John 6:38 _____

John 17:20 _____

Hebrews 7:27 _____

The responsibilities Jesus Christ assumed in His earthly ministry parallel those of the priests. He worshiped in the temple, He instructed the people in God's laws, He blessed the people, He determined God's will, He interceded for the people, and He sacrificed at the altar. Indeed, He sacrificed Himself at the altar. Either this man assumed responsibilities that were not given to Him, a crime punishable by death (remember the Korahites?), or He was a Priest!

Who is the only one who can ordain a priest (Heb. 5:1-4)?

_____

Read Hebrews 5:5-6. Did Christ fulfill this utmost qualification to be called only by God?   ❏ yes   ❏ no

From what order of the priesthood was Christ called?

_____

Turn to Genesis 14:18-20. Verse 17 refers to the first war mentioned in God's Word. Discover every detail you can find about the roles and relationship of Melchizedek and Abram by checking the correct answer to each question.

What was Melchizedek's position?
   ❏ king of Salem   ❏ king of Sodom   ❏ king of kings

What was his other position?
   ❏ prophet   ❏ priest   ❏ prince

Of exactly whom was he priest?
   ❏ Yahweh   ❏ the God of Israel   ❏ the Most High God

What did Melchizedek bring with him?
   ❏ bread and wine   ❏ good tidings   ❏ a word from God

What have we already learned to be the symbolism of

the bread? _____

and the wine? _____

What did Melchizedek do to Abram?
   ❏ knelt before him   ❏ received him   ❏ blessed him

What did Abram give to Melchizedek?
   ❏ tithes of all   ❏ his blessing   ❏ his fortune

How many times do these verses refer to the Lord as the Most High God?   ❑ two   ❑ three   ❑ four

Hundreds of years later, yet hundreds of years before it was fulfilled, what did the Lord swear in Psalm 110:1-4?

_____

Carefully read Hebrews 7:1-3 and record every detail that made Melchizedek unique.

_____

_____

Zechariah 6:12-13, KJV, says: "And speak unto him, saying, Thus speaketh the LORD of hosts, saying, Behold the man whose name is The BRANCH; and he shall grow up out of his place, and he shall build the temple of the LORD: Even he shall build the temple of the LORD; and he shall bear the glory, and shall sit and rule upon his throne; and he shall be a priest upon his throne: and the counsel of peace shall be between them both." These verses describe the Messiah, the Kinsman Redeemer of the nation Israel, who would be both Priest and King! No earthly priest was ever called to fulfill both positions except Melchizedek and Jesus Christ. Yet every time Aaron put on the turban and the robe, he cast a shadow of both of them. The turban was the royal diadem, or headpiece. The robe was the priestly garment. Together they symbolized the culmination of the priesthood in the blessed Messiah.

> The Messiah would be both Priest and King!

Hebrews 7:1-2 interprets the name Melchizedek for us by expressing that he was the king of two things. What are they?

_____

Read Psalm 76:1-2.

Salem is none other than Jerusalem, the place from which shall come peace! We have the unique perspective to see through whom that peace has and will come.

Remember that Abram was the father of the great nation of Israel. He had no apparent equal on this earth. Yet he clearly perceived this unique one as his superior, offering tithes to Melchizedek and receiving his blessing. Furthermore, Melchizedek was not just any priest. He was the priest of the Most High God—supreme and sovereign Ruler of all the universe!

The range of Melchizedek's priesthood did not encompass one nation alone, but through him all people could be blessed. This most fascinating royal priest was none other than a type, or picture, of Christ, foreshadowing the true King-Priest to come. Likewise, through Him all nations would be blessed!

Hebrews 7:11 asks an important question. Write your own paraphrase of the verse.

_____

_____

_____

According to Hebrews 7:15-16, what was the basis on which the next "Melchizedek" or royal Priest would be named?

_____

On that basis, who was the only one who could possibly be named "a priest forever, in the order of Melchizedek" (v. 17)?

_____

Read Hebrews 7:24.

Christ's indestructible life did not simply allow Him to assume a title of honor. It allowed Him to burst open every believer's grave and shout, "Where, O death, is your victory? Where, O death, is your sting?" (I Cor. 15:55). "Blessed and holy are those who have part in the first resurrection. The second death has no power over them, but they will be priests of God and of Christ and will reign with him for a thousand years" (Rev. 20:6). Hallelujah!

God chose you in Christ "before the foundation of the world" (Eph. 1:4) and knew you before you were born (Ps. 139). Have you recently questioned God's plan for your life or His timing? ❏ yes ❏ no

Has this study encouraged you to feel differently? ❏ yes ❏ no If so, how have you changed?

_____

_____

_____

Day 3
The Open Door

Today's Treasure

"FOR THIS REASON HE HAD TO BE MADE LIKE HIS BROTHERS IN EVERY WAY, IN ORDER THAT HE MIGHT BECOME A MERCIFUL AND FAITHFUL HIGH PRIEST IN SERVICE TO GOD, AND THAT HE MIGHT MAKE ATONEMENT FOR THE SINS OF THE PEOPLE. BECAUSE HE HIMSELF SUFFERED WHEN HE WAS TEMPTED, HE IS ABLE TO HELP THOSE WHO ARE BEING TEMPTED."

Hebrews 2:17-18

Begin today's study by reading Today's Treasure and praying that God will speak to you through His Word.

In day 2 we penetrated the very heart of the Book of Hebrews. One continuing theme of this precious book is the superiority of Jesus Christ. Chapter 1 expresses that the Son of God is greater than the angels. Chapter 3 states that Jesus Christ is greater than Moses. Chapter 5 exclaims that Jesus Christ is greater than Aaron. In day 2 we saw proof that Christ was appointed God's Priest, a position enacted continually through His earthly ministry. Today and tomorrow we will learn that Christ's assumption of His role as Priest only began during His earthly ministry. Christ's priesthood will continue as long as human beings inhabit this earth—a reality that makes Him far superior to Aaron.

Carefully read Hebrews 7:26-28 and list every way you see Christ's priesthood as superior to Aaron's.

_____

_____

_____

Read Hebrews 2:17-18; 4:15. Why was it necessary for Christ to be made flesh before He could completely fulfill His role as Great High Priest?

_____

_____

_____

Jesus was tempted, but He never sinned. He is available to help you overcome temptation. What does 1 Corinthians 10:13 promise?

_____

Do you realize what it means to us that Christ was willing to become a man and be tempted as we are tempted? Based on the Scriptures you have recorded, picture the impact this one element of His priesthood has on you.

1. God became flesh so that He could dwell among us.
2. Jesus faced every temptation known to humanity so He could identify with us.
3. God the Father provided a door of escape for every temptation.
4. Only Christ was in a position to unlock the door of escape by facing every temptation as a man without sin.
5. Christ not only unlocked the door of escape from every temptation but also became the Door: "I am the door. If anyone enters by Me, he will be saved" (John 10:9, HCSB).
6. Any who have walked through the door of salvation from the sin of unbelief are also invited to walk through the door of salvation from daily temptation.
7. Because Christ has faced our every temptation without sin, we never face a temptation that has no door of escape.
8. Any door Christ has opened cannot be closed: "I have placed before you an open door that no one can shut" (Rev. 3:8). Neither Satan nor anyone else can make us fall to temptation. The door always remains open for our escape.
9. Although the door is open for our victory over sin and God's blessing flows only from our willingness to walk through it, a provision is already in place for the sin of failing to choose it. The consequences of our lack of obedience are left to help train us to walk through that door next time!
10. He who *walked* through the door of escape, thus *becoming* our means of escape as well, *leads* us through every door of escape and *prays* for us as we follow.

My friend, every provision has been made for us to be victorious over temptation! This will not be the one day, or the one moment, or the one circumstance from which there is no way out. Every door of escape has been unlocked. Christ made absolutely sure of it by unlocking it personally.

Occasionally, I recall a conversation I had with a woman who confessed to me that she had become involved in an extramarital affair. Her face was etched with frustration as she cried: "I begged God to make me stop! Why didn't He?" I felt no need to respond to that question. The defeated expression on her face revealed that she was already painfully aware of the answer. God had provided a way, but she had refused it.

A difficult sequence begins to unfold the moment we do not resist the first temptation. Let's put ourselves in this woman's place to determine the point at which we can fail to appropriate God's provision for our escape.

Satan started weaving the web the first moment you realized that you and this man enjoyed each other's company. You experienced a spark that made it appealing; yet you had the distinct feeling that you had better run.

The alarm was loud. An open door stood before you. But you hesitated. Then you refused it, offering your thoughts permission to proceed. Little by little the relationship progressed. *Harmless, you reasoned. It must not be a big deal. I no longer have the feeling that I need to run away.* The alarm grew increasingly faint. Satan had done everything he could to weave a web you could not escape; but no matter how

Because Christ has faced our every temptation without sin, we never face a temptation that has no door of escape.

he tried, he could not slam that door. It remained open. Each time you refused to go through it, however, your strength to resist drained.

This cycle of temptation, hesitation, and participation is as old as the garden of Eden, and it is not limited to sexual temptation. Two things about a believer's temptation never vary: (1) We always have an open door, a way out. (2) Every door we refuse to walk through makes the next one even harder to enter.

If a person is inhabited by the Holy Spirit, an alarm sounds. How can I say those words so dogmatically? Because the Holy Spirit's job is to convict us of sin, and He is never late for work. Remember, being tempted is not sin; refusing to take the way out is sin. Either way, it is a matter of resistance. We resist either the sin or the Holy Spirit.

The obvious key to victory is walking through the first door of escape. Every time we refuse another door, we lose more sensitivity to the Holy Spirit. He never goes away, but the less sensitivity we have to Him, the less power we have until, finally, we find ourselves fighting the battle on our own, absolutely powerless against temptation. In the flesh we always do what comes naturally, and what comes most naturally to every one of us is sin.

♥ Can you cite a time when you narrowly escaped a sin that could have ruined your life? If it is extremely personal, write your comments vaguely. The important part is to acknowledge the One who opened before you a way of escape.

_____

_____

_____

Read 2 Samuel 11:1-6; 12:1-10,13-14,19-20.

We can compare David's temptation with our own because, you may recall, he was one of the few persons to be anointed with the Holy Spirit prior to Acts 2. He was equipped with an alarm system just as we are. For him and for us, additional steps were available in the cycle: repentance and restoration.

Using the following headings, catalog David's sin from the time he opened the door to sin until his restoration in 2 Samuel 12:20. The point of hesitation will be more vague; however, you can surmise rather easily when the hesitation must have occurred.

Temptation: _____

_____

Hesitation: _____

_____

Participation: _____

_____

Repentance: _____

_____

Restoration: _____

_____

Now read Psalm 51:1-4,7,10-12, David's prayer of repentance after his sin with Bathsheba. Answer the following questions.

Was David aware of his sin at all times?   ❏ yes   ❏ no

Against whom was his sin? _____

Why do you think the sin was so specifically against God?

_____

_____

One reason David's sin was specifically against God was because God would have given him a way out the moment he asked. David's refusal to ask was an affront to God's power that was available to him.

What prospect was worse than any other judgment God could render, according to verse 11?

_____

Verses 13-15 speak of activities that could not be restored to David until he had come to true repentance. What are they?

_____

_____

What are "the sacrifices of God" (see v. 17)?

_____

God poured His abundant grace on David and forgave his sin. Although God removed his guilt, He did not remove the repercussions. If only David had walked through that first door! Thank You, God, that in every temptation You provide an open door. When I am tempted, remind me to run through it!

God never convicts us of sin to make sure we know how wretched we are, for He calls us the righteousness of God in Christ. Rather, God convicts us through His Holy Spirit because He is grieved when fellowship between us is broken. Learn to develop thankfulness toward a keen conviction of sin and pray for it in the lives of your children. God's heart cry is "Come home!"

Day 4
The Right Hand of God

Today's Treasure

"WE DO HAVE SUCH A HIGH PRIEST, WHO SAT DOWN AT THE RIGHT HAND OF THE THRONE OF THE MAJESTY IN HEAVEN, AND WHO SERVES IN THE SANCTUARY, THE TRUE TABERNACLE SET UP BY THE LORD, NOT BY MAN."

Hebrews 8:1-2

Begin today's study by reading Today's Treasure and praying that God will speak to you through His Word.

Last week we began considering our Great High Priest's supremacy over Aaron. Today we will continue the same theme as we focus our attention on the revolutionary words of Hebrews 8.

The first words of this chapter indicate that the divinely-inspired writer has arrived at a pivotal point. He can proceed no further without stating his reason for writing. Today's Treasure provides a synopsis of the entire Book of Hebrews. Let's attempt to understand the book's great significance to its immediate audience: the Hebrew Christian. First, consider what the writer means by "such a high priest."

Hebrews 7:26, part of the text from our previous lesson, provides a beautiful simplification of these passages: "such a high priest" meets our needs. Aaron could fulfill his duty to the letter of the law. He could work His hands to the bone and never miss a sacrifice, but he could not truly meet the people's need. He was powerless to make unrighteous persons righteous. How could he? He could not even make himself righteous. But "we do have such a high priest, who sat down at the right hand of the throne of the Majesty in heaven" (Heb. 8:1).

Take a closer look. Why was it significant that our Great High Priest "sat down," according to Hebrews 10:11-14?

_____

_____

Why did He sit specifically at God's right hand? The right hand represents the point from which God releases His unparalleled power. The right hand of God, as opposed to the hand of God, is a fascinating study. Look at several examples.

Read each of the following verses. Then fill in the letter beside the corresponding teaching on the significance of God's right hand.

_____ 1. Psalm 17:7   a. His right hand purchased the hill
_____ 2. Psalm 44:3   country where He led His children.
_____ 3. Psalm 45:4   b. It displays awesome things.
_____ 4. Psalm 77:10   c. He saves by His right hand.
_____ 5. Psalm 78:54   d. His right hand holds me.
_____ 6. Psalm 80:15-17   e. It gave His children the land.
_____ 7. Psalm 139:10   f. His right hand planted the vine.
                            g. We must remember the years of
                                God's right hand.

Notice that each reference is ultimately fulfilled in Christ Jesus, who sits at God's right hand. Christ is the saving hand of God. Christ is the One who holds us, who said, "No one can snatch them out of my hand" (John 10:28). Christ is the One who teaches us through His Spirit—the One whom Mary called Rabboni (see John 20:16). Christ is the One who leads us to the holy mountain of God and who purchased our promised land with His own blood. In Christ's resurrection God displayed His mightiest work. Therefore, we must remember the years of the One who sits at God's right hand.

We have more to learn about God's right hand, where Christ resides. In an ancient courtroom the judge's right side was also the position of the defense lawyer or advocate. "My dear children, I write this to you so that you will not sin. But if anybody does sin, we have one who speaks to the Father in our defense—Jesus Christ, the Righteous One" (1 John 2:1).

Perhaps Christ had many reasons to sit at God's right hand, but let's examine what might have been His most personal motivation.

What does Psalm 16:11 tell you about God's right hand?

_____

By what name does Hebrews 8:1 refer to God? _____

Not *His* Majesty but *the* Majesty! The word *Majesty* used in this passage is translated from the Greek word *megalosune*. *Mega* means *large*. *Megalosune* means *greatness*. A more pointed way to translate the word *Majesty* is "very God." Why is it so important that Christ sat down at the right hand of the Majesty in heaven? Hebrews 8:2 provides the answer to this question: because heaven is the true tabernacle, the one the Lord Himself built!

MAJESTY

very God

Carefully read Hebrews 8:6-7.

These verses begin a comparison between the old covenant and the new. The concept of the new covenant should not have been a surprise to the Hebrew Christians to whom this book was written. Was it not their own beloved prophet Jeremiah who first decreed God's precise intentions?

What will be different about the new covenant? Check each of the following specified in Hebrews 8:8-13.
- ❏ He will put His laws into their minds.
- ❏ He will establish a completely new set of laws.
- ❏ He will write His laws on their hearts.
- ❏ He will be known by all.
- ❏ He will judge their unrighteousness.
- ❏ He will be merciful to their unrighteousness.
- ❏ He will remember their sins at the judgment.
- ❏ He will remember their sins no more.

The old covenant was obviously external and the new covenant is internal. How does God enable us to internalize that new covenant? The key is in Hebrews 8:6. On what is the new covenant founded or established?
- ❏ God's Word ❏ a better sacrifice ❏ better promises

Remember that the continuing theme of the Book of Hebrews is supremacy. Christ is better than the angels, Moses, Aaron, the patriarchs, and the prophets. Now we see further progression of the theme, with God stating that the new covenant is better than the old because the new covenant is founded on better promises. The same Greek word used each time for *better* is *kreissonos*, meaning *more profitable, nobler, more excellent*.

What can we conclude so far? The new covenant is established on more profitable and valuable promises. The Greek word for *promises, epaggelia*, is primarily a legal term denoting a summons or a promise to do or give something. The same Greek word is used in 2 Corinthians 1:20, in which we will find the key that unlocks Hebrews 8.

"No matter how many promises God has made, they are 'Yes' in Christ. And so through him the 'Amen' is spoken by us to the glory of God" (2 Cor. 1:20). Every promise of God finds its yes in Jesus Christ! Jesus Christ is God's yes!

Every time the Israelites slaughtered another animal, God shook His head no. It was not enough. The offering was accepted only on the basis that a yes would finally come. That afternoon on Calvary God cried out with agony mingled with relief, "Yes!" At that very moment all of God's promises found their fulfillment in Christ. The old covenant was based on a shadow. The new covenant was based on a Savior. Christ made it possible for an external covenant to be obsolete and a new covenant to be injected straight into the point of our need: the heart.

His perfect Spirit enables the internalizing of the new covenant in every receiving heart. We needed a yes, and He met our need.

Do you sometimes wonder how God could seem so different in the Old Testament compared to the New Testament? We know that He is "the same yesterday and today and forever" (Heb. 13:8). What could have happened? He is the same God. He simply has a different answer: yes!

Test God's new program for a moment. Think of any promise and determine whether His yes is Christ.

Will He heal you from the ravages of sin? Read Isaiah 53:5. If your answer is yes, how does this verse say He will do it?

_____

Can He make something good come from something bad? Read Romans 8:28. What is your answer?

_____

Now read Romans 8:29. What is His purpose?

To _____ us to the _____

of His _____!

If you have accepted Christ as your Savior, will He always be with you? Read Romans 8:38-39. If so, where is God's love found?

_____

Will He bless you? Read Ephesians 1:3. If your answer is yes, how does this verse say He will do it?

_____

Will He meet your needs? Read Philippians 4:19. If your answer is yes, how does this verse say He will do it?

_____

We could go on and on. All of God's promises in Christ are yes! Since Calvary, God stands before us 100 percent in the affirmative. He died to say yes! You may be asking yourself, *Is she saying that God never says no?* He certainly does, but His no is given only so that He can say yes to something better. God's no is a street sign to direct you to an oncoming yes. He says no to premarital sex so that He can say yes to the blessed intimacy of marriage. He says no to addiction so that He can say yes to freedom. If He has been forced to say no to you lately, rejoice! He is directing you to a point at which He can extend to you a resounding yes! Keep driving in His direction. A better yes is just around the corner.

♥ Think of a past personal need that God undoubtedly met in Christ—perhaps the need for acceptance, intimacy, approval, a friend, someone you could trust, or someone to fill a terrible void left by loss. How did God obviously meet this need in Christ?

_____

_____

_____

Do more people know what Christians do not believe than what we believe? Does the world view us as a squelched, restricted, mindless group of people who serve a God who says only no? May this be the generation that seizes every opportunity to attest to a God who says yes—yes to salvation, yes to forgiveness, yes to abundant life, and yes to a mansion in glory. Christ is God's yes!

Day 5

Heaven, the Blessed Adoption Agency

Today's Treasure

"YOU DID NOT RECEIVE A SPIRIT THAT MAKES YOU A SLAVE AGAIN TO FEAR, BUT YOU RECEIVED THE SPIRIT OF SONSHIP. AND BY HIM WE CRY, 'ABBA, FATHER.'"

Romans 8:15

Begin today's study by reading Today's Treasure and praying that God will speak to you through His Word.

Although today we will conclude the weeks specifically devoted to the Hebrew priesthood, in week 8 we will have far more to learn about the priests' duties regarding the innermost room of the tabernacle.

Our study in the past few days has centered in the Book of Hebrews; however, today we will return to the original chapter from which we started. I earlier omitted a portion of Exodus 28 so that we could study it today, since it describes the attire the high priest must wear. In week 6, day 5 you recorded some of the high priest's garments. Maybe you noticed that the clothing we studied was for the high priest alone.

Whose garments are described in Exodus 28:3-4? _____

The garments God described in the next 35 verses are only for Aaron and the high priests who follow him. Look back in verse 1, which lists four sons who will aid Aaron in the tabernacle. What are they to wear? Let's find out.

> **Carefully read Exodus 28:40-43.** Notice that the sons' garments obviously differ from those of the high priest. With the exception of the embroidered sash (which also could have been white), the sons were wholly dressed in fine linen.

> Do you recall the representation of fine linen (see Rev. 19:8)?
> ❑ the purity of saints
> ❑ the bride of Christ
> ❑ the righteous acts of the saints

> **Now read Exodus 28:29.**

Aaron was to bear over his heart the names of the sons of Israel. Do not miss the beautiful shadow of sonship so majestically portrayed through the priesthood. Just as Aaron was a type, or picture, of Christ, our Great High Priest, the sons who were permitted to serve with Aaron are types, or pictures, of New Testament believer-priests—you and me!

> **Read the familiar words of 1 Peter 2:9.** I pray that as you read them this time, you will glean a much greater blessing.

> According to this verse, what kind of priesthood are we?

> _____

> Of what order was Christ's priesthood (see Heb. 5:6)?

> _____

> What two positions did this unique priest fill (see day 2)?

> _____

> What positions will we also fill, according to 1 Peter 2:9?

> _____

We are also priests after the order of Melchizedek!

> **Rejoice in reviewing Revelation 1:5-6** in light of what you have studied thus far today.

What has Christ made us? _____

_____

We were granted this wonderful position because of sonship! Sonship carries with it countless wonderful and inexhaustible truths.

Read Romans 8:13-17. What kind of sons are we as Gentiles?

_____

What name may we call our God? _____

Who testifies that we belong to God? _____

What relationship do we have with Christ? _____

Read Romans 8:17-18. You might say these verses offer good news and bad news. The bad news to believers may be that we must "share in his sufferings" (v. 17). But what is the good news (v. 18)?

_____

Read Hebrews 12:4-11. What is the exhortation or "word of encouragement" verse 5 addresses?

_____

What is one major way God reveals sonship to us?

_____

What does it mean if we are not disciplined?

_____

Meditate on verse 10. What is discipline's eventual outcome (v. 11)?

_____

_____

_____

How contrary our reception of God's discipline is to His holy intention! Are you like me, often interpreting the Lord's discipline as proof that He must not love you, that He is angry with you, that you are illegitimate or a castaway? In our seven years with Michael, Keith and I certainly experienced the impact of an adoption-like mentality on discipline. Michael required twice the tough, consistent discipline his "sisters" did. It was not because they were better than he was but because he shared neither a genetic nor environmental makeup with them.

You see, Michael was not an infant when he came to live with us. As an older child, he came with an established set of habits and tendencies. He did not share our same "Moore-isms." He did not understand our expectations nor did he often care to try. For a long time, he wanted to share the benefit of our home without sharing our nature. Does that make sense? Don't we often respond similarly to our adoption into God's family? I certainly do.

I remember so often saying to Keith, "I want to love Michael to wholeness." He had been through enough in my estimation. I never wanted to chastise him. I never wanted to have to enforce authority on him. Thankfully, God's will broke through my ignorance. If we had not followed God's undeniable directive to discipline him, our home would have turned to shambles. God's spiritual house on Planet Earth would also be in shambles without divine discipline. As adopted children of God, perhaps we need more discipline at times than anyone to conform to our Father's house.

♥ **Recall a time when God disciplined you. Why did He? Name at least two different reasons based on Hebrews 12: 1-13.**

_____

_____

Read 1 John 3:1-2.

These verses overwhelm me every time I read them. As God's children, we are the recipients of lavish love—a love that covers the lack of recognition this world system gives us, a love that motivates us to keep trusting even when we have no idea what God is doing. When everything else in our lives is a frightening fog, we can be sure of one perfect promise: when we shall see Him, we shall be like Him; for we shall see Him as He is!

A popular magazine recently published an article written by the illegitimate daughter of a well-known actor who is now deceased. Her words testified to the deep sense of loss and detachment she experienced because her father never acknowledged her.

You are not illegitimate, my beloved sister. You have been planned and purposed. Your Father has acknowledged you as His child. "Let the little children come to me, and do not hinder them, for the kingdom of heaven belongs to such as these" (Matt. 19:14).

> As God's adopted children, perhaps we need more discipline at times than anyone to conform to our Father's house.

Viewer Guide

A Heart That Intercedes

Fill in the following blanks based on the King James Version of Hebrews 7:25:

"Wherefore he is able also to _____ them to the _____ that come unto God by him, seeing he ever _____ to make _____ for them."

Part 1: The Promise of Hebrews 7:25a

- "Able": Greek transliteration, *dunamai*, which means "is powerful to."

- "Save": Greek transliteration, *sozo*, which means "to save, i.e., deliver or _____ (literal or figurative):— _____, preserve ... do well, be (make) _____."

"Christ's salvation is a complete deliverance, no matter what the need of the sinner." Expositor's Commentary

- "uttermost": Greek transliteration, *panteles*, is comprised of two Greek words: *pas*, which means _____ and *telos* which means _____, "from a primary *tello* (to set out for a _____ point or _____) ... result ... _____."

- The Greek transliterated phrase *eis to panteles* appears in one other place: Luke 13:11 (read Luke 13:10-17). Consider the following translations: "She was _____ unable to bend back"—Lenski; "_____ unable"—New International Commentary of the New Testament; "not able to straighten up _____ _____," and further, " _____ unable" —Word Biblical Commentry

Part 2: The Passion of Hebrews 7:25b

- Romans 8:27 tells us this intercession is according to the _____ of God.
- "Purpose"—Greek transliteration, *boule*, "will, project, intention, as the result of _____; counsel, decree, aim, or estimation, as it denotes deliberation and reflection."[1] "*Boule* as the _____ _____ of inward 'deliberation' ... _____ ... Secondly, *boule* denotes the _____ result of inner deliberation."
- The verb form of this same Greek word, *boule*, is used in I Corinthians 12:11 concerning God's assignment of our _____ _____.

In light of these meanings, let's explore Luke 22:41-42; 22:31-32.

---

1. *Hebrew-Greek Keyword Study Bible: New International Version* (Chattanooga: AMG Publishers, 1996), 1600.

Video sessions are available for download at *www.lifeway.com/women*.

Hearts Beyond the Veil

DAY 1 • RADIANT INTIMACY

DAY 2 • A ROOM WITH A VIEW

DAY 3 • THE ARK OF THE TESTIMONY

DAY 4 • GOD ON THE MOVE

DAY 5 • THE MEETING PLACE

WEEK 8

Having studied the ministry of the priesthood in the holy place and having received access through our Great High Priest, we will seize the invitation to step beyond the heavy veil to behold the holy of holies. We will move from the place of fellowship to the place of pure intimacy. Here in the holy of holies God kept His promise that He would meet with persons. It was the place of perfect dimensions—the place that housed the ark of the testimony. In the holy of holies we will seek answers to the following questions.

Principal Questions

1. What important task did the cherubim have in Genesis 3:23-24?
2. What might have been the significance of the cube-shaped room?
3. By what authority do you dare enter the holy of holies?
4. What was the significance of the mercy seat?
5. What was the posture of the angelic creatures in Ezekiel 1:11?

Perhaps you will wonder as you complete this week's study how a God so holy could be so committed to reconciling sinful humanity to Himself. Our God is both universal and personal, terrifying and tender. Come and meet Him in the holy of holies.

Day 1
Radiant Intimacy

Begin today's study by reading Today's Treasure and praying that God will speak to you through His Word.

For the past several weeks we have studied the priests' consecration and calling. We have also examined the holy place, the center of their communion with God in fellowship, worship, and prayer. Recall that three furnishings adorned the holy place: the lampstand, the table that held the bread of the Presence, and the altar of incense. Today we will focus on the veil just beyond the altar of incense, the heavenly partition that separated the holy place from the holy of holies itself.

Read Exodus 26:31-33 and answer the following questions.

What were the colors of the veil? _____

_____

What figures were to be embroidered into the veil? _____

How was the veil to be hung? _____

_____

What article was to be placed beyond the veil?

_____

At this point in our study we are quite familiar with the four colors employed strategically through the tabernacle. These same colors were woven into the gate at the entrance to the outer court, the door of the holy place, the covering overhead in the holy place, and the high priest's garments. Today we will examine the fifth designation for the holy hues: the veil.

Every entrance was embroidered with the same colors, but this is the first time we have seen cherubim, a class of winged angels, embroidered in an entrance. The only other place we have seen the cherubim was overhead in the covering of the sanctuary, or the holy place.

I find it intriguing to think that the psalmist may have been thinking of the cherubim in the tabernacle covering when he wrote: "I long to dwell in your tent forever and take refuge in the shelter of your wings" (Ps. 61:4).

Today's Treasure

"WE, WHO WITH UNVEILED FACES ALL REFLECT THE LORD'S GLORY, ARE BEING TRANSFORMED INTO HIS LIKENESS WITH EVER-INCREASING GLORY, WHICH COMES FROM THE LORD, WHO IS THE SPIRIT."

2 Corinthians 3:18

161

Psalm 91 states, "He will cover you with his feathers, and under his wings you will find refuge" (Ps. 91:4). However, the cherubim wrought in the veil seem to possess a different meaning.

Restate the major purpose of the veil. _____

_____

The cherubim were intricately involved in the veil's ability to accomplish its designated responsibility: to separate the holy place from the holy of holies.

 What important task did the cherubim have in Genesis 3:23-24?

_____

What was the task of the angels in Luke 2:8-14?

_____

The cherubim woven into the veil appear to possess a dual role that combined both of these responsibilities. They announced God's presence, which resided behind the veil in the holy of holies. In addition, they denied access to that holy presence. They were both proclaimers and protectors.

So great was God's glory that entrance behind the veil for the masses had to be withheld, or they would die. The veil not only protected God's dwelling place but also protected the people yet unprepared to stand in His presence. On our side of the completed work of Calvary we sometimes forget that God unveiled His glory through a progressive disclosure.

Remember that before the tabernacle structure was constructed, only one person had been allowed to partake of God's glory, and he had to go up to do it. Humanity had to meet with God by going up because God had not yet met with humanity by coming down. For the remainder of the lesson today we will consider the impact of God's glory on this one who was invited to go up and the necessity of a veil to cover the glory he received.

Let's turn back to the "parenthesis" God placed between the commandment to build the tabernacle and its actual construction (Ex. 32–34). Countless riches are braided throughout these three chapters, but we will look now at the last occurrence Scripture recorded before Moses gave God's instructions to the entire assembly.

Read Exodus 34:28-35 and answer the following questions, keeping in mind that this is the second time God had given Moses the Commandments on stone, the first ones having been destroyed at the feet of an idolatrous people. Check the correct answers.

God's glory had to be withheld, or they would die.

What mountain had Moses climbed to meet with God?
❑ Mount Horeb   ❑ Mount Zion   ❑ Mount Sinai

How long had he been there?
❑ 6 sabbaths   ❑ 7 days   ❑ 40 days and nights

What mark did God's glory leave on Moses?
❑ a veil   ❑ a new reverence   ❑ a radiant face

What was the response of Aaron and the congregation to the mark of God's glory?
❑ fear   ❑ great interest   ❑ pleasure   ❑ jealousy

What measure did Moses take to lessen the people's intimidation?
❑ He helped them grow accustomed to his radiance.
❑ He tried to keep his distance.
❑ He wore a veil.

No wonder Moses did not eat or drink! He was in the very presence of the Bread of life and the Living Water!

In these beautiful passages we can discover the effects of God's glory in the life of one He invites to approach.

1. A change took place. Moses' face was radiant after returning from God's presence. He bore an undeniable mark of God's glory. Likewise, we can never partake of God's glory without His presence evoking a change in us. Sometimes I believe this is exactly why we avoid His presence. Change would be inevitable, and we so often resist change.

2. Moses was not aware that his face was radiant. Although a change had been wrought, Moses was not aware of its obvious mark. How typical of God's methods! As God perfects us, He keeps us protected from the pride that might otherwise develop by veiling to some extent our progress in our own eyes. You see, the light of the glory of His presence shines two ways: it sheds light on the knowledge of God so that we can learn to see Him more clearly, but it also sheds light on us so that we can see our own sin more clearly. Remember, the closer you approach the light, the brighter it shines on you. This is the marvelous two-edged sword of intimacy. We see Him more clearly, and we see ourselves more clearly. It is the perfect safeguard against pride. You can mark His word on this: true intimacy breeds true humility!

3. Although Moses was not aware of the marked change God's presence evoked in him, others were. Intimacy with God shows! Just as Aaron and the congregation were intimidated by Moses, persons around you may be also as God marks you with His glory. You will sadly discover that your own brothers and sisters in Christ may have a harder time dealing with God's glory in you than your unbelieving friends and coworkers. Others may react negatively for one major

God protects us from pride by veiling our progress.

reason: radiance to one is confrontational to another. Others are drawn to it like magnets. They are authentic seekers of the Way.

4. The mark of radiance on Moses finally faded. The greater the gap of time since he had climbed the mountain, the more his radiance dissipated.

Do you begin to see what the veil of the tabernacle covered? If Moses' face had to be veiled simply from the secondhand absorption of God's radiance, imagine what God's glory must have been like firsthand.

♥ Read 2 Corinthians 3:7-18, which extends a blessing to you, and write a paragraph describing what these verses say to you.

_____

_____

_____

_____

Can you possibly keep from going up to that holy mountain today? May these words He gave me entice you:

> I hear You call, "Come meet with Me,
> See that which eyes are veiled to see,
> And ears in vain will please to hear
> Except your heart should draw you here!
>
> "Abandon deeds down at My feet.
> No crowns as yet, no judgment seat.
> Surrender here all noble plans.
> Just lift to Me your empty hands.
>
> "I'll fill them with the richest fare
> And circumcise your heart to dare
> To reach beyond all earthliness,
> For on this mount you're Mine to bless.
>
> "With gentle hands till heart is stretched
> I'll have My Word upon it etched
> 'Til only knees can catch the fall
> Of one who cries, 'You are my all!'"

Conclude by reading the wonderful words of Psalm 43:3-4.

Day 2

A Room with a View

Read Today's Treasure and ask God to speak to you through His Word.

Before we take our first step inside the holy of holies, let's reconsider the dimensions of the holiest of all rooms made with human hands. Recall our study in week 5, day 1, when we examined the dimensions of the tabernacle proper. The tabernacle proper was the structure that housed both the holy place and the holy of holies. The rectangular building was 10 cubits wide and 30 cubits long.

Draw a diagram like the one you drew on page 94, approximately one-third as wide as it is long.

Today's Treasure

"Prophecy never had its origin in the will of man, but men spoke from God as they were carried along by the Holy Spirit."

2 Peter 1:21

Mark the dimensions in cubits on your diagram and divide the tabernacle proper into its two rooms. The front two-thirds, or 20 cubits, of the tabernacle proper was designated for the holy place; the back one-third, or 10 cubits, for the holy of holies. Draw a line to represent the veil that divided the holy place and the holy of holies. Now look at the dimensions of the holy of holies.

What shape do you see? _____

What might have been the significance of the cube-shaped room?

_____

Recall that the frames or boards of the tabernacle proper were also 10 cubits tall (see Ex. 26:16). As you can see, the holy of holies was a perfect cube, exactly as tall as it was wide. If every detail of the tabernacle was to be constructed by a heavenly pattern, the dimensions of the room that inhabited the very presence of God's glory must be extremely significant. We will devote our study today to learning the significance of the perfect perimeters of the holy of holies.

With what portion of Scripture did Christ begin to explain Himself (Luke 24:13-27)?

_____

Remember that Moses wrote of Christ! As we have seen through our study of the tabernacle, every detail in this marvelous structure speaks of Christ and our subsequent relationship with Him. From what you have already learned, you can predict that we will capture an intimate look at our Savior in the holy of holies. We can expect to see our Savior's finished work in this holy room.

Four adjoining walls surrounded and embraced the holy contents of this innermost room. Only one piece of furniture was present; yet from any one of the four walls the structure could be seen from a different perspective. It was the same structure no matter where the priest stood, but it could be viewed at ground level from any one of four walls or perspectives.

What does Psalm 18:30 tell you about God and His Word?

_____

Every piece of information we need to know about God is contained in this one small book.

Over the past 25 years, two realizations have reduced me to tears with increasing frequency: God is so awesome I can hardly believe I have the privilege of knowing Him, and God's Word is so perfect I can hardly fathom it.

John 21:25 says, "Jesus did many other things as well. If every one of them were written down, I suppose that even the whole world would not have room for the books that would be written." Do you realize what that means? Consider a set of encyclopedias, which fill several shelves. Each volume usually contains a scholar's synopsis of several hundred years of modern history. Now hold your Bible in your hand. This is the entire Word of the God of all creation! Every pertinent piece of information we need to know about Him and our relationship with Him is contained in this one relatively small book. You see, ours is a God of few words.

When you consider His Word from this perspective, you come to realize that every one of the 66 books He inspired as a part of the whole is vital. As we learned from Luke 24:27, the Old Testament continually points forward to Jesus' life. The New Testament Letters point back to His life on earth and forward to His life to come. But the Gospels point straight to His earthly life as He lived it.

One perfect life may be viewed from four divinely-inspired perspectives—Gospel glimpses from ground level!

The walls that witnessed the ark of the covenant from four different angles draw a wonderful representation of the Gospels, which witnessed Jesus' life from four different angles. Nothing in Scripture is accidental or coincidental. Just think about it: God chose no less and no more than four Gospels. They were adjoined in sovereignly-ordained order. If you lined the four Gospels around Jesus' life, they would provide a perfect, four-sided perspective forming four embracing walls. Actually, it is one Gospel expressed from four angles. As we combine the four, a perfect room emerges from which to study the life of Christ.

Each of the following Scriptures expresses the theme of a Gospel. In what light does each inspired Gospel writer reveal Jesus Christ?

Read Matthew 2:1-2. The theme of Matthew is Christ as—
❏ servant   ❏ man   ❏ king   ❏ God

Read Mark 10:43-45. The theme of Mark is Christ as—
❏ servant   ❏ man   ❏ king   ❏ God

Read Luke 4:1-4. The theme of Luke is Christ as—
❏ servant   ❏ man   ❏ king   ❏ God

Read John 1:1,14. The theme of John is Christ as—
❏ servant   ❏ man   ❏ king   ❏ God

Consider the audience each Gospel targeted:
1. Matthew targeted Jews—religious people.
2. Mark targeted Romans—average business people.
3. Luke targeted Greeks—philosophers.
4. John targeted all of the above.

The Gospels presented our Lord Jesus Christ as King (Matthew), Servant (Mark), 100 percent man but God (Luke), and 100 percent God but man (John). Through the Gospels all audiences could find languages they understood. They extended the life of Christ to all neighboring peoples (Jews, Romans, and Greeks) and "to the ends of the earth" (Acts 1:8). Through them we witness our Savior's life from four different ground-level perspectives.

Something else is evident when you meditate on the holy of holies. From wall to wall and from ceiling to floor it measured 10 cubits in every direction. As I drew it and looked at it, God immediately brought to mind certain Scriptures.

In Ephesians 3:16-19, what did Paul hope we would understand about the love of Christ?

How wide and long and high and deep—with His lavish love Christ embraces us equally in four perfect directions. This verse about the completeness of Christ's love for us might be applied like this: God's love for me extends in every direction. Because I am His child, all that is behind me must be worked toward good, even when I have failed (see Rom. 8:28). In addition, everything ahead of me belongs to God. My future is entirely His, and His love extends through circumstances I have not yet known (see Jer. 29:11). No matter how deep I sink into a pit of despair, His hand can extend that much deeper to lift me out (see Ps. 40:2). No matter what heights this human experience can boast, God's ways are higher. Every day I spend with Him, I am lifted out of insignificance to ascend and take my place in God's high calling in Christ Jesus (see Isa. 55:9; Phil. 3:14).

God's Word states that this life is only a breath, a disappearing vapor, very brief. And we get only one opportunity to experience Him as mortals relating to an immortal Savior. Will you agree to experience Him in His fullness? Will you revel in your God through the breadth, length, depth, and height of this human experience? Can you say to Him, "I want to experience every part of You that is possible on this side of heaven"? If you can, then you will "know this love that surpasses knowledge—that you may be filled to the measure of all the fullness of God" (Eph. 3:19).

> No matter how deep I sink into a pit of despair, God's hand can extend that much deeper to lift me out.

To undergird what you have read today, read each verse below. Then label each with the word past, future, depths, or heights to complete this sentence appropriately: "Christ is Lord of my ..."

Read Psalm 40:2. Christi is Lord of my ...
❏ past ❏ future ❏ depths ❏ heights

Read Isaiah 55:9. Christ is Lord of my ...
❏ past ❏ future ❏ depths ❏ heights

Read Jeremiah 29:11. Christ is Lord of my ...
❏ past ❏ future ❏ depths ❏ heights

Read Romans 8:28. Christ is Lord of my ...
❏ past ❏ future ❏ depths ❏ heights

Read Philippians 3:14. Christ is Lord of my ...
❏ past ❏ future ❏ depths ❏ heights

♥ Which of the Scriptures in the activity above most nearly addresses your circumstances right now and why?

_____

_____

Day 3
The Ark of the Testimony

Begin today's study by reading Today's Treasure and praying that God will speak to you through His Word.

Stop right here. Only the high priest may enter farther. Have you gained access to the holy of holies, based on the position of the One appointed Great High Priest?

 By what authority do you dare enter the holy of holies according to Hebrews 10:19-22?

_____

_____

If you have this confidence, then you may advance. Step beyond the altar of incense and lift the thickness of the veil. Humbly fall on your knees and crawl under the veil. Then stand if you can before the most awesome structure ever constructed by human hands—the ark of the covenant!

Minutes have passed since I wrote that last word. I have been staring straight ahead with retracted hands, pondering the arrival of a moment for which we have waited eight weeks. Now that we have arrived, I have no words with which to proceed. God's own words penetrate my thoughts: "Do not come any closer. … Take off your sandals, for the place where you are standing is holy ground" (Ex. 3:5). I pray that by His mercy and with His help I can guide you into truth as I attempt to teach you about the ark of the covenant.

Before we can begin to describe what we see in the holy of holies, recall the principle of a God-given name. When God ascribes a name to anyone or anything, He expresses something specific about the recipient's character, nature, and destiny.

By what name does God introduce the object in the innermost

room (see Ex. 25:22)? _____

The Hebrew word for _testimony_ is _eduwth,_ which means _witness._ This divinely-inspired structure, constructed after a heavenly pattern, possessed a God-given destiny: be My witness! For the next several days we will ask that the ark of testimony fulfill its sovereign purpose, through the Holy Spirit's power, by witnessing to us of its Master Designer.

Today's Treasure

"THERE, ABOVE THE COVER BETWEEN THE TWO CHERUBIM THAT ARE OVER THE ARK OF THE TESTIMONY, I WILL MEET WITH YOU AND GIVE YOU ALL MY COMMANDS FOR THE ISRAELITES."

Exodus 25:22

Although later we will examine the Hebrew meaning for the exact translation of our word *ark*, also referred to as *the ark of the covenant, the ark of God,* and *the ark of the Lord,* every ark to which Scripture refers has a common purpose.

Find these two examples and note the use of each ark.

Genesis 7:7 _____

Exodus 2:3 _____

In the latter reference the King James Version uses the word *ark*. The word *tebah* means "a box, chest—ark, basket." No matter what name your version calls the basket, the purpose remains the same. Preservation was the common purpose of the arks in Scripture.

Although we will discover a far more specific definition for the ark of the testimony, we have already derived a wide definition for it: the ark of the testimony was to preserve God's witness. Are you beginning to see why this divine object was in a place of such priority?

Now turn back to Exodus 25:9-10. What is the first object God commanded to be made for His dwelling?

_____

Without a doubt, the ark of the testimony had a priority position in the tabernacle. Let's expand on a question we asked in the beginning of week 4: Why did God give directions about the innermost place first? He began with the place of His presence because communication starts with God and ends with people. God always approaches us before we can approach Him!

Read each Scripture and write beside it the letter corresponding to the information it states about God's method of reconciliation.

_____ I. John 6:44-45,65   a. God works in us to please Him. We do not devise acceptable actions on our own.

_____ 2. I John 4:19   b. No one comes to Christ unless the Father draws her.

_____ 3. Romans 3:10-12   c. No one can come to God as righteous. No one seeks Him on her own.

_____ 4. Philippians 2:13   d. We love God because He first loved us.

Our relationship with God always begins where He is because He is the originator of all relationships. Let's consider this truth in immediate terms. Based on the Scriptures we read above, I can confidently say that I did not approach God with this Bible study. He approached me. On my own accord I can do nothing that pleases Him! Furthermore, you did not approach God with the desire to do this Bible study. He approached you. It is God who works in us both to will and to do His good pleasure.

♥ **Think back on either your initial salvation or restoration after a time of wandering. Describe ways God drew you to Himself.**

_____

_____

_____

_____

How, then, can we approach God? On the basis that He first approached us. And because God approached us with His will for this Bible study, He is obligated to use it as a tool through which we can approach Him. Our approach is always based on His approach. And His approach is always for the expressed purpose of our approach. This agenda has been in effect since creation, and it will continue until He approaches us in the air and in the twinkling of an eye invites us to approach Him there (see I Thess. 4:16-17).

The ark of the testimony was the place where God's approach began in the tabernacle of His presence. God said, "Make this tabernacle and all its furnishings exactly like the pattern I will show you" (Ex. 25:9). If you have this truth engraved in your heart, you will never forget the divine significance of the tabernacle in the wilderness. It was not just a sacred building. It was not simply a place of sacrifice or a center of worship, as important as these facts are. It was tangible evidence of intangible truth. It was a heavenly picture drawn on an earthly canvas! God's Word gives us a glimpse of the heavenly object the ark of testimony illustrated.

What appears in the heavenly temple in Revelation 11:19?

_____

The Apostle John had the unfathomable experience of getting to see the "true tabernacle set up by the Lord, not by man" (Heb. 8:2). Proceeding from "the ark of his covenant" were "flashes of lightning, rumblings, peals of thunder, an earthquake and a great hailstorm."

The earthquake and great hail signify God's impending judgment, but what was the origin of the lightning, voices, and thundering according to Revelation 4:1-5?

_____

Our approach to God is always based on His approach to us.

Could it be that the true ark of the testimony, from which the earthly ark was patterned, was none other than God's throne? I dare not be dogmatic on a subject so far above my understanding, but this is certain: in the earthly tabernacle made divinely with human hands, the ark of the testimony was doubtless the throne of His glory. It was the focus of His dwelling, the seat of reconciliation.

Let's stop here for today and try to absorb this information before we see the actual construction of the ark of the testimony.

Conclude by reading aloud Psalm 103 as praise to the Lord. Please do not skip this exercise. You will miss a blessing.

Over the next few days we will ask God to share intimately with us what was innermost in His holy tabernacle. Therefore, with all that is within you bless His holy name!

Day 4
God on the Move

"Go and tell my servant David, 'This is what the Lord says: Are you the one to build me a house to dwell in? I have not dwelt in a house from the day I brought the Israelites up out of Egypt to this day. I have been moving from place to place with a tent as my dwelling.'"

2 Samuel 7:5-6

Begin today's study by reading Today's Treasure and praying that God will speak to you through His Word.

Today we will delve into the Scriptures in which the Master Designer decreed His unalterable instructions for the ark of the testimony. His commands are distinct yet brief, so please read them carefully.

Read Exodus 25:10-22 and answer the following questions by checking the correct answer or answers.

What two materials were used to build the ark of the testimony?
❑ bronze ❑ acacia wood ❑ gold ❑ silver

What were the dimensions of the ark?

_____

Where were the rings fastened?
❑ to the posts ❑ to the cherubim ❑ to the corners or feet

How was the ark transported?
❑ by poles or staves ❑ by the Spirit ❑ by ox cart

In verse 15, what specific instructions were given for the poles?
- ❑ They must be solid gold.
- ❑ They must not be removed.
- ❑ They must not be touched by unclean hands.

Notice the dimensions of the mercy seat in verse 17. Now read verse 10 again. What is the physical relationship between the chest and the mercy seat (KJV) or atonement cover (NIV)?
- ❑ The mercy seat is exactly one-fourth of the ark.
- ❑ The mercy seat and the ark were molded from the same piece of gold.
- ❑ The mercy seat was the same size as the ark, fitting on top of it as a lid.

What were to be at the ends of the mercy seat?
- ❑ cherubim   ❑ engravings   ❑ swords   ❑ veils

How were the cherubim's wings to be fashioned?
- ❑ spread upward
- ❑ covering the mercy seat
- ❑ straight out to the sides

How were the cherubim to be positioned on the mercy seat?
- ❑ looking upward to heaven
- ❑ facing one another
- ❑ looking toward the mercy seat

What was the significance of the mercy seat as stated in verse 22?

_____

Recall the representations of the two materials used to design the ark of the testimony. The acacia wood speaks of Christ's incorruptible humanity. The gold represents His deity. Together they represent the unity of incorruptible man and God. Only One can fill such a position: our Lord Jesus Christ.

According to verses 10-11, the ark was formed in three layers: gold on the outside, wood in the center, and gold on the inside. The gold on the outside represented God the Father. The wood in the center represented the One who became incorruptible humanity and thus the center of our salvation: God the Son. The gold on the inside could represent only the Holy Spirit, "Christ in you, the hope of glory" (Col. 1:27).

The gold molding around the edge of the ark formed a wreath or a crown exactly like those around the edges of the golden altar of incense and the table of the bread of the Presence.

What appears on Christ's head in Revelation 19:12?

_____

As you have discovered, the two poles remained in the golden rings of the ark at all times. The immovable poles served two major purposes, which we will discover.

Read I Chronicles 13 and write a brief synopsis of this passage.

_____

_____

_____

_____

What went wrong to incur such wrath? Discover the answers by reading about a more successful voyage of the ark that's recorded in I Chronicles 15:1–16:2.

Reason 1 (see I Chron. 15:2,12-13) _____

_____

Reason 2 (see I Chron. 15:15) _____

_____

How was the ark to be carried? _____

How was it carried the first time in I Chronicles 13:7?

_____

Reason 3 (see I Chron. 13:10) _____

_____

The poles were constant reminders of the proper transport of the ark of the testimony. It was to be moved only by the Levites, God's assigned servants. The ark was to be carried on human shoulders. It was never to be conveniently transported on wheels or hooves. The ark was never to be touched by unclean hands.

David learned a very valuable lesson that day—and he learned it the hard way.

From what source did David learn the proper way to handle the ark (see I Chron. 15:13,15)?

_____

He sought the Word of the Lord! When all else fails, read the instructions. Better yet, before all else fails, read the instructions! How many mistakes I have made in noble endeavors by moving on impulse rather than according to God's Word.

♥ Think of times you have acted on your own impulses rather than seeking direction from God's Word. What should your plan of action be when you have decisions to make?

_____

_____

_____

_____

We have discovered the first purpose of the immovable poles: proper transport. Now let's consider their second purpose.

Read 2 Samuel 7:1-6. Why did David want to build a more permanent dwelling place for the ark of God, according to verse 2?

_____

In one word, what was God's response to David? _____

What was the wonderful reason God would not allow David to build a permanent dwelling for the ark of the Lord (v. 6)?

_____

Do you understand why the tabernacle had to be a tent? Because God chose to be on the move with His people! What cause for celebration! God refused to be boxed inside a permanent dwelling, because He demanded the right to take every step His people took as they wandered through the wilderness. For this dispensation of time the ark of the testimony was the sovereign center of God's earthly presence. No matter where the Israelites went, the poles bore constant witness that God would be their traveling companion, continually testifying: "God with us! Emmanuel!"

The tabernacle had to be a tent because God chose to be on the move with His people!

Conclude today's lesson by basking in several promises from your constant Traveling Companion. Record the assurance you receive from each verse.

Isaiah 30:21 _____

_____

Isaiah 42:16 _____

_____

Isaiah 58:8 _____

_____

Listen carefully. God often whispers.

The Meeting Place

Today's Treasure

"HEAR US, O SHEP-HERD OF ISRAEL, YOU WHO LEAD JOSEPH LIKE A FLOCK; YOU WHO SIT ENTHRONED BETWEEN THE CHERU-BIM, SHINE FORTH."

Psalm 80:1

Begin today's study by reading Today's Treasure and praying that God will speak to you through His Word.

Today we will continue our study of the construction of the ark of the testimony. Although this lesson will conclude week 8, we are far from finishing our study of the holy of holies. Week 9 will also be devoted to the innermost room of the tabernacle.

We concluded day 4 by examining the poles permanently installed in the ark's four gold rings. Let's return to Exodus 25 and proceed with our construction. Immediately after God instructed Moses about the poles, He continued by commanding, "Make a mercy seat of pure gold" (Ex. 25:17, HCSB).

Although we'll consider the critical implications of the mercy seat in week 9, today we will focus our attention on the sacred cover's appearance. The mercy seat was to be adorned with a cherub on each end. God's command was clear that the angelic figures and the mercy seat were to be beaten from the same piece of gold. The cherubim stood facing each other from the ends, with wings spread upward, overshadowing this sacred center of mercy. The golden cherubim's gaze was set firmly on the mercy seat. "There, above the cover between the two cherubim that are over the ark of the Testimony, I will meet with you" (Ex. 25:22).

Many scholars believe that the mercy seat and the two cherubim represent the Trinity. I could not find ample scriptural basis for agreement. Psalm 61:4

confirmed for us that the cherubim overhead in the holy place indeed represented the "refuge" of God's "wings." However, the angelic figures over the mercy seat apparently represent exactly what they appear to: heavenly hosts gathered around God's throne. This conclusion can be drawn from several significant passages that describe a similar angelic posture.

What does each Scripture say about angels?

Psalm 80:1 _____

Psalm 99:1 _____

Isaiah 6:1-3 _____

Read Isaiah 37:16. I pray that these words will become very dear to you.

A woman named Kathy used to attend my Sunday School class. She is legally blind. She sat in exactly the same place every Sunday: first seat, second row. I grew so accustomed to her presence in this locale that I would almost have a hard time teaching without her. Each class began the same way. We read through the entire text; then we began dissecting it. Countless times as I read aloud to the class, my eyes were drawn to that first seat, second row. If you could have seen what I saw in that spot, you would know the reason. Kathy did not read the Scriptures. She experienced the Scriptures.

Every Sunday I had the privilege to witness the raptured face of a woman cast with sweet abandon into the words of Scripture. When I looked at Kathy, I realized that she was no longer simply sitting in our classroom. Her attention had been unmistakably drawn into the scene we studied. In the split second it took me to notice the chills on her arms because of her beloved Savior's Word, I was covered with them as well. Kathy "read" the Word in such a way that it would be impossible for her to depart unchanged. I testify to a woman who honestly practiced Psalm 1: she delighted in the Word of her God. Oh, that we might be so "blind"!

As you read the next Scripture, read it as Kathy would. Partake of Scripture. Meditate on the words. Then close your eyes and picture the scene. Just imagine what it might have been like to behold the glory described so beautifully in these passages. Don't just read it. Experience it!

Delight in reading Ezekiel 1:1-14,24,28.

Did you imagine their faces? Did you picture the brightness of their countenance? Did you hear the sound of their wings? Before my acquaintance with this chapter of Ezekiel, I always assumed that the sound of angels' wings was very hushed and that if we were quiet enough in worship, we could almost hear the gentle brush of their wings nearby. But Ezekiel 1:24 says that the sound of angels' wings is like the roar of rushing waters! Have you ever been to Niagara Falls? The sound is deafening!

When God decides to open our spiritual ears, we will not have to close our eyes and strain to hear. The sound will be overpowering!

Notice Ezekiel's response in 1:28. Now read God's request of him in 2:1. Now enjoy 2:2.

 What was the posture of those angelic creatures (1:11)?

_____

Read verse 12. Where did the creatures go? _____

_____

As we have seen, the Word plainly teaches that God is enthroned between heavenly hosts. Therefore, I believe that it is safest to interpret the cherubim overlooking the "throne" in the holy of holies as pictorial evidence of those who live to surround His Highness with praise in the true sanctuary.

Let's reconsider the "throne" they surveyed. Day 3 stated that we would define the word _ark_ with greater clarity as we continued our study. The emphasis on the cherubim presents us with the perfect opportunity to learn the Hebrew meaning of this exact English translation.

The Hebrew word for _the ark of the testimony_ is _arown_. It differs from the Hebrew words used for Noah's ark and Baby Moses' ark. Although all three arks share the common purpose of preservation, the Hebrew word _arown_ stretches the intent even further, meaning _chest_ or _coffin_. Why would a coffin serve as the earthly throne of God's glory? Because God's mercy rests only on God's "death."

The mercy seat was a fitting cover for a coffin. Had there been no plan for death, there would have been no possibility for mercy. How fitting that both the first and last objects in the tabernacle pointed to access by death. Whether in God's approach to persons or in our approach to God, there is no approach at all without death—the death of "the Lamb that was slain from the creation of the world" (Rev. 13:8).

How the heavenly hosts must adore God's precious Son, as anxious as they were to shout His blessed birth announcement, as compelled as they were to minister to His every need in the wilderness! How they must have begged the Father for release the day the nails were driven into His flesh!

 What new appreciation does this give you for Christ's words in Matthew 26:53-54?

Both the first and last objects in the tabernacle pointed to access by death.

_____

Read Luke 24:1-8 and grasp the significance of the angels' presence in this crucial scene. How many men whose clothes "gleamed like lightning" did the women see?

_____

Where were the women standing? _____

_____

Notice there was not one angel but two. Let's discover their role and position at Christ's tomb, or coffin.

Read John 20:10-13. Record the angels' role and position.

_____

_____

Can you imagine the divine appointment as God called out the names of two of His cherubim and beckoned them before the throne, then sent them to earth to guard the most precious body that ever lived? Surely as the body of their beloved lay in that tomb, those two angels stood constant guard, one at the head, one at the feet, facing one another with wings outstretched, feet practically melted into position, eyes cast solidly in one direction. Surely their gaze never wavered from the One they adored. Their eyes were fixed securely on His own. Not a single angelic muscle must have twitched, awaiting the Father's promise.

Then those eyes—those penetrating eyes that saw the pain of a leprous man, the eyes that set free a woman at a well, the eyes that saw a "rock" instead of a fumbling disciple—those piercing eyes began to open. And with the sound of mighty, rushing waters, their wings propelled them straight into the heavens with the dearest cry a pair of spiritual ears would ever hear: He is risen!

Viewer Guide

Hearts Beyond the Veil

Exodus 26:33 introduces our lesson today as we move from the holy place to the most holy place, the home of the ark of the covenant. We have only one way of getting there. We must find our way through the veil.

The Most Holy Place

1. We have an _____ behind the _____ (Heb. 6:13-20).

   The "two unchangeable things" (v. 18):

   • The _____ of God

   • The _____ by which it is _____

2. We have an _____ behind the veil (Heb. 10:19-25).

   • We have _____ (v. 19). "Therefore, brothers, since we have _____ for free _____ to the heavenly sanctuary by the means of the blood of Jesus."

• We have "a _____ and _____ way." Three Greek words for *new:*

    a. *Neos:* new and _____

    b. *Kainos:* new but _____

    c. *Prosphatos:* "etymologically meaning '_____ _____'; …
    the word simply means 'new,' 'fresh,' 'recent.'" "With respect to time,
    the way is 'new' in the sense of recent … With respect to quality, it
    expresses the _____ of the new _____
    that will not become old."

• We have an open curtain (Matt. 27:51).

• We have faith, hope, and love (1 Cor. 13:12-13).

The Heart of the Testimony

DAY 1 • THE MERCY SEAT

DAY 2 • THE GARDENER'S SHEARS

DAY 3 • THE TEN COMMANDMENTS

DAY 4 • FINISHED WORK

DAY 5 • A CROSS IN THE DESERT

WEEK 9

Our previous week's study invited us beyond the veil into the innermost room of God's sanctuary, the holy of holies. In week 9 our eyes will focus on the mercy seat (KJV) or atonement cover (NIV) on which His glory dwelt and on the contents that were encased beneath its weight. God ordained that three objects would be memorialized in the ark of the testimony. Each object speaks to us as clearly as it spoke to the children of Israel thousands of years ago. This week we will also behold the finished work of God's tabernacle and will witness the inspection of each component by Moses, then by God Himself. We will seek answers to the following questions.

Principal Questions

1. What does Isaiah 64:6 say about our righteousness?
2. What is God's foremost instrument for cleaning and pruning us?
3. What happened to the first set of the Ten Commandments?
4. How did Moses respond to the people's obedience?
5. What was the first action God commanded to be done after the tabernacle was completely furnished?

In this climactic point in the life of Israel we see all work cease except Christ's work. Week 9 will emphatically underscore the only basis on which God will grace a sanctuary with His presence.

The Mercy Seat

Begin today's study by reading Today's Treasure and praying that God will speak to you through His Word.

In week 8 we studied the veil that separated the holy of holies from the holy place, the divine dimensions of the innermost room, and the golden cherubim that graced the ends of the mercy seat. Today we will focus specifically on the mercy seat, on which the cherubim gazed.

Refresh your memory by reading Exodus 25:17. Of what material was the mercy seat made?

_____

How significant was the atonement cover on the ark of the covenant? What does each of the following Scriptures tell you about it?

Leviticus 16:2 _____

Numbers 7:89 _____

The mercy seat was the focal point of God's manifested glory to His people! The Hebrew word for *mercy seat* is *kapporeth*, which means *lid* or *cover of the sacred ark*. The Hebrew word *kaphar* is a derivative of that word, meaning *to cover the sins, to reconcile, to pardon, to cancel*, or *to make atonement*. I counted 69 instances in the Old Testament in which *kaphar* is translated *atonement*. Perhaps this term is familiar to you. Its Anglo-Saxon roots lend us the meaning of the word: *to make at one, to reconcile*. Somehow here on the mercy seat God would express the ministry of reconciliation. Let Scripture teach Scripture as we turn to the New Testament interpretation of the mercy seat.

Read Hebrews 9:1-5.

Look carefully at the term *mercy seat* in verse 5 (or *atonement cover*, NIV). The Greek word used in Hebrews 9:5 for *mercy seat* is *hilasterion*.

Read Romans 3:23-26.

Depending on which version you are using, note either the word *propitiation* or the words *sacrifice of atonement*. You are looking at the English translation of exactly the same Greek word, *hilasterion*, that is translated *mercy seat* in Hebrews 9:5. In other

KAPHAR

to cover the sins, to reconcile, to pardon, to cancel, to make atonement

ATONEMENT

to make at one, to reconcile

Jesus Christ is
the mercy seat.

words, the Greek text would read like this: "God presented [Jesus Christ] as a [mercy seat], through faith in his blood" (Rom. 3:25). Jesus Christ is the *hilasterion*. *He* is the mercy seat. *He* is the manifestation of God's glory. *He* is the location of reconciliation. *He* is the minister of reconciliation. *He* is the at-one-ment. Only through His death could the prayer be answered that "they also [may] be one in Us" (John 17:21, HCSB).

Another use of the same Greek word is found in 1 John 4:10. You'll probably remember that we have looked at this verse before, but let's consider it again in the context of today's lesson.

Read 1 John 4:10, substituting the phrase *mercy seat* **for the term** *propitiation* **or** *atoning sacrifice.*

God sent His Son to be the mercy seat for our sins! What was our condition when Jesus Christ became the mercy seat, the place of atonement, the bridge between Father God and humans?

Carefully read Romans 5:1-2,8 and check the correct answers.

According to verse 1, what condition did our mercy seat, Jesus Christ, extend to us on the cross?
❏ oneness with God ❏ peace with God ❏ favor with God

According to verse 2, what have we gained by faith?
❏ grace ❏ access ❏ holiness ❏ love ❏ peace

According to verse 8, what was our condition as God worked His ministry of reconciliation through the death of His Son?
❏ righteous in His sight ❏ covered by His blood ❏ sinners

In the depths of our depravity Christ died for us. He did not wait for persons to get as close as possible through obedience to the law and righteous living. Never once did He proclaim to His Father: "Close enough! This one made it!" In the breadth of our separation from God, Christ died for us. He died for people who yelled, "Crucify Him!" He died for those who ripped His flesh with whips. He died for those who slapped Him and spit on Him, for those who mocked Him, embedding a crown of thorns in His brow. He died for those who humiliated Him by stripping away His garments. He died for the soldier who pounded the nails into His flesh. He died for the one who gave Him vinegar to drink. He died for the 11 who ran for their lives. In the moment in all of history when humanity could not have been farther from God, Christ died for us.

Christ died not just for the depths of that generation's depravity: "My prayer is not for them alone. I pray also for those who will believe in me through their message" (John 17:20). He who knew all things died in advance for the most depraved deed I would ever commit. Although I was not present in that crowd that dreadful day, my sins most assuredly were.

So horrendous were the sins that hung on Christ that day, His Father was forced to look away. His Holiness had to forsake His own Son so that through His sacrifice Christ could intercede on our behalf. Jesus experienced the excruciating pain of being forsaken by God so that we might not have to. And because He did, "we have peace with God" (Rom. 5:1).

At this moment I must ask God to halt the whirlwind of memories that swirl in my mind—the depths of my own depravity that hung on the cross that day. I am tempted to wonder, *If I had only understood the penalty of my sin, would I have attempted to be much better?*

You see, I do not have a testimony like the ones many believers have. I cannot tell of my depravity before my salvation experience and of its falling behind me the moment I was saved. I was a small child when I trusted Christ as Savior. Every sin I can remember committing occurred after I was saved, even though His Holy Spirit lived inside me! Like my mother Eve, I partook of the forbidden fruit in spite of all the Holy Spirit's power God could breathe to stop me. Sadly, humanity would have been no better if it had depended on Adam and Beth.

A time surely comes, in the innermost places of our hearts, when we secretly wonder: *Could I have been good enough for Christ to avoid the cross? If I could do it all again, knowing all I know now, could I live an unstained life?*

 What does Isaiah 64:6 say about our righteousness?

_____

Even at our best, our salvation rests only on God's great mercy. It rests between two cherubim on a golden throne called the mercy seat.

> **Conclude today's lesson by reading each of the following verses and filling in the blank with its corresponding letter.**
>
> _____ 1. Micah 7:18   a. We have ministry because we have mercy.
>
> _____ 2. Luke 1:50   b. God is rich in mercy.
>
> _____ 3. 2 Corinthians 4:1   c. He saved us because of His mercy.
>
> _____ 4. Ephesians 2:4-5   d. God delights in mercy.
>
> _____ 5. Titus 3:5   e. His mercy extends to those who fear Him.

♥ No matter what your background is, you have reason to be thankful that you no longer bear the burden of your sins. We could name pages of things for which we could thank God for His sacrifice and forgiveness through Christ. What five things would be at the top of your list?

No wonder the psalmist cried out, "I will sing of the mercies of the LORD for ever" (Ps. 89:1, KJV)! Ask God to refresh your mind regarding the great mercy He has shown you; then sing with the psalmist all day long because "his love endures forever" (Ps. 118:1)!

Day 2
The Gardener's Shears

"I HAVE TOLD YOU THIS SO THAT MY JOY MAY BE IN YOU AND THAT YOUR JOY MAY BE COMPLETE."

John 15:11

Begin today's study by reading Today's Treasure and praying that God will speak to you through His Word.

Over the last two weeks, we have tried to develop a basic understanding of the appearance of the ark of the testimony. Now let's lift the heavy, golden mercy seat and take a glimpse at what is inside.

Read Hebrews 9:4 and list the three contents of the ark of the

covenant. _____

_____

Each of the three contents has extreme significance, much of which we have studied in previous weeks. During this lesson and the next we will consider each component in the order Hebrews 9:4 lists them.

God's Word points out two major purposes for the manna. Refresh your memory by noting each according to the following Scriptures.

Exodus 16:7 _____

Deuteronomy 8:3 _____

What does John 6:35,51 tell us? _____

_____

Jesus Christ was the perfect manifestation of God's glory! Even the angels proclaimed at His birth, "Glory to God in the highest" (Luke 2:14). God's precious baby Son was the highest and best of all His glory manifested to humanity, the manna sent down from heaven, sustenance straight from God's arms literally to fill our hungry souls.

You'll recall that Numbers 17 tells the story of Aaron's staff budding, representing the tribe of Levi and God's selecting this family to be priests to the nation of Israel and Aaron as the first high priest. Just as God sovereignly chose Aaron to be the *first* high priest to intercede and serve in a sanctuary made with hands, He chose the *last* High Priest to serve in a sanctuary made without hands and to intercede on behalf of His people.

Superior to the first, the last High Priest is Jesus Christ, our Great Intercessor. The budding rod was to be placed in the ancient ark to show the authenticity and preservation of the Aaronic priesthood long after Aaron would depart. Jesus Christ, our Great High Priest, has also left a "budding rod" to be a constant witness to His authenticity and authority in His earthly physical absence.

As we noted in week 5 in conjunction with the almond branches on the lampstand, "A tree is recognized by its fruit" (Matt. 12:33). Let's take this point a step further by considering how the budding rod foreshadowed not only the Great High Priest to come but also the fruit that would be produced to preserve His witness after His physical departure from earth.

Read John 15:1-11. What is the task of the Gardener?

_____

In the middle of His perfect Word our God included a gardening lesson. He took on the role of the Gardener, gave Christ the role of the true Vine, and assigned us the role of branches. According to John 15, the Gardener has one main task: to create an environment in which the best crop can be produced. The conditions for fruit bearing are twofold: (1) The branches must stay attached to the vital lifeline of the Vine so that they can be nourished. (2) The branches must be pruned so that they can produce a greater crop of fruit.

The little I know about gardening I learned from my mother, who had an emerald thumb. No doubt, her attention to pruning distinguished her garden from many others. She had an absolute goal in mind for the outcome of each bush. First, she planted deeply. Then, as the plants began to leaf, flower, and produce fruit, she pruned away anything that did not conform to the final image she had in mind.

When she came to my house, she couldn't walk by my flowers without giving them a thorough inspection. She would say, "Now Beth, you've got to clip away those dead flowers, or they will keep other buds from blooming." She also pointed out countless sucker shoots that needed to be removed. Once I proudly showed her a zinnia bush that had one branch at least a foot longer than the others. She said: "You're going to have to clip that one off. It's growing out of control and is sapping energy from the rest of the plant. Look how the bush is misshapen. Now get a sharp pair of shears …"

The woman knew what she was talking about. Her yard looked like the garden of Eden. When I read John 15, I found out why: she and God shared the same gardening techniques! God has a perfect image planned toward which He is growing us.

Romans 8:29 tells us what that image is: _____

God's responsibility as the Gardener is to promote that image any way He desires because "this is to my Father's glory, that you bear much fruit" (John 15:8).

The budding rod foreshadowed the fruit that would be produced to preserve Christ's witness after His physical departure from earth.

According to John 15:2, He performs His task by pruning. What is He pruning? Dead works and sucker shoots! Dead works are services that will not stand up under the cleansing fires of Christ's judgment—those that are not products of pure motivation, resulting in a loss of reward.

Sucker shoots are activities and energy consumers that grow wildly out of control and contribute nothing to God's intended image for us. Anything that saps energy from our growth toward His Son's image is a sucker shoot. It may be something for which we receive great recognition. Goodness knows, sucker shoots like to be noticed! But they are not consistent with the overall work God is doing. I offer no list of possible sucker shoots. Only the Gardener can identify what activities in our lives are wastes of time, with little eternal purpose.

Reread John 15:3. What is God's foremost instrument for cleaning

(pruning) us? _____

God uses another instrument to conform us to His image. You will find one of many references to this instrument in James 1:2-4.

What is this method? _____

God, our Gardener, has two major gardening tools for increasing our crop and for conforming us to His Son's image: His Word and circumstances. Which do you prefer? Me too! Do you know why we prefer to be pruned by God's Word?

Read Hebrews 4:12. How does this verse describe God's Word?
❏ trustworthy   ❏ unchanging   ❏ sharp   ❏ complete

The shears of God's Word are sharp! When God uses His Word as our pruning instrument, it is a lot less painful because it is sharp and quick. But circumstances can be a different story. I also believe that God favors pruning us through His Word rather than through circumstances. I do not think that God wants to see us in pain any more than we want to experience it. He knows, however, that sometimes there is no other way.

I am convinced, based on the authority of Scripture, that if we allow God to prune us more often by His Word, we avoid a portion of our pruning through circumstances. Without a doubt, we will be pruned one way or the other.

What does Philippians 1:6 promise?

_____

God has promised to finish what He started when He saved us, and that necessitates pruning. But sometimes we could help make our pruning processes less painful by heeding His Word, by being "doers of the word and not hearers only"

(Jas. 1:22, HCSB). This way our lives can sometimes be matured and purified on the basis of what He has told us rather than what He is forced to show us.

Please do not misunderstand; you and I could not avoid being matured by circumstances no matter how hard we tried, because through circumstances God often gives us the field experience to live what we have learned. However, based on John 15, at other times God provides opportunities for our maturity based strictly on what He has written in His Word.

When we refuse to learn the precept in the Word, He is sometimes forced to transfer that lesson outside the Word. Although I would not trade the "field trips" He has given me, at times I would rather stick with the Textbook, wouldn't you?

♥ Reflect on the maturing process through which God is taking you. What lesson did you learn the hard way that you could have learned more easily by heeding God's Word?

_____

_____

Name a situation you avoided simply because you obeyed God's Word and never participated in the unauthorized practice.

_____

No matter which tool God uses, His Word is still the key to our growth in His image. Allowing our Gardener to prune us through His Word sometimes helps us avoid pruning through our circumstances. But even when it does not, the Word makes our circumstances far more bearable.

Let's take a look at one last element of God's gardening procedures.

When God has successfully pruned us with His Word and has caused our crop to flourish, what result will we reap (John 15:11)?

_____

What can be our response to pruning by circumstances (Jas. 1:2)?

_____

What is the result of a branch that cooperates and grows in the purposeful atmosphere of its Gardener? Joy, pure joy! What is the result of a branch that refuses to cooperate with God's inevitable gardening tools? Crop failure.

We are the staff our Great High Priest left behind to testify to His authority and authenticity in the midst of a perverse generation. People will know us by our fruit.

Day 3
Day 3
The Ten Commandments

Today's Treasure

"'TEACHER, WHICH IS THE GREATEST COMMANDMENT IN THE LAW?' JESUS REPLIED: ' "LOVE THE LORD YOUR GOD WITH ALL YOUR HEART AND WITH ALL YOUR SOUL AND WITH ALL YOUR MIND." THIS IS THE FIRST AND GREATEST COMMANDMENT. AND THE SECOND IS LIKE IT: "LOVE YOUR NEIGHBOR AS YOURSELF." ALL THE LAW AND THE PROPHETS HANG ON THESE TWO COMMANDMENTS.'"

Matthew 22:36-40

Begin today's study by reading Today's Treasure and praying that God will speak to you through His Word.

In our previous lesson we focused on the first two contents preserved in the ark of the testimony: a golden pot of manna and Aaron's rod that budded. Today we will focus our attention on the third object.

Read Hebrews 9:4 and name the third object: _____

The first thing I ever remember associating with God was the Ten Commandments. For a young child oblivious to the leadership of the Holy Spirit, who internalizes God's law in our hearts, the Commandments provided a concrete standard. Before I came really to know a God I could not see or touch, the Ten Commandments were words I could both see and touch. For a spiritual toddler unaware of impending dangers, they were the stern voice of the Parent saying, "Yes, that's it" or "No, no, no!"

As an adult, I turn to Exodus 20 and find that the Commandments have the same effect. They have not changed in all of these years. Their tone has not softened. No words have been deleted. No conditions have been added. And somehow I am comforted. Maybe it is because I live in a generation spray painted with grays, and I sometimes long for a little black and white. Like children, without boundaries we have no security.

My husband and I attended a parents' night at the beginning of our oldest child's first year in junior high. Each teacher briefly described what we could expect our child to experience. Math has never been my best subject, but this time I was more confused than ever. The math teacher said: "This year we will not be nearly as concerned with the answers as with the methods. In fact, sometimes your child may find that there is more than one right answer."

New math, she called it. I did not even like old math when it was new. I could not quite put my finger on what disturbed me about it until Keith and I were on the way home. I suddenly exclaimed: "An absence of absolutes! That's what bothers me! You could always depend on math to be black and white, to have one right answer. You were either right or wrong. Science is always changing. Now history seems to be changing. Not math too! Where are the absolutes?"

Read the Ten Commandments afresh in Deuteronomy 5:6-22.

Aren't you thankful for absolutes, for black and white? Some things are right, and some things are wrong. Period.

Some things are right, and some things are wrong. Period.

Count how many commandments pertain to a relationship with God and how many pertain to relationships with others.

_____ lengthy commandments specify conduct between persons and God, and

_____ brief commandments specify conduct among humans.

Which set did God prioritize by listing first? _____

_____

Look at Today's Treasure. List in order the two commandments Jesus considered to be most important.

_____

_____

How do you think all the law and the prophets could hang on these two commandments?

_____

How does Luke 2:52 say Jesus grew? _____

_____

We can be rightly related to others only when we are rightly related to God! Otherwise, what do we have to motivate us? If Keith and I had not had relationships with the Lord, our marriage would have grown cold long ago. What motivation would we have had to work toward a good marriage? The world is certainly not promoting it!

If I had not had the Lord, I would never have nurtured a constant desire to be a better parent. I would have had no voice whispering inside me: "Your time will come. For now your personal life must be part-time, and their little lives must be full-time." I would simply have heard the world's loud roar: "Go get 'em, girl! You only go around once!" And with a husband and children to worry about, why in the world would I even care about anybody else?

To be perfectly honest, if God were not caring through us, we would probably not care about others. Without being rightly related to God, we are not motivated to make right relationships with others a priority.

So are these ancient laws worth our attention? A number of years ago a newspaper article recorded a venomous interview with a well-known broadcasting mogul. "Sick to death" of Judeo-Christian demands for television, he charged that the Ten Commandments are archaic and offered an updated job description: the Ten Voluntary Suggestions. Just picture God saying: "It's entirely up to you, but may I suggest that you don't murder anyone or steal or cheat on your spouse if you don't want things to get complicated? And there's the possibility of getting AIDS. Oh, well, think it over and do what you must."

God is not the only one who never changes. Human nature never changes. With all my heart I believe that human nature cries out to be stopped, to be saved from itself, to be confronted by a standard, to discover pure black and white, to realize the importance of absolutes. God delivered those words to Moses without apology or hesitation.

Read Deuteronomy 5:22-29 and check the correct answers.

Did the people have any doubt that it was God's voice they heard?
❑ yes   ❑ no

What did they fear would happen if they heard His voice again?
❑ They would die.
❑ They would be blinded.
❑ They would be terrified.

What request did they make of Moses?
❑ Let them rest from His presence for a while.
❑ Ask God to have mercy on them and not to consume them.
❑ Listen to God for them and tell them what He said.

How did God respond to their request?
❑ He found their request to be good and acceptable.
❑ He was angered by their request.
❑ He called them a stiff-necked people.

Why did God want the people to fear and obey Him?
❑ because He is God and worthy of reverence
❑ because they would otherwise die
❑ because He wanted it to go well with them and their children

♥ Are you obeying all of the Ten Commandments, or just the ones that you find covenient? Ask God to reveal areas of your life where you have strayed from His laws.

If we could only accept that God's commands are for us, not against us. The Ten Commandments were not only given to provide a pure standard for living. They were also given to evoke fear and reverence for the Holy One, who possessed the authority to give them, so that obedience and blessing might result.

Let's receive a firsthand history lesson on the Ten Commandments from someone who was there. Pull up a chair in the midst of a people preparing to enter the land of promise. Just as Moses seized the moment for a background check, let's do the same.

According to Deuteronomy 9:1–10:5, what happened to the first

set of the Ten Commandments? _____

_____

Think about it for a moment. Why didn't God become angry with Moses for breaking the Ten Commandments in a rage after such divine deliverance?

I think He meant to carve an unforgettable picture in their hard heads. They had broken the law. It would forever remain broken until Someone could find a way to keep it.

How did God write the Ten Commandments (see Deut. 9:10)?

_____

Now read John 8:2-11. What was the basis of the scribes and the Pharisees' challenge that the woman should be stoned?

_____

After writing on the ground with His finger, Jesus stood and

replied: _____

_____

Was this not the same finger that wrote the Ten Commandments? Was the perfect, sinless One not the only one who had the right to point a finger at someone else's sin? Did He?   ❑ yes   ❑ no

What did Jesus say He came to do to the Law and the Prophets (Matt. 5:17)?

_____

Instead of pointing a finger at this pitiful woman's sin, Christ, in effect, pointed a finger at Himself—the One who came to fulfill the law so that through Him all might be free of it.

The manna, the budding staff, the Ten Commandments. All three were preserved in the ark—the coffin. Only through the death of One to come would there be true bread on which to live, a Great High Priest to intercede, and glorious liberty through the fulfillment of the law.

Day 4
Finished Work

"'MY FOOD,' SAID JESUS, 'IS TO DO THE WILL OF HIM WHO SENT ME AND TO FINISH HIS WORK.'"

John 4:34

Begin today's study by reading Today's Treasure and praying that God will speak to you through His Word.

Listen carefully. Where are the sounds of the workers measuring the boards and erecting them in place? Where are the sounds of the instruments hammering the gold—sounds we not only heard but also felt, like the inner echo of a drum in a parade? Where are the voices of the women busily sewing the priestly garments? Where is the bleating of the goats as their coats are sheared for the sanctuary covering? Where are the reprimands of the mothers chasing their curious children from the workplace? Conspicuously absent are the sounds to which we have grown so accustomed. Ashes smolder where once a blazing fire roared to melt the gold that overlaid the many precious objects. The vibrant sounds of activity have been replaced by the hush of anticipation. All construction has ceased.

♥ Do you find it difficult to persist in a task until it is finished? What is God's guarantee for you in Galatians 6:9?

What did the Israelites do according to Exodus 39:32?

_____

If you built a house, what would you expect to be the last step in the process?

_____

God had commanded Moses about every detail of the tabernacle of testimony, and Moses had delivered every word to the children of Israel. All instructions had been given and carried out. "Thoroughly equipped for every good work" (2 Tim. 3:17), they had lacked absolutely nothing. The freewill offerings of joyful donors had been superabundant. After they had used all they needed, baskets still overflowed, just like the loaves and fish after Jesus' miracle (see Matt. 14:20). The people had been invited to give part of themselves to build a proper dwelling for their God. The Holy Spirit had anointed a craftsman to transform human offerings into divine design. Now the time had finally come for inspection. Imagine the Hebrews' emotion after toiling before God's perfectionist requirements!

Designated carriers transported the holy articles with greatest care before God's chosen servant. How Moses' heart must have pounded! He knew above all others that if he missed the tiniest deviation from God's command and allowed a defective piece to be carried into the sanctuary, it could mean death for all of them. He must have an eye like an eagle and a taste for the heavenly.

Number the tabernacle contents in the order Moses inspected them from first (I) to last (7) according to Exodus 39:33-43.

_____ the priests' garments _____ the golden altar
_____ the bronze altar _____ the ark of the covenant
_____ the lampstand _____ the coverings of skins
_____ the table and bread of the Presence

How did Moses respond to the people's obedience? _____

_____

Moses blessed them. The word *barak,* or *blessed,* means that he saluted them by dropping to his knees. In those few moments when he was on his knees, can you imagine the thoughts that must have raced through his mind? Exactly one year had passed since Yahweh had led them from slavery, since the Red Sea had rolled out a carpet of dry ground and had beckoned them to cross. In those precious moments as his tears must have moistened the dry desert ground, the progression of the previous year's events surely flew through his mind like pages blowing off a calendar. Let the following interpretations of several significant dialogues lead you to ponder this climactic moment.

Moses: *Who, me?*
God: I'll be with you.
Moses: *But I'm slow of speech!*
God: Who gave man his mouth?
Moses: *He'll never budge!*
God: I'll make you like God to Pharaoh …
Moses: *But he refuses to listen!*
God: … so that My wonders may be multiplied in Egypt!
Moses: *Slay a lamb and do what?*
God: You heard Me. And have your sandals on your feet and your staff in your hand. Be ready the instant I tell you. Now go-o-o-o-o-o-o!
Moses: *Have I ever told You I can't swim?*
God: Have I ever told you I made the seas?
Moses: *It sure is dark out here.*
God: I'll cover you with a cloud by day and fire by night.
Moses: *We sure could use a pot of stew.*
God: I'll rain down bread from heaven for you.
Moses: *We're about to die of thirst!*
God: See that rock?
Moses: *We should have packed for a longer stay.*
God: Your clothes will not wax old on you.
Moses: *This quail is coming out our noses!*
God: Do you still want to go back to Egypt?

God:	Moses, come up here!
Moses:	*Who, me?*
God:	Up on top of this mountain.
Moses:	*Can they come too?*
God:	Just you. I want you to build Me a place for My name.
Moses:	*Your name? In what kind of place does an I AM dwell?*
God:	A heavenly place.
Moses:	*But how will we build a heavenly place, since we have never seen . . .?*
God:	You won't. I will.
Moses:	*Huh?*
God:	Through you.
Moses:	*Whatever You say.*
God:	Now hold the tablets steady and let Me jot down a few things.
Moses:	*Yes, Sir.*
God:	Now take it down and tell them all I've told you. By the way, you may not like what you see when you get there.
Moses:	*No sweat. I'm ready to go!*

Moses:	*Aaron! What have you done?*
Aaron:	I just pitched a few earrings in a fire and look what popped out!

Moses:	*Say, God. About those tablets . . .*
God:	Get back up here.
Moses:	*What do You mean we're going without You?*
God:	I'll kill them if I go on!
Moses:	*I'll kill 'em if You don't! If You're not going, don't send us away from here. Look at them. They're mourning.*
God:	OK, Moses. I will do as you've asked.
Moses:	*We will build a place for Your name.*
God:	I will accept no disobedience this time, Moses.

Moses:	*My gracious Lord, I am honored to report that Your people have done just as You commanded them.*
God:	Is everything ready?
Moses:	*Yes, my Lord. It is finished.*

It had been the worst year of his life and the best year of his life. Funny how often that happens when the Lord is your God. Oh, Moses was proud—proud of a stiff-necked people who for at least a few moments stiffly stared upward. He stood and gazed into the faces of a people smiling with a strange mix of exhaustion and exuberance. Never before had one group of people made him so angry—or so proud. It was worth it, every second of it. Moses, an unlikely ambassador of Jesus Christ. While one pled for their lives, another bled for their lives. Yes, it is finished.

Day 5
A Cross in the Desert

Read Today's Treasure and pray that God will speak to you through His Word.

The inspection was complete. The time had finally come to place all of the components in the tabernacle, to make the sum of the pieces one whole.

Read Exodus 40:1-8 and complete the following.

Yesterday you placed the objects of the tabernacle in the order Moses inspected them. Now number the objects below in the order God commanded for them to be placed in the tabernacle.

_____ the hanging at the court gate   _____ the basin
_____ the ark of the covenant   _____ the altar of incense
_____ the veil covering the ark   _____ the table
_____ the altar of burnt offering   _____ the lampstand

Who was commanded to set up the tabernacle? _____

On what day was the tabernacle furnished? _____

According to Moses' example in verses 20-33, draw a diagram of the entire tabernacle on the next page, labeling each object. Then check it against the one provided on the inside back cover.

What was the first action God commanded to be done after the tabernacle was completely furnished and why (see vv. 9-11)?

_____

_____

What was God's next commandment, according to verses 12-16?

_____

Review your list. What was the first object put in the tabernacle?

_____

What was the last object hung in place? _____

Today's Treasure

"MAY I NEVER BOAST EXCEPT IN THE CROSS OF OUR LORD JESUS CHRIST, THROUGH WHICH THE WORLD HAS BEEN CRUCIFIED TO ME, AND I TO THE WORLD."

Galatians 6:14

Label the tribe of Judah at the court gate. Now draw a straight line all the way from the court gate to the mercy seat.

This line should have been inserted through the bronze altar, the bronze basin, and the altar of incense, bringing the line to its final destination: the mercy seat.

Now draw a second line on your diagram from the golden lampstand to the table of the bread of the Presence. What do you see?

_____

In exactly the same formation as the tribes encamped around the tabernacle, God looked at a cross. And when He saw the cross, He saw reconciliation. I can almost hear Him say: "Not on the basis of your freewill offerings, not on the basis of your good works, not on the basis of your obedience, not even on the basis of your burnt sacrifices but only on the basis of the cross will I come and dwell among you." And indeed He did.

Read Exodus 40:34-38.

When God looked at the finished work of the tabernacle, He did not see a sanctuary made with hands. He saw the heavenlies, a work finished "before the creation of the world" (John 17:24), not a shadow but the true Tabernacle.

The tabernacle was acceptable. And because it was, God did just what He had promised. He filled the designated dwelling place with His glory—a glory unlimited by the veil. Yahweh God filled the tabernacle to the uttermost! So rich was His glory that even Moses could not stand in His presence. God crowned the tabernacle with a cloud, making it fit for a royal priesthood. Far beyond their expectation, His acceptance of their invitation was abundantly above all they had asked or thought.

Perhaps it was a bittersweet moment as God made His earthly descent. The gap was quickly closing between the time He provided Abram a substitute for the death of his beloved heir and the time He would provide His own beloved Heir as a substitute for all who would make the great exchange. Yet He graced the tabernacle with His glory and filled their hearts with awe and wonder, the surest signs that we have witnessed God's glory. The same blinding glory that made Isaiah cry out in agony and that made Ezekiel drop to his face culminated in a cloud before all Israel. But it was only a glimpse. Read Solomon's words at a similar gathering to dedicate the temple as a dwelling for His name: "Will God really dwell on earth? The heavens, even the highest heaven, cannot contain you. How much less this temple I have built!" (I Kings 8:27).

Read God's reply to Solomon in I Kings 9:1-3.

No, the fullness of the Divine Nature could never be confined to the perimeters of even the most glorious dwelling made with hands. But "my eyes and my heart will always be there" (I Kings 9:3)—eyes to see a cross instead of a crude building made with hands, a heart to love "the world that he gave his one and only Son, that whoever believes in him shall not perish but have eternal life" (John 3:16).

That day when His Majesty's glory descended on that remote wilderness dwelling, God fell in love—with His whole heart.

♥ According to Paul's testimony in I Corinthians 2:1-2, what were the only things Paul claimed to know?

Just as the tabernacle found its acceptance ultimately in the cross of Christ, you have found complete acceptance on the same unfailing grounds. Recall your salvation experience and describe your excitement in knowing that He is present with you.

199

Viewer Guide

The Heart of
the Testimony

Today we get to celebrate the finished work of the Old Testament tabernacle and
see how God demonstrated His approval. We will then track the glory of God
amid earthly dwelling places and behold glimpses of God's perfect order.

Some Revelations of God's Glory

Read Exodus 40:12-38. Consider the following revelations of God's glory based
on this segment and those which follow.

1. The _____ for the glory of God.

   • The _____: Note the repetitive clause in verses 19, 21,

   23, 25, 27, 29, and 32. *Word Biblical Commentary* translates the Hebrew,

   "_____ as Yahweh had commanded Moses."

   • The _____

2. The _____ of the tabernacle with the glory of God (vv. 34-35).

   The Hebrew *sakan* transliterated "settled" means to _____ or

   _____. The term "_____" in relationship to God's

   glory was derived from *sakan*.

3. The _____ of the (manifest) glory of God (2 Chron. 5:1-14).

4. The _____ of the glory of God (Ezek. 10:1-8,18-19;

   11:16-25). Trace each sighting in this space:

   • Ezekiel 10:3—the _____ court

   • Ezekiel 10:4—the _____

   • Ezekiel 10:19—the entrance to the _____ _____

   • Ezekiel 11:23—above the _____ _____

   of the temple

5. The glory of God associated with _____ temple (Luke 2:21-32).

   Note the translation, "A LIGHT OF REVELATION TO THE GENTILES,

   And the _____ of Your people _____" (v. 32, NASB).

6. The _____ of the glory of God.

See Acts 1:8 and hear Zechariah 14:1,3-9.

Conclude with Ezekiel 43:1-7 and Philippians 2:9-11.

Mended Hearts, Eternal Ties

DAY 1 • A PEEK AT THE PROMISED LAND

DAY 2 • HOME TO JERUSALEM

DAY 3 • THE TRUE TABERNACLE

DAY 4 • THE NEW TABERNACLE

DAY 5 • THE INTIMACY OF THE HOLY OF HOLIES

WEEK 10

Week 10 brings an end to our journey together. This week we will see one of history's greatest leaders find rest in God's arms. We will trace the future of the tabernacle and the ark of the testimony. We will bridge the gap between the shadow and the true, as the One who was depicted in a structure made with hands becomes the One who "became flesh and made his dwelling among us" (John 1:14). We will discover what the Old Testament tabernacle means for the New Testament believer. And finally, we will be faced with the ultimate challenge: how will we respond to the God we have met each step of the way in the sanctuary of old? Before facing that final challenge, let's seek answers to the following questions.

Principal Questions

1. How did God intervene and save the lives of Joshua and Caleb?
2. What did the people do "throughout the lifetime of Joshua"?
3. Who is the true Tabernacle?
4. What does the New Testament tell us about God's tabernacle now?
5. In the Gospels, how many were invited into the innermost chambers of Christ's glory?

Week 10 will draw many general conclusions about the Old Testament tabernacle, but only you can draw conclusions for your life. Come with me as we behold the culmination of God's dwelling among humans.

Day 1
A Peek at the Promised Land

Read Today's Treasure and pray that God will speak to you through His Word.

Through the tabernacle God indeed dwelled among His people. On their journey to the land of promise, God's glory accompanied their every step. The priests continued their daily ministrations in the courtyard and the holy place, and the high priest met each annual Day of Atonement with great fear.

God had issued His commands for a place for His name, and the people had constructed it just as the Lord commanded. God's glory therefore descended as He promised, for God cannot break His Word. Never before had a generation of people been so abundantly graced. By God's mercy He deemed the sanctuary, made by heavenly design, a fit place to entrust His presence. The tabernacle was established, and the wheels of its occupation were set in motion.

If you feel as I do, you aren't quite ready to let go of the tabernacle. You may wonder: What happened to it then? How long did it last? Did God's people remain faithful to His presence? For the sake of closure, both day 1 and day 2 of this week's study will trace the remaining history of the tabernacle of testimony. Today's lesson contains much reading. Please do not shortchange your learning experience now. Read the chapters faithfully; they are crucial to our conclusion.

Today let's build a background for answering this question tomorrow: What happened to the ark after the Israelites departed from the wilderness? Only a few short years after their exodus, God guided the Israelites to the edge of the land He had promised.

Read the verses indicated from Numbers 13–14 and answer the following questions.

According to Numbers 13:1-2, who was to explore the land of

Canaan? _____

According to 13:18-20, what questions were the spies to answer? Check the questions that apply.
- ❏ How are the water supplies?
- ❏ Are they strong or weak?
- ❏ Who are their leaders?
- ❏ What gods do they serve?
- ❏ Are they many or few?
- ❏ Does the land have trees?

How many days did they explore the land (v. 25)?
- ❏ 70 days ❏ 7 days ❏ 40 days

"THEN HAVE THEM MAKE A SANCTUARY FOR ME, AND I WILL DWELL AMONG THEM."

Exodus 25:8

203

What good news did the spies bring (v. 27)?

_____

What bad news did the spies bring (v. 28)?

_____

Who silenced the people before Moses, and what did he say?

_____

Nevertheless, the people argued with Caleb and reacted in a way typical of our human nature. According to 13:32, what did the majority of the explorers do with their negative feelings?
- ❏ They spread a negative report among the Israelites.
- ❏ They refused to return to Canaan.
- ❏ They threatened to kill Caleb.

What was the result of the rumor they spread, according to 14:1?
- ❏ They became furious.
- ❏ They wept all night.
- ❏ They did not believe the report.

What were their exact words in 14:2? _____

_____

What were Joshua and Caleb's responses in 14:5-9? Check each correct answer.
- ❏ They drew swords against the opposing Israelites.
- ❏ They tore their clothes in grief.
- ❏ They assured the people that the land was good.
- ❏ They asked who would follow them to Canaan.
- ❏ They said God would lead them in if He was pleased.
- ❏ They told them to quit crying.
- ❏ They told them not to rebel against the Lord.
- ❏ They told them not to be afraid of the people of Canaan.
- ❏ They told them that their enemy's protection was gone.
- ❏ They told them that the Lord was with them.

What did the people prepare to do to Joshua and Caleb (v. 10)?

_____

How did God intervene and spare their lives (14:10)?

_____

What question did God ask Moses (v. 11)?
- ❏ What will it take to make these people obey Me?
- ❏ How long will these people treat me with contempt?
- ❏ What do you want Me to do with these stiff-necked people?

What was God prepared to do with the people (14:12)?

_____

What was God prepared to do with Moses?

_____

What was the basis of Moses' plea for God to spare their lives?
- ❏ God's reputation   ❏ the Egyptians' reputation
- ❏ the Israelites' reputation

What was God's reply in verse 20?
- ❏ He would not listen to Moses.   ❏ He would pardon.
- ❏ He would increase their wandering for one hundred years.

How many times had the Israelites tempted, or tested, God (v. 22)?
- ❏ 70 times 7   ❏ 40   ❏ 7   ❏ 10

Continue reading verses 20-35. God forgave the sin, but He did not remove the sin's repercussions. State in your own words the verdict of the righteous Judge about the promised land.

_____

What would happen to their children?
- ❏ Their carcasses would fall by their fathers.
- ❏ They would bear their fathers' guilt.
- ❏ They would enjoy the land their fathers had rejected.

What happened to the Israelites who went into battle without the Lord's presence (vv. 40-45)? They were ...
- ❏ returned after great defeat.   ❏ attacked.
- ❏ shamed.   ❏ rewarded.

A trek that could have taken only a few short years turned into 40 before God let a new generation, under Joshua and Caleb's leadership, enter the land of milk and honey. As the years neared completion, Moses delivered an address to the people of Israel that is found in Deuteronomy 31.

♥ Has fear ever kept you from walking through a door God obviously opened for you? What have you learned to help you the next time God opens a door?

Check the answers according to Deuteronomy 31:2-3,16-18.

How old was Moses? ☐ 100 ☐ 120 ☐ 140

What did Moses promise the people (v. 3)?
☐ The Lord will send His angel before them.
☐ The Lord will give them a better leader.
☐ The Lord will go before them and will destroy the nations.

What prophecy did God deliver to Moses about the Israelites in the land of promise (vv. 16-18)?
☐ These people will flourish in the promised land.
☐ These people will demand a king.
☐ These people will forsake Me for foreign gods.

Deuteronomy 32 records the descriptive song of Moses that God placed within His faithful servant's heart. When Moses finished reciting the words to the people of Israel, he solemnly warned them to take his words to heart (see v. 46).

In Deuteronomy 32:47 Moses explained why they must take seriously God's inspired Words. What is the reason?

_____

_____

Numbers 20:1-13 records Moses' refusal to uphold God's holiness. What was God's specific instruction about the rock in verse 8?

_____

_____

How did Moses respond to God's instruction (see vv. 10-11)?

_____

_____

Because Moses responded to God's commandment with anger and disobeyed Him before the congregation, Moses did not enter the promised land (see v. 12). These are difficult passages to understand, but the main theme of God's revelation is obvious: "I am holy, and no other is holy." He had to extend the same judgment to His chosen servants that He gave to the other rebels. A tiring patriarch growing increasingly weary of a stiff-necked people would not be the one to lead them into the promised land. Oh, but how God loved him.

Read Deuteronomy 34. Who buried Moses? _____

We have been with him so long that it hurts, doesn't it? Take heart in verse 15 of Psalm 116: "Precious in the sight of the LORD is the death of his saints."

Are you standing at your own Kadesh-barnea? Have you found yourself on the brink of the place for which God has long been preparing you? A location? A place of service? A circumstance? A position? Something for which you sense He has been preparing you for a long time?

Now that you see God fulfilling His promise to use you and have gone through excruciating preparation toward that end, are you filled with fear? An overwhelming feeling of unreadiness? A sudden emotion that this may not be what you wanted? A little sorry you volunteered to go wherever and do whatever? Do you feel like a grasshopper beside the task? God will deal with those feelings and will bring them to a place of dismissal if you confess them to Him and invite Him to give you the courage to accept His personalized plan for you.

If only the Israelites had cried to God like the struggling father, "Help me overcome my unbelief" (Mark 9:24), their carcasses would never have fallen in the wilderness. How God must grieve over two common approaches to His unfolding plan: those who want position without preparation and those who refuse to leave the comforts of preparation to take the position. If the truth were known, Joshua may have suffered a few butterflies himself. Remember, he saw the giants in Canaan with his own eyes! There was one major difference between Joshua and Caleb and the other spies: their God was bigger than their obstacles. Is yours?

God banished Joshua's fear with the words of Joshua 1:1-9, His encouragement for one precious man who stood at the crossroads between preparation and position, promise, and possession.

Take the land, beloved.

Day 2
Home to Jerusalem

Reading Today's Treasure and ask God to speak to you through His Word.

On day 1 we witnessed the unbelief of a generation whose carcasses were doomed to fall in the wilderness. We also grieved over the death of one of history's greatest leaders: "No one has ever shown the mighty power or performed the awesome deeds that Moses did in the sight of all Israel" (Deut. 34:12). Then, like a ray of golden sunlight through blackened clouds of sin and death, the faith of two simple men led to the eventual gathering of the mightiest army in all of Hebrew history.

Today's Treasure

"JOSHUA TOLD THE PEOPLE, 'CONSECRATE YOURSELVES, FOR TOMORROW THE LORD WILL DO AMAZING THINGS AMONG YOU.'"

Joshua 3:5

Read Joshua 3:5. In what primary way did Joshua direct the people to prepare themselves to possess God's promised land?

_____

Some things never change. God desires to do wonders among us; but to give Him the freedom to intervene in our lives so magnificently, we must be sanctified!

What role did the ark of the covenant play in Joshua 3:2-6,11-17?

_____

The nation of Israel was about to be surrounded by pagan peoples. Assuming a posture of separation—of peculiarity, or distinction—would again be necessary. Again, circumcision, the sign of the Abrahamic covenant, was enforced as an ongoing reminder of their consecration. In many ways it was a new beginning for the nation Israel: "Today I have rolled away the reproach of Egypt from you" (Josh. 5:9). God had commanded the Israelites to take the land. As Joshua prepared for the battle, he rose to behold an imposing figure standing before him. So powerful was the appearance of this mighty Warrior that he could ask only one question: "Whose side are you on?"

Tony Evans of Oakcliff Bible Church in Dallas, Texas, paraphrases the Warrior's response: "I didn't come to take sides. I came to take over!" Little in human experience is as sweet as victory after a miserable season of defeat.

Consider this newspaper article titled "And the walls came tumbling down." Keep in mind that this article was not in the religion section.

> The walls of Jericho did come tumbling down as recounted in the Bible, according to an archaeological study. "When we compare the archaeological evidence at Jericho with the biblical narrative describing the Israelite destruction of Jericho, we find remarkable agreement," said archaeologist Bryant G. Wood of the University of Toronto. ... "Scholars by and large have written off the biblical record as so much folklore and religious rhetoric," Wood said. However, he said extensive ceramic remnants and a carbon-14 sample ... support the biblical account. "The correlation between the archaeological evidence and the biblical narrative is substantial," he said. As described in Joshua 6, Joshua's army marched around the city for a week, blowing rams' horns, and on the seventh day combined shouting with the piercing horns, "and the walls fell down flat."[1]

Imagine that. Throughout Joshua 7–18 the Lord's army took one piece of land after another. It enjoyed the ecstasy of victory when it obeyed God in battle and the agony of defeat when it failed to follow its Victor. The land divisions began, and the Israelites settled into a strange land that God had called their own.

The tabernacle, or tent of meeting, was erected at Shiloh, about 30 miles north of Jerusalem. Shiloh remained the Israelites' religious center for over a century after the conquest. The door of the Shiloh tabernacle was where Hannah, Elkanah's barren wife, received word from Eli the priest that she would give birth to a child: "In the course of time Hannah conceived and gave birth to a son. She named him Samuel, saying, 'Because I asked the LORD for him'" (I Sam. 1:20). The account continues with the tender words "After he was weaned, she took the boy with her, young as he was … and brought him to the house of the LORD at Shiloh" (I Sam. 1:24). "'I prayed for this child, and the LORD has granted me what I asked of him. So now I give him to the LORD. For his whole life he will be given over to the LORD.' And he worshiped the LORD there" (I Sam. 1:27-28).

Note the key facts I Samuel 3:19-21 tells you about Samuel:

"[The LORD] let none of his words fall to the ground" (I Sam. 3:19). Can you imagine what it would be like for God to make such a statement about your growth? How I wish that this were my testimonial. Instead, how often I have tripped on the very words I have let fall to the ground!

"The LORD continued to appear at Shiloh" (I Sam. 3:21). God once again delivered His Word through a prophet at the tent of meeting. God dwelled among His people in the land of promise. Meanwhile, His dismal prophecy to Moses was being fulfilled. The tabernacle remained in Shiloh much of the dreadful period of the judges, when God's mighty nation ignored His stern warning and bowed to the idols of the heathen.

♥ What do you think I Samuel 3:19 says about Samuel's ability to speak for the Lord? How does your life reflect your viability as God's spokesperson?

Read Judges 2:7-8,10 and check the correct responses.

What did the people do "throughout the lifetime of Joshua"?
❑ grumbled against the Lord
❑ battled their enemies
❑ served the Lord

How old was Joshua when he died?   ❑ 110   ❑ 120   ❑ 140

What was the following generation like after Joshua's death?
❑ They were faithful to do all Joshua had commanded.
❑ They did not know the Lord or the works He had done.
❑ They were stiff-necked and demanded a king.

Read Judges 18:30-31, two crucial verses in Israel's history. Remember, Israel's strength was contingent on obedience to its Commander in chief. What disobedience do these verses record?

_____

_____

First Samuel 4 records the beginning of the end of an intact tabernacle of testimony. Even though the ark was eventually returned, God's presence had abandoned the tabernacle in Shiloh. First Samuel 21:1-6 records that the tabernacle was eventually moved to Nob to avoid the Philistines' threat to Shiloh. The worn and misused tent was nothing but a shell without the glory of the God who had once graced it. God revealed Himself through chosen, faithful servants but never again in a sanctuary until He raised up "a man after his own heart" (I Sam. 13:14). Having prepared a homemade tent for God's divine furnishings, King David deeply desired a glorious dwelling for the name of the Lord. As we witnessed earlier, God granted that special request through David's son Solomon.

First Kings 8 contains the last Old Testament reference to the sacred relics built by a stiff-necked people in a remote wilderness. What happened to the ark of the testimony (vv. 1-13,21)?

The ancient objects had found a new home no longer in a portable tent made to travel. They had finally come home, home to a place they had never been, home to Jerusalem.

"Then the Lord awoke as from sleep, ... then he rejected the tents of Joseph, he did not choose the tribe of Ephraim; but he chose the tribe of Judah" (Ps. 78:65,67-68). Praise God for His magnificent stubbornness and for His marvelous jealousy! Why didn't He give up on them? Because "he who fashioned and made the earth, he founded it; he did not create it to be empty, but formed it to be inhabited" (Isa. 45:18). He created humankind for fellowship. And fellowship we would—whatever the cost. It appears that God had a plan—straight from the tribe of Judah.

Day 3
The True Tabernacle

Today's Treasure

"THE LORD HIMSELF WILL GIVE YOU A SIGN: THE VIRGIN WILL BE WITH CHILD AND WILL GIVE BIRTH TO A SON, AND WILL CALL HIM IMMANUEL."

Isaiah 7:14

Begin your study by reading Today's Treasure and praying that God will speak to you through His Word.

What Luke expressed to us in immediate terms in chapter 2 of his Gospel, John the beloved expressed to us in broad and ultimate terms: "The Word became flesh" (John 1:14). The Greek translation for *Word* in this verse is *Logos.* Christ was the actual and literal embodiment of God's perfect Word—God's living, breathing, audibly speaking Word. The preincarnate Word in John 1:1 became the visible, incarnate Word in John 1:14.

"The Word became flesh and made his dwelling among us." Are you ready for this? The Greek word for *dwelt* is *skenoo* and it means *tabernacled:* "The Word became flesh, and [tabernacled] among us." Let the Holy Spirit bring all of this together for you as you read the following Scriptures.

> "Have them make a sanctuary for me, and I will dwell among them. Make this tabernacle and all its furnishings exactly like the pattern I show you" (Ex. 25:8-9).
> "A sanctuary that is a copy and shadow of what is in heaven" (Heb. 8:5).
> "Beginning with Moses and all the Prophets, he explained to them what was said in all the Scriptures concerning himself" (Luke 24:27).
> "The Word became flesh and made his dwelling among us" (John 1:14).

Christ, the Son of God, the complete embodiment of God's Word, came to tabernacle among us. He looked on humanity's losing battle with sin and pitched His divine tent in the middle of the camp so that He could dwell among us. "We beheld his glory" (John 1:14, KJV).

What was the purpose of the tabernacle of testimony, built by heavenly design in the wilderness? It was to be a dwelling place in which to behold God's glory among people! How much greater, then, was God's glory displayed in the true Tabernacle! Is it any wonder, when they announced the long-awaited birth of the One and Only, the heavenly hosts cried, "Glory!" as they proclaimed, "the glory as of the only begotten of the Father" (John 1:14, KJV)?

This Tabernacle was planned before the foundation of the world was established (1 Pet. 1:20), long before the first sin in the garden of Eden. Before God breathed a soul into the first man, the blueprint for a Tabernacle had been designed—One that would somehow, someway miraculously encase the Creator of all the universe inside the parameters of human flesh.

> "Sacrifice and offering you did not desire, but a body you prepared for me; with burnt offerings and sin offerings you were not pleased. Then I said, 'Here I am—it is written about me in the scroll—I have come to do your will, O God'" (Heb. 10:5-7).

"The Word became flesh and [tabernacled] among us" (John 1:14). Can you imagine the excruciating transformation of going from having absolutely no limitations to being imprisoned inside about 170 pounds of human flesh? How many times do you suppose He would have liked to burst out of that tent and to unleash His awesome power? We have nothing with which to compare the confinement of omnipotent, omniscient, and omnipresent God in flesh.

God's Son left a position of sympathy and for 33 years inhabited a shell of empathy, feeling what humans feel. He scraped His knee as a child. He laughed with friends as an adult. He felt pain when the hammer slipped and hit His thumb. He experienced exhaustion. He longed for solace. He knew frustration. He experienced anger. He suffered temptation. He knew what it was like to be

♥ **What does it mean to you that Jesus had the power to escape His circumstances but chose to endure suffering for our sake?**

211

Christ Jesus
is the true
Tabernacle.

used and abused. He knew the pain of sheer dread. And He was altogether too well acquainted with the nature of His portable abode, His flesh, His tent, His tabernacle. It was a temporary dwelling, a seemingly unfit place for God's Son to dwell. Like the tabernacle of testimony, somehow its exterior did not seem to match its interior. But after all, everything about His life seemed that way.

The King of kings and Lord of lords, the only Begotten of the Father was born in a stable, raised by a poor carpenter, teased by his brothers, and was virtually homeless, practically penniless. He was deserted by His friends, insulted in a mock court, beaten, stripped, bruised, then crucified. To us it is a scenario that makes little sense. To God it was the only scenario that made any sense. He had to become flesh and tabernacle among us. Yes, Christ Jesus is the true Tabernacle.

Walk back through the tabernacle with me. Check off each Scripture as you read of its fulfillment. Christ is the ...
❑ Door (John 10:9).   ❑ Basin (John 13:8b).
❑ Bread of the Presence (John 6:35).   ❑ Lampstand (John 8:12).
❑ Altar of incense (Heb. 7:25).   ❑ Veil (Heb. 10:20).
❑ Mercy Seat (Rom. 3:25-26).   ❑ Tabernacle (John 1:14).

To me it would have been sacrifice enough for God to humble Himself and walk side-by-side with us. Yet had He done it my way, we would still be lost. I cannot relate to my Savior's perfection or His agony on the cross. The closest I can crawl into that pivotal scene is to imagine that tender mother's emotion. What must she have thought as she stood below her own suspended vulnerability? I doubt she was in total control of her silent pain. Why else would her Son have been so moved in the midst of His ripping war with death that He cried to His friend words like these: "Take care of her! Hold her and promise Me you'll be there for her!" I feel certain she, like us, would have cried out for her own death to escape the excruciating sight of His, yearning to hide her eyes yet powerless to do so.

When my children were babies, I rocked them for hours and often thought about that chosen mother. She had no idea what awaited that soft, cuddly baby. The thought would invariably make me hold my own even closer. I also wondered how different things might have been if God, in His perfect sovereignty, had allowed Mary to know the fate of her firstborn Son. However, my overwhelming thought is simply this: thank God it was not I.

"For now, My child, but for a while, cuddle Him all you can.
Gather hay from the loft, sing a lullaby soft: 'Sleep, Baby, blessed God-man.
So much work must we do when time becomes due. Rest for now, my darling; don't cry.
Stars, shine bright! Dance on His face tonight! Look up, your redemption is nigh!'

"He is God's Son, the only One through whom men can be restored.
Dry your tears; incline your ears. Your pain is not ignored.
Hail His Majesty, the Prince of peace, the bright and Morning Star,
Bow each knee and tongues proceed. Praise Him wherever you are!"

Day 4
The New Tabernacle

Read Today's Treasure and pray that God will speak to you through His Word.

Since the garden of Eden, God has desired to dwell among His prized creation. After sin cast humans from God's dwelling place, He enacted a plan to make His dwelling place with humans. Through the Old Testament tabernacle God testified of a true Tabernacle to come. God graced the tabernacle in the wilderness with His glory; but the true Tabernacle He had planned would enclose not simply God's glory, as awesome as it is, but God Himself. The true Tabernacle would be the habitation of a far greater degree of glory: "In Christ all the fullness of the Deity lives in bodily form" (Col. 2:9). We cannot even fathom it.

Christ took the true Tabernacle back to its rightful place: to the heavenlies, where He belongs. However, because the price had been fully paid and believing humanity had been saved to the uttermost, people were now reconciled to God and deemed fit for fellowship through the cross. Much too high a price had been paid for any person not to have an invitation to salvation. Therefore, Christ purposed that He would never be separated from humanity again; so as long as the unredeemed continued to walk on this earth, God's Tabernacle would walk among them.

Who would that be? I think you know the answer, but let's allow God's Word to impart the truth to our souls.

Today's Treasure

"DO YOU NOT KNOW THAT YOUR BODY IS A TEMPLE OF THE HOLY SPIRIT, WHO IS IN YOU, WHOM YOU HAVE RECEIVED FROM GOD? YOU ARE NOT YOUR OWN; YOU WERE BOUGHT AT A PRICE. THEREFORE HONOR GOD WITH YOUR BODY."

1 Corinthians 6:19-20

 What does each verse tell you about God's tabernacle or dwelling place in this present period of time?

I Corinthians 3:16 _____

I Corinthians 6:19 _____

2 Corinthians 6:16 _____

Ephesians 2:21-22 _____

How many times in the past 10 weeks have you wished for a time machine to get a glimpse of the wilderness tabernacle? Every time you drew one of those diagrams, I'm sure! I cannot show you the actual Old Testament tabernacle, but I can do better: I can show you the New Testament tabernacle. Have you received Christ as your Savior? Then take a long, hard look in the mirror and consider the words of I Corinthians 3:17: "God's temple is sacred, and you are that temple."

You are that temple! You are looking at a sacred dwelling place! That body you might like to trade in for a newer version is sacred! Take a good look at how God approaches the shell that encases your spirit and your soul.

Read Psalm 139:13-18. I know that you have read it before, but read it again! You will see it from a different perspective in the context of today's lesson.

Recall the detail to which the tabernacle of testimony had to conform: to absolute precision, no deviation. In fact, the dwelling had to be so perfect that only the Holy Spirit could build it to suit holy God. Remember the crucial inspection each object had to pass before the Hebrews dared transport it into the tabernacle? This Contractor was a perfectionist.

♥ Has it been difficult for you to look in the mirror and accept that you are "fearfully and wonderfully made" (Ps. 139:14)? Why or why not?

And He is the same One who built you. If that sounds trite, you have grown cynical. You can confidently tell your children that they are "fearfully and wonderfully made" (Ps. 139:14), but you may have a hard time believing it about yourself. He is God. He could have chosen to dwell anywhere in the universe. He could have made His sanctuary in the farthest galaxies, in the majestic mountains, in the deep oceans, or in the vast Grand Canyon. But He chose to live in you and me. You are now the way He dwells among the people of this world. He dwells there in your tent. We often observe two common yet erroneous attitudes toward the physical body: making it too small a priority and making it too important.

Review Today's Treasure. Verse 19 states the fact; verse 20, the follow-up. How must we respond to the reality that we are the temple of Holy God?

The Word emphatically teaches that our physical bodies are important to God (Rom. 12:1). He loves the bodies He gave us! He specifically chose them and sovereignly assigned them, like it or not.

Some Christians think God doesn't care whether our bodies are in shape or, frankly, what we do with them. That is simply not true. I'll always remember the words of a very good friend who lost a precious two-year-old son in an accident. I returned a few weeks after the funeral to minister to her in her tremendous pain. Instead, I learned a lot myself. She told me that as she stood over the casket, many well-meaning family members and friends said: "Ginny, walk away from it. He's not in there anymore." Some of those same persons even dissuaded her from visiting the grave site to take fresh flowers: "He's not there, Ginny. He's with Jesus."

She said: "Beth, I knew he wasn't in there anymore. I knew that better than anyone. I also know that his little soul and spirit are not in that grave. I know that! But the body that came from my own, that I held and kissed, the hair I washed and brushed, the hand I secured in mine as we walked across the street, the face I cherished, and the frame I rocked were in there. And I loved them!"

Those were the most honest words I have ever heard a grieving person utter.

If my friend—a mother made of flesh and blood who has relatively limited capabilities to love—could make such a statement, how much more our limitless Heavenly Father loves His children, our bodies and all! We are the works of His hands!

In addition, God has to live inside us, too. Anyone who thinks the body has no impact on the soul should test how easy it is to focus spiritually the next time she has the flu. Or imagine sitting comfortably in a Bible study after having used your body as an instrument of immorality the night before. Until we die or God meets us in the air, we are inseparably linked to these bodies; and each part has a major impact on the others.

Of what three components are we made (see 1 Thess. 5:23)?

_____

Is one component less important than the others? ❑ yes ❑ no

Why or why not? _____

Is it as important that we present our bodies "blameless at the coming of our Lord" as our souls and spirits? ❑ yes ❑ no

Explain: _____

_____

_____

As some care nothing about their bodies, others care only about them. This is also an unhealthy, unbiblical extreme. To treasure a decaying tent more than an eternal spirit and a soul is futile. The balance is this: a healthy, holy tabernacle provides the best possible environment in which a healthy, holy soul and spirit can thrive.

The tabernacle had to be maintained with such care because it enclosed the very glory of God—a motivation that must remain ours as well. This discussion is not about looks, size, or weight. It is about authority. Can you openly acknowledge God as Master over your entire being? "May God himself, the God of peace, sanctify you through and through. May your whole spirit, soul and body be kept blameless at the coming of our Lord Jesus Christ" (1 Thess. 5:23).

We are dwellings through which Christ desires to tabernacle among His people—a gathering place where He may reveal His glory. After all, isn't that our purpose: "everyone who is called by my name, whom I created for my glory, whom I formed and made" (Isa. 43:7)?

We are not on this planet in the midst of a perverse generation by accident. God predestined this society to be the one in which He would tabernacle specifically through us. We have been chosen to reveal His glorious presence to this dark generation. He has entrusted it to us: "Guard the good deposit that was entrusted to you—guard it with the help of the Holy Spirit who lives in us" (2 Tim. 1:14).

Be faithful to guard the trust.

> A healthy, holy tabernacle provides the best environment in which a healthy, holy soul and spirit can thrive.

Day 5
The Intimacy of the Holy of Holies

"Blessed are those you choose and bring near to live in your courts! We are filled with the good things of your house, of your holy temple."

Psalm 65:4

Read Today's Treasure and pray that God will speak to you through His Word.

I can't begin to express what your dedication to this study and to all studies of God's perfect Word really means. I will simply let the Logos say it for Himself: you have been "a workman who does not need to be ashamed" (2 Tim. 2:15).

As I share these next words, my heart overflows: "The secret things belong to the LORD our God, but the things revealed belong to us and to our children forever" (Deut. 29:29). No matter what happens to you, whether you lose your health, your job, your home, or even your spouse, the words He has given you these weeks belong to you forever. You have put countless hours into God's Word. It can never be taken from you. It is yours to keep and share with your children!

For the last time in our study, draw a basic diagram of the tabernacle of testimony.

Could it be enough for you simply to stand in that outer court any longer? As a member of the royal priesthood, do you yearn to enter that holy of holies and "consider everything a loss" (Phil. 3:8) just to know Him? How deep you will allow God to draw you into His dwelling place is a choice only you can make. We will conclude our study by accepting the challenge of several designated groups who dared to enter Christ's tabernacle of intimacy.

Read 1 Corinthians 15:6. What number is given? _____

By what name does God call these people? _____

What does that mean? _____

Five hundred is the largest specific number we have in Scripture to represent the brethren, or believers in Christ. Oh, yes, there were far more; but this is the largest recorded number that represents a general group of believers. We know only one fact about the depth of their intimacy with Christ: they were saved. Let's allow the 500 to represent those who accepted God's marvelous gift of salvation. In other words, they passed through the gate and stood at the bronze altar.

On your diagram label this group at the bronze altar by the name of *500 fellow heirs*.

According to Luke 10:1-2, how many are numbered? _____

What insight do we receive about their depth of intimacy?

_____

These 70 (or 72, NIV) were set apart for service. They accepted the invitation to approach more deeply in the tabernacle of intimacy. Let's call these the *70 field harvesters*.

Because God sanctified them for service, place them on your diagram at the location of consecration: the basin.

Read Matthew 26:17-30. Who was sitting at the table with Jesus?

_____

How many were there? _____

Twelve will represent the next step in the tabernacle of intimacy with the living God. These were the ones who sat at His table, ate with Him, conversed with Him, and followed Him. The Twelve fellowshipped with Him.

Write *Twelve who fellowshipped* on your diagram beside the holy place, the sanctuary of fellowship.

A final group gathered farther in the tabernacle of intimacy with Christ.

 Read Matthew 17:1-8; Mark 14:32-52. How many were invited

into the innermost chambers of Christ's glory? _____

Peter, James, and John witnessed the true power of the resurrection at Jairus's home. The same three had their vision refocused on the mount of transfiguration, which I like to call Mount Perspective. They were invited to fellowship in the agony at Gethsemane. Perhaps these three alone truly went into the holy of holies with their Savior on this earth. Why just those three? Because God pierces the deepest intents of the heart. He knows who really yearns and searches for Him.

Mark these on your diagram inside the holy of holies as *the favored three.*

God did not love them more than He loved every person He died for, but their yearning hearts and willingness to risk the cost of intimacy gave them positions of favor. They discovered that He was their "very great reward" (Gen. 15:1).

What are the qualifications of those who learn to experience Christ in the holy of holies? Those who are unafraid to let Him display His awesome resurrection power before their very eyes. Those who can shake off the grave clothes of the former life and enjoy the freedom of the resurrection. Those who are not satisfied with the seen things of this world. Those who are willing to have all earthly perspectives stripped away and to allow God to renew their minds to a fresh capacity for understanding. And those who are willing to fellowship in His sufferings. Yes, as hard as it may be to accept, if you stop short of a willingness to fellowship in His sufferings, you stop short of the indescribable experience of His holy of holies.

Do you want to know Him just for the sake of knowing Him, for the joy of kneeling in His awesome presence? Then you may enter the holy of holies.

Read Philippians 3:10.

My friend, how He beckons you. How He longs for you to enter through the veil He tore for you. We have only this one experience to know Him as mortals. We can live our lives on the outer perimeters of our salvation, in Christ but not with Christ, or we can accept the challenge to enter and behold His glory.

Look back at your diagram. Would you dare to make that a circle of four in the holy of holies? Will you be like the shepherds who received the invitation of the angels and "came with haste" (Luke 2:16, KJV)? Can you live with the mediocrity of life in the outer court when you have been invited to dwell in the

If you stop short of a willingness to fellowship in His sufferings, you stop short of the indescribable experience of His holy of holies.

excellence of the innermost place? If you dare enter, you will never be the same. Nor will anyone around you.

Oh, our God, give us the courage to enter the holy of holies—truly to know and experience You deeply. Teach us to meet You in this tabernacle until the glorious day when we stand in a new tabernacle: "I heard a loud voice from the throne saying, 'Now the dwelling of God is with men, and he will live with them. They will be his people, and God himself will be with them and be their God. He will wipe every tear from their eyes. There will be no more death or mourning or crying or pain, for the old order of things has passed away.' He who was seated on the throne said, 'I am making everything new!' Then he said, 'Write this down, for these words are trustworthy and true'" (Rev. 21:3-5). Come, Lord Jesus!

♥ **What it would mean for you to dwell in the holy of holies?**

HEAVEN

How infinite Your grace for us
As You've prepared a place
Beyond our mere imaginings
With no familiar trace.

We'll find our custom-built abode
Beyond the pearly gate,
Step-by-step down streets of gold,
Oh, I can hardly wait!

Yet Lord, I feel I must express
What heaven means to me.
It's not the mansion of my dreams
That I receive for free.

You see, Lord, if You'd given me
A hut beneath a tree
Or led me to a country shack
Where I'd forever be,

I'd make my home there happily
For always and a day
If You'd make just one promise:
You too would come and stay.

Because, my Lord, one thing is sure,
So search my heart and see—
It's not reward my heart leaps for:
You are heaven to me.

I. "And the walls came tumbling down," *Houston Chronicle*, 22 February 1990, sec. A, 11.

Viewer Guide

Mended Hearts, Eternal Ties

Today we not only complete our series but also we glance ahead at prophecies describing how God will complete *His*. In our final hour of Bible study, let's behold the beauty and consistency of God once more.

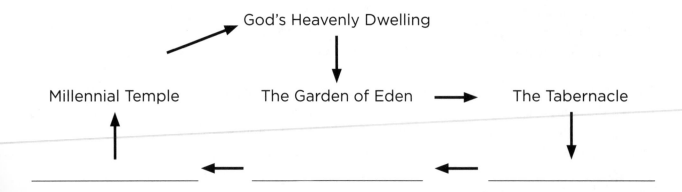

Part 1: The Present Dwelling Place

Read Acts 2:1-4,17,38-41.

- _____ _____: Exodus 40:34 reads, "Then the _____ covered the Tent of Meeting, and the glory of the LORD _____ the tabernacle." Remember that "_____ was in the cloud by night" (v. 38).

- _____ _____: I Kings 8:10-11 reads, "When the priests withdrew from the Holy Place, the cloud _____ the temple of the LORD. And the priests could not perform their service because of the cloud, for the _____ of the LORD filled his temple." (Cross reference 2 Chron. 7:1-3.)

- _____ _____: Acts 2:2-4 reads, "Suddenly a sound like the blowing of a violent wind came from _____ and _____ the whole house where they were sitting. They saw what seemed to be tongues of _____ that separated and came to rest on each of them. All of them were _____ with the Holy Spirit."

"The manner in which God's presence comes to fill the _____, _____ and _____ enhances the plausibility that Luke is describing Pentecost as the _____ for this new age."[1]

Part 2: The Final Dwelling Place

Read Revelation 21:1-6.

- The _____ plan: "Behold, the tabernacle of God is with men" (Rev. 21:3, KJV).
- The _____ (a _____) and the _____ (_____) (Rev. 21:10-18; I Kings 6:20-22)
- The _____ _____ (Rev. 21:22-27)
- The eternal _____ (Rev. 22:1-6)

1. G. K. Beale, *The Temple and the Church's Mission* (Downer's Grove, IL: InterVarsity Press, 2004), 211.

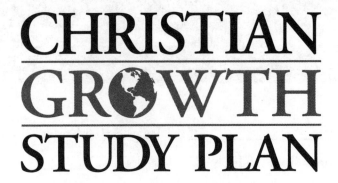

CHRISTIAN GROWTH STUDY PLAN

In the Christian Growth Study Plan, this book *A Woman's Heart: God's Dwelling Place* is a resource for course credit in the subject area Personal Life of the Christian Growth category of plans. To receive credit, read the book, complete the learning activities, show your work to your pastor, a staff member or church leader, then complete the following information. This page may be duplicated. Send the completed page to:

Christian Growth Study Plan
One LifeWay Plaza, Nashville, TN 37234-0117
FAX: (615)251-5067; E-mail: cgspnet@lifeway.com
For information about the Christian Growth Study Plan, refer to the Christian Growth Study Plan Catalog. It is located online at www.lifeway.com/cgsp. If you do not have access to the Internet, contact the Christian Growth Study Plan office (1.800.968.5519) for the specific plan you need for your ministry.

A Woman's Heart
COURSE NUMBER: CG-0114

PARTICIPANT INFORMATION

Social Security Number (USA ONLY-optional) | Personal CGSP Number* | Date of Birth (MONTH, DAY, YEAR)

Name (First, Middle, Last) | Home Phone

Address (Street, Route, or P.O. Box) | City, State, or Province | Zip/Postal Code

Email Address for CGSP use

Please check appropriate box: ☐ Resource purchased by church ☐ Resource purchased by self ☐ Other

CHURCH INFORMATION

Church Name

Address (Street, Route, or P.O. Box) | City, State, or Province | Zip/Postal Code

CHANGE REQUEST ONLY

☐ Former Name

☐ Former Address | City, State, or Province | Zip/Postal Code

☐ Former Church | City, State, or Province | Zip/Postal Code

Signature of Pastor, Conference Leader, or Other Church Leader | Date

*New participants are requested but not required to give SS# and date of birth. Existing participants, please give CGSP# when using SS# for the first time. Thereafter, only one ID# is required. **Mail to:** Christian Growth Study Plan, One LifeWay Plaza, Nashville, TN 37234-0117. Fax: (615)251-5067.

Revised 4-05